GW00669654

A VOICE, A LIFE

A VOICE, A LIFE

Autobiography

by

JOAN HAMMOND

LONDON
VICTOR GOLLANCZ LTD
1970

ISBN 0 575 00503 3

Printed in Great Britain by
The Camelot Press Ltd, London and Southampton

DEDICATION

To my parents—my Fairy Godmother—my lifelong friends—a loyal public—and countless others, to whom I shall be forever grateful for a full and joyful life.

ACKNOWLEDGEMENTS

My thanks and indebtedness to: Bill Newman (E.M.I. Records) for compiling my discography; to Jane Henderson, who succeeded in making the first draft from my rough typewritten and long-hand pages, and from whom I received inestimable advice; to Odette Inglis who painstakingly completed the finished MS.; to Lolita Marriott and Estrées Walker for helping me in my research and checking of my diaries, and above everything, for their persistent encouragement, which kept me on the job; to Pauline Grant, whose liaison work at twelve thousand miles distance was invaluable; to Margaret Walkom, for her interest and co-operation at the end of the road, i.e. proof reading.

I am most grateful to Squadron Leader D. M. Barrett, R.A.F., Ret'd, to Miss Monica Starke of the Red Cross, to Mr Percy T. Hanson and to Miss Sylvia Darley for permission to reproduce the letters printed in the Appendix.

CONTENTS

LIST OF ILLUSTRATIONS

Desdemona in *Otello* (*Photo: Paul Trenoweth*)

Elizabeth in *Don Carlos* (*Photo: Angus McBean*)

Rusalka in *Rusalka* (*Photo: Michael Boys*)

Leonora in *Fidelio* (*Photo: Angus McBean*)

Salome (*Photo: Angus McBean*)

Madam Butterfly (*Photo: Angus McBean*)

Tosca (*Photo: Angus McBean*)

Following page 192

Durban: with Bobby Locke, the golfer (*Photo: Lynn Acutt*)

Royal Festival Hall, 1953, with Ivie Price and the Earl of Gowrie (*Photo: General News Features*)

Johannesburg, 1947: the author and Lolita Marriott inspecting a gold-mine

Moscow, 1957, with Ivan Koslovsky and Constance Shacklock

London, 1969, with John Whittle and Robert Leslie following the presentation of the Gold Disc

The author at The Old Cottage, Bucks, with some of her pets (*Photo: Paul Wilson*)

Australia House, London, 1964, at a reception for the Australian Prime Minister

The author setting off for a bird-watching picnic in Australia

PART I

Kaleidoscope

THE ROAR OF SURF, of heavy seas pounding the shore, the calm undulating swell after a storm, the feel of hot sand on bare feet, the prow of a yacht surging through the waves, maybe dancing as through a curtain of foam, a horse's mane flying in the wind—these things are woven into the fabric of my childhood. And more: the smell of the bush and the leaves of gum trees twinkling silver after the rain, and boronia and the wattle; sunrise and sunset, trees, birds, animals—the whole of nature's riotous pageant. Then the glory of a great symphony or opera, the simplicity of a lovely song, the sometime beauty of prose and poetry, of art. Children's playtime laughter, the trust and companionship of good friends—all these I love.

A career should conform to a pattern rather like a menu—hors d'œuvre, entrée, main dish, sweet and savoury; corresponding, perhaps, to childhood, adolescence, young adulthood, maturity, and old age. When viewed in retrospect some careers do seem to follow this pattern. Such was mine. Whether or not this autobiography does is for you to decide.

My mother was born in Cowes on the Isle of Wight, home of the Royal Yacht Squadron and where, towards the end of my singing career, I so often took my own yacht.

My father was a Londoner. When he and my mother married he had a rapidly growing electrical business in the City. Business was good, contracts plentiful, and they lived in a rambling old house overlooking Wimbledon Common. Life for them had all the ingredients of a well assured future.

But the long cold northern winters were affecting my mother's health. She had already lost two of her sisters with tuberculosis, and the fear of it was ever present. So my father, who lived for the day and was never one to concern himself greatly with security, decided that they would move to the other side of the world.

They chose New Zealand. There would be a good climate, good business prospects, a whole new world to conquer. My father had a gay, devil-may-care attitude to it all, and he was full of confidence. My mother was more sceptical. She knew that the electrical business in London was bound to expand, but she did want to escape the rigours of European winters, and New Zealand sounded as good as anywhere else. Perhaps she was infected by father's inherent belief in the goodness of things. Anyway, passages to New Zealand were booked on the Shaw Savill liner *Athenic*. With their two sons, Noel and Leonard, aged one and two years respectively, another baby on the way, high hopes but not too much money, they sailed away to their brave new world.

The *Athenic* took a course round the Cape of Good Hope and across the Southern Ocean to Tasmania. It was not an easy passage, and the weather was no help. There were storms which delayed the ship, and the voyage took longer than had been anticipated. My mother, expecting her third child, had considerable cause for uneasiness, and by the time the *Athenic* reached New Zealand it was becoming urgent to find somewhere for the third birth in the family to take place.

My father was astonished to find how difficult it was to rent or buy suitable property in New Zealand. Thus the first small crack appeared in the façade of his land of promise. Driven by a situation which made action imperative, he at last rented a small house in Christchurch, and there, on 24 May 1912, I was born.

My father was finding New Zealand something less than the mecca for which he had hoped. The climate did not seem much superior to that of England, and business prospects were not good. With a young wife and three very small children it was imperative that he should take some positive action. What about Australia? With his usual optimism he envisaged a land of sunshine and promise where he could house his family with freedom to grow and expand. A few weeks after my birth I was christened in New Zealand at a small seaside resort called Sumner, which is near Christchurch. As we were strangers in a strange land where we knew nobody, my parents were also my godparents.

My father went on ahead to Sydney, to look around and to prepare for his family's arrival. He liked Australia from the start. The climate was good, the business prospects were bright and, though it was difficult, it was not impossible to find the sort of home he wanted for his family.

After six months we were able to join him in Beecroft, a suburb of Sydney. The house was sizeable, with good grounds where we children could play, and the garden gave directly on to bushland. I quickly took advantage of all this although at the time I was too small to be aware of it. I was three years old: the summer night had been very hot, and just before dawn I got out of bed, evidently having decided to "go walkabout". I did not bother about bedroom slippers, and soon I did not bother about my nightdress either. It was in the way and kept catching on twigs and brambles. So I took it off, and that was how I was found several hours later by my parents, who realised only too well the dangers of bushwalking in the nude. A bite from a funnel-web spider can cause almost instantaneous death, and another dreaded spider, the red-back, is a great danger, not to mention the venomous snakes. I was blissfully unaware of these perils, and in any case I was accompanied by our dog, which probably gave me a feeling of security. It was because of the dog that I was found before many hours of daylight had elapsed. A neighbour had seen him and recognised him, though she did not know me. By calling the dog and finding him, I was found too. As well as being my first "walkabout" it was the beginning of my lifelong rapport with animals.

Guy Fawkes' fireworks' night is not observed in Australia as it is in England, but no self-respecting Australian is going to miss the chance of having a private fireworks show, or the opportunity of watching a big display of set pieces. So Empire Day, now called Commonwealth Day, was set aside as "cracker night". It was also my birthday, the 24th of May, and crackers would be exploding excitingly on the neighbouring streets and gardens, with an occasional rocket tearing into the sky in an effervescent fizz, to explode in a bomb-burst of drifting coloured stars. We had our own bonfire and display of fireworks in the garden, and when my father told me that cracker night was held in honour of my birth-day I was filled with joy and wonder. I believed him with all the enchantment of a child believing in Father Christmas.

We did not stay very long in Beecroft. My father had chosen a site in the Lindfield-Killara area of Sydney's North Shore, where he meant to build a house which would conform in every way to his ideal of a family home.

The new house was called "Walbrook", after the Ward of Walbrook in the City of London where my father had had his electrical business. It was a big house where there was plenty of room for the activities of my two elder brothers, myself and the younger brother Tony who had arrived to complete our family. There was a small ballroom where later I was able to do all my singing and violin practice. Outside we had a tennis court and a large cricket lawn which gave on to bushland, so, as my interest in sport grew and developed alongside my music studies, I was able to indulge in them all untrammelled and without causing any annoyance to anyone.

My father's business was flourishing, and he passed on the advantages to his growing family without stint. The move from England had proved to be a wise one.

I was blessed with parents who denied me nothing, and who gave me every sort of encouragement and opportunity to follow my love of sport and music. They allowed me to develop freely and naturally, so that as the early years went by and my interests became more selective and concentrated on singing, the violin and golf, they exerted no pressure, nor did they try to influence me to specialise in one or the other. They gave me complete freedom to grow and expand, and for their wisdom in this I am forever grateful. A background of love, security and encouragement is the most essential of any child's needs, and these I was able to accept as a birthright.

My first school was a co-educational establishment called Morven Garden School, where I started as a boarder when I was seven years old. My happiest times were spent in the playing fields or in the music rooms, for I was already learning to play the violin. We had singing lessons too, and when I had been at the school about a year I can recall being brought out in front of the singing class because, as the teacher said, I was the only one singing in time and obeying her instructions. I was so elated at being held up as an example of anything good that I did my best not to let her down. There seemed to be some quality in the voice that appealed to people, and after that I was often called upon to sing where there were a few of us together. This would be at playtime, between classes, even in the dormitory, with varying degrees of approval or disapproval from the staff. But the other children seemed to enjoy it and I certainly did. It gradually became an established pattern which went on through the years, long after I had left that school.

Many years later I was singing for a group of friends in an hotel in Canberra. We were in a golfing party during the first tour of the British ladies' team in 1935. Not all my songs were classical, but we were a bit surprised when the telephone rang. My friend Lolita Marriott answered it. Looking angry, she covered the mouthpiece with her hand and turned to us.

"It's the reception desk. Another guest, a member of Parliament or something, says he wants you to stop that noise, Joan. The cheek of it!" she added crossly. "Who does he think he is?"

I stopped my noise and we fell to talking instead.

In the years to come there was a pleasant sequel to this incident. I was on tour for the Australian Broadcasting Commission, and after one of my concerts I received a beautiful bouquet. Inside was a note: "Some years ago I complained about the noise you were creating at the Hotel Canberra. Now I should like to thank you for the many hours of glorious 'noise' you have given me since." The note was signed "A devoted admirer".

By the time I was twelve years old the love of violin playing had become very great, and I made considerable progress in my studies. It seemed to me that a violin speaks, that it sings, but that its eloquence can only be released by the player. I longed to be a really good performer. Then fate intervened with a move that changed the pattern inexorably, as fate does.

It was holiday time and my father had bought us a new bicycle. I was riding round the quiet roads of Lindfield, and I had established

B

a sort of track where there was very little traffic. I was just completing my fourth run, and perhaps I had become a bit careless. I took a bend too wide, and there, coming towards me, was a car. I avoided a head-on crash, but I was flung to the road and my left arm was brutally entangled in the spokes of the car's wheel. Lying there in the road thus enmeshed I was completely numb, but I remember that the distraught chauffeur lifted me into the back of the car, and that he covered my arm. He drove me to the nearest doctor, who after a quick look said that I must be taken to a hospital in Killara, where an immediate operation would have to be performed. I could only ask for my mother and beg them, please, would they take me home.

It was thought at first that the arm would have to be amputated at the elbow, but a brilliant young surgeon had been rushed to the hospital, and it was his initial care that averted what for me would have been a tragedy.

Mother had gone into Sydney on a shopping trip that day, and it happened that both she and father caught the same train back to Lindfield. The station-master met them and told them about the accident, but by the time they reached the hospital the operation was already in progress. This was the first of five operations on the arm. The final one was for a skin graft.

Bicycles were never mentioned in our family again.

This mishap cost me a year of active life. When I was able to use my left arm again it was found to be nearly two inches shorter than the right arm, and movement was greatly restricted. Youth happily overcomes obstacles of this kind, even if considerable pain is involved. I was unable to play the violin for a year because the agile finger movements required were impossible, but nothing was going to keep me from playing hockey, or any other game in which both arms participate equally. A shield with a thick inner padding of cotton wool was devised to protect the still tender wound. I felt very self-conscious about wearing it, but when it was pointed out to me that a blow to the wound could easily cause serious trouble, I overcame my susceptibilities and never played without it.

The scars are very ugly, both on the arm and on the thigh from which the skin graft was taken. I still feel very self-conscious when I wear a swimsuit. Youth has no regard for such sensitivity, however, and I vividly remember the shock of hearing another girl remark on "that horrible looking scar". Until then I had not realised what an impact it would have on other people. When I could resume my interrupted education I went to a different school. This next one was the Presbyterian Ladies' College, known to us as P.L.C. Many of the secondary schools in Australia are run under the auspices of a religious denomination, though the pupils are not required to be practising members of that particular religion. P.L.C. is at Pymble, also close to our home at Lindfield, but I was a boarder at the school.

At this new school my whole interest was centred, as usual, on sport and music. I loathed mathematics, and to this day I have difficulty in believing that two and two make four. This may be why I am still acutely embarrassed whenever it is necessary to discuss money. School to me meant games. It meant swimming, tennis, hockey and netball teams, athletics. Swimming I particularly loved, and while at P.L.C. I won the Bronze Medal and Bronze Bar for life-saving. Later the Silver and Gold medals followed. Reaching the "A" teams and winning many swimming and diving championships crowned everything, and were enough to make me think my education was complete. The only real award I won was the yearly singing prize.

My extra music subjects at P.L.C. were singing, violin and piano, the last being a bad third; my art subjects were charcoal drawing, painting with water colours and later with oils, but I was rather wayward in these subjects. I could not work up any interest in bowls of fruit or Grecian heads. I liked to draw sailing ships, or rocky shores. For a time I succeeded in avoiding maths lessons by arranging tuition in my extra subjects to coincide with them. If this failed, I would disappear into one of the music rooms and practise the violin, and there were a few times when I contrived to slip into the pool and have a swim. Eventually I was found out, and of course the worst part of the punishment was being given several psalms to learn by heart after school. This really cut to the bone, for it meant I had to miss games. But it had a salutary effect as well, for it sharpened my memory and this has stood me in good stead ever since, whenever it has been necessary to learn by heart.

Later in life I naturally regretted that my excessive love of sport had caused me to waste so many opportunities.

Miss Nancy Jobson—known as Job—was headmistress at P.L.C. during most of my time there. We were very lucky to have such a warm, understanding person in charge of our young lives, and her method of dealing with me was to make me a prefect, presumably in the hope that I would live up to the responsibility and behave accordingly. This was excellent psychology on her part. Up until that time I had made a point of sitting next to a particular girl in church on Sundays because in hot weather she nearly always fainted, thus providing me with an opportunity to help her out of church and take her back to school in a taxi.

I was one who was supposed to attend the Church of England church, which was at the top of a steep hill. The Presbyterian Church was much closer, and some of us managed to join the girls who were going there, keeping our faces down so that Miss Jobson would not notice us. She was not so easily taken in. "Chins up, girls!" she would say, and as we raised our heads she noticed which of us were in the wrong group. We were then sorted out accordingly.

After being made a prefect I had to put childish pranks behind me. Perhaps my improved behaviour was instrumental in persuading Miss Jobson to give her consent when my mother asked permission to take me to a performance of Massenet's opera *Thaïs*, which was being given by the Melba-Williamson Company. My mother was always anxious for me to hear as much opera as possible, and although *Thaïs* was not the ideal choice, it was the only opera for which she could get seats. I loved the work, and the performances of Lina Scavizzi as Thaïs and of John Brownlee as Athanael have remained in my memory ever since. It was the first opera I had ever heard, and I gave a glowing account of it to my friends when I returned to school the next day.

I shall always remember Miss Jobson with affection, not only because she re-directed my wayward behaviour, but because she was a wonderful headmistress. She was a real friend whose interest in her pupils remained constant long after they had left school. I corresponded with her throughout my travels and up to the time of her death.

I resumed violin playing and it was hoped that the exercise would help to strengthen the fingers of my damaged arm. It was a very painful process but I stuck at it, determined to do all I could to improve the circulation in my left hand and to firm up the muscles. I still loved the instrument, though it was becoming a forlorn hope that I could ever achieve my ambition to become a first-class performer. At week-ends when I went home, and during the holidays, I played golf at Palm Beach. My father had built a cottage there, and in front of it was a nine-hole golf course. I was rather a curiosity because I was completely self-taught, and my grip on the clubs was unorthodox because of my arm. Otherwise my golf was not affected by the injury unless the weather was very cold. Then my arm would ache badly because the circulation was affected. I gripped the clubs in the only way I could, and that is how I play to this day, with both hands straight down the shaft. It is known as the old St. Andrews' grip.

My game developed quickly in those early years because I played so much with men. They were my father's friends, and they were all good players. Inspired by them I made enormous efforts to drive to a greater length in order to keep up with them and to putt more accurately. They gave me great encouragement, and playing with them extended my game enormously.

While at P.L.C. I had a very good holiday arrangement whereby I often spent winter holidays with a friend whose people owned a property at Narrabri, in the northern part of New South Wales, and she often spent summer holidays with me at our Palm Beach cottage. It was this friend and her family who introduced me to droving, which meant sitting in the saddle for long hours just mooching along, but becoming very stiff in the process. Stiff or not, there was deep content in helping to pitch the tents at night and make the camp fire. We would throw potatoes into the glowing ashes to cook while the billy boiled.

The taste of this simple food, eaten as it was under the night sky, with good friends for company and a pleasantly tired body, was an unforgettable experience for me. Often I would sing for a while before we turned in for the night.

Everyone works when on a station, and I used to take tea, morning and afternoon, to the men who might be miles away fencing or rounding up sheep. I carried a saddle-bag with the food and mugs in it, and held the reins with my right hand and the billy in the left. The horse would go up to the numerous gates and stand while I leaned down to undo them, and then wheel round to allow me to shut them. But on the homeward journey it was quite a different matter. He brought me up to the first post and I trustingly undid the latch, but before I could say "Whoa" he was round that post and had left me sitting on it for a brief second before I completed the act and fell to the ground. A nasty, painful lesson, followed by a long walk to the next gate, where the horse was waiting for me impatiently. After that I knew he would instinctively head for home, and I was wise to his capers.

I used to sometimes stay with a friend who lived at Scone, and she also was keen on riding as her people owned a number of horses.

Scone was the home of polo, and it was while staying with my friend that I was induced to try the game. The experience was a most unhappy one for the unfortunate pony, who could follow the ball with an eye as sharp as that of an eagle. The way he wheeled and chased the ball was amazing. The first time I played I found myself going straight ahead after he had made a sharp right turn, and the results were again most painful. We got to know each other better after that, but I hit his forelegs more often than the ball, and this possibly hurt me more than it hurt him. I had tried the game, but I was satisfied that the health of the horse was more important than my desire to continue to learn to play.

Around this time something happened which gave me a sharp introduction to fear, a word which had barely entered into my vocabulary at that time.

I was surfing at Palm Beach, and was out beyond the breakers waiting as usual for the best and biggest wave to bring me in.

Suddenly I saw the fin of a shark cutting slowly through the water ahead of me. Simultaneously I heard the warning bell ringing on the beach. I was treading water at the time, and I knew that the safest action was to make as big a splash as possible, for sharks have the reputation of being the most cowardly of all sea-creatures. But my body was frozen with fright. I was panic-stricken, expecting at any second to feel those cruel teeth tearing my flesh. Then a magnificent wave came in, and suddenly, galvanised into action, I caught it and rode it until it was spent. When I had got the last wriggle out of it I stood up in about two feet of water. I was alone in the sea—everybody else had rushed out—and there was still a deep channel between me and the beach. I swam across it at racing speed.

Soon after this there was a shark tragedy at another beach. The worry of it all was more than my mother could bear.

"Joan," she said, "you'll have to promise me you'll never swim out beyond the breakers again. With all these sharks around it's really too dangerous."

I had had a severe shaking, and I was willing to agree that surfing could be risky, especially if there was a deep channel between the swimmer and the beach.

"All right," I said. "I'll try not to do it again."

"Now promise me, dear?"

"Well, I won't promise but I'll stay closer to the beach."

It was all to no avail, I am afraid. I did not mean to break my word, but to be on the beach on a hot day with a perfect surf running was too much for me. My former fears were thrown to the seaweed and I would swim out beyond the breakers, to wait for the ideal wave to bring me in.

My father had given me a cabin cruiser, which was named *Alawa*, an aboriginal word meaning "I camp here". I kept it at Palm Beach, and it afforded me tremendous pleasure. I spent as much time as possible aboard her, and I also went sailing on other people's yachts. I learnt such a lot from the yachtsmen who visited that beautiful stretch of water known as Pittwater.

This sailing experience proved very useful, because on most afternoons during the summer months my younger brother Tony and I used to race in a twelve-foot boat on Sydney Harbour. The boat was called *Stormalong*, and she was a lovely, lively craft. As far as I remember we carried off four trophies with her.

Twice we were caught with too much sail by a "Southerly Buster", the cool strong wind-change which comes up without warning. We capsized. We clung to the gunwale for an hour on one occasion before being towed ashore. It was what I called a "wet bottom" hobby, but exhilarating fun. Luckily Tony had two friends with whom he could sail her if I had to play golf. That often happened.

In the summer holidays the days were never long enough for all my activities. I became a sort of human fish, spending hours in the surf either body-shooting or surf-board riding. The surf was a magnet which drew me to it day after day. I played golf on the nine-hole course in front of our cottage, which was later to become the Golf Clubhouse, or I was sailing. I knew no other way of life and I took it all for granted.

During those last terms at P.L.C. it must have been apparent that the time was fast approaching when I should have to make a decision between sport and music. Throughout my schooldays they had run neck and neck, but I was not aware of any sense of conflict at that time. I loved it all so much: the outdoor activities, singing anywhere and everywhere, doggedly continuing with my violin studies in the hope of strengthening my arm. In this enchanted period of my life it did not seem possible that there could ever be hard times ahead, times when I should have to work long hours and contribute out of my small earnings to the family coffers. Those golden days were touched with magic, and it was almost as if I knew I must make the most of them. Financial clouds were gathering on the horizon, though as yet they made no shadow.

I left P.L.C. in 1928 and began my studies at the New South Wales Conservatorium of Music in Sydney, known as the Con. Students were not allowed to take singing as a first subject, and rightly so. My first subject was the violin, with singing second.

Soon I was given a place in the second violins of the Sydney

Philharmonic Orchestra. I was greatly excited about this, but I also realised that the sustained effort required to get through a whole evening's orchestral programme would be a test, the first real test my violin playing had had since the accident to my arm. When it came to my first appearance on the stage of the Sydney Town Hall, I was terribly anxious not to let the rest of the orchestra down. Up until that time I had had to rest the arm periodically because of the pain. Maybe I had hoped subconsciously that on this night, which was so important to me, a miracle would occur and I would be able to play through.

There was no miracle. Sheer brute pain forced me to rest my arm, and each time I did so I felt that every eye in the audience must be trained on me, wondering why I had stopped playing. I felt stripped, stripped and acutely ashamed of my handicap.

When the concert was over I knew that I must abandon forever any idea of playing the violin professionally. I kept on for a time with two small amateur orchestras, and with a chamber group, but my serious violin playing days were over before they had properly begun, and I knew it. My last appearance was at a charity concert in which I played a violin obbligato and sang the Bach-Gounod Ave Maria. I'm sure it was a musical mess.

My singing studies were progressing apace, and my first professional appearance was rather unusual in as much as I was heard but not seen. It is strange to recall that the last time I sang in public, just before my enforced retirement in England following a coronary, I was also heard but not seen.

For this occasion Dr Arundel Orchard, who was then the Director of the New South Wales State Conservatorium of Music, had included the Symphony in F major by Vaughan Williams, known as the Pastoral, in a subscription concert to be given in the Conservatorium Hall. In the last movement a solo voice is heard singing in free style. Dr Orchard was having some difficulty in finding a singer who could sing the unaccompanied passages and still be in tune when the orchestra picked up the theme. He came to the studio where I was having a lesson with my teacher, Mr Spencer Thomas, and listened outside the door for some time. What he heard evidently caused him to think I should be suitable for the solo part. The next day the music was sent to me, and after the first rehearsal the part was mine.

Two great duo pianists, Lindley Evans and the late Frank Hutchens, both on the teaching staff at the Con, also took a great interest in my voice. They were giving duo piano recitals throughout Australia, and whenever possible they engaged me as their assisting artist. They also insisted on my being included in a broadcasting tour for the Australian Broadcasting Commission. This was wonderful experience for me, for the tour included Melbourne, Adelaide and Tasmania. I was very lucky to be taken under their collective wing, for they both had great personal charm, and a light-hearted approach to life which earned them the devotion of students and musicians, as well as of the general public. They brought happiness to everybody.

Another unique couple who helped to mould my musical career were the sisters, Lute and Jean Drummond. Lute was an excellent musician and linguist, and worked as an independent coach. Jean was already a sick woman when I first met her. She would often interrupt coaching lessons in order, she said, to keep Lute from getting too excited by my young voice. It was her role to restrain her ebullient sister. They both foresaw a future for me, and they did everything they could to help me.

I also attended Lute's German, French and Italian classes, and she gave me many unusual arias to learn at this stage: Marietta's Lied from *Die Tote Stadt* by Korngold, the "récitative et air de Lia" from *L'Enfant Prodigue* by Debussy, "Depuis le Jour" from Charpentier's *Louise*, and Marguerite's aria from the *Mefistofeles* of Boito. "Troppo, Signore" from Cilea's opera, *Adriana Lecouvreur*, was another unhackneyed one.

Lute also introduced me to Puccini with the aria, "In quelle trine morbide", from *Manon Lescaut*, and she was responsible for the very catholic taste I acquired in both opera and song. My repertoire included the works of Duparc, Debussy, Strauss, Schubert, Wolf and Marx. There were contemporary English composers too; Delius, Quilter, Bax, Vaughan Williams and Armstrong Gibbs. There was one ballad I particularly liked, and that was "The Green Hills o' Somerset" by Eric Coates. I often sang it at school and at various friendly gatherings, and it has played an important part in my career.

So much singing activity had softened the blow of knowing I could never be a first-class violinist, but it also left room for plenty of golf, which was becoming an increasingly major interest with me, and in which I was having some success. If it was strange to have, virtually, two careers running parallel in my life, I was hardly aware of it. There was room for everything, and although my father had had to dispose of some of his property in and around Sydney, the effect was not very noticeable. We still lived at "Walbrook" and life was wonderful.

It was in 1929, when I was seventeen, that I won my first golf championship event. The Ladies' Golf Union had arranged a Junior State Championship of New South Wales, and it was the inaugural event. I won the title that first year, and again in 1930, when I also reached the final of the senior State Championship. My opponent was Miss Odette Lefebvre, now Mrs Inglis. We were the first young women to take up golf which at that time was regarded as an older person's game. When we reached the final we made history. The press claimed it as being the greatest final in the history of Associates' golf in New South Wales. After this we met on many occasions as adversaries, but we each expressed the hope that the other would carry on and win if one of us was knocked out. Odette is to this day one of my closest friends. In 1931, our first final, she beat me in a wonderful match.

It proved to be a sad day of losses for me. In order to be nearer to the Royal Sydney Golf Club where the championship was being played, I had gone to stay with friends at Rose Bay. This saved me a very early start each day from Lindfield. The night before the final, my mother telephoned to say that my small dog was ill with tick poisoning. The tick is a loathsome little thing, and it is the curse of Sydney's North Shore. It fastens itself on to the animal's body and injects a poison which causes paralysis, starting in the hind legs and eventually swelling the tongue so that the animal chokes. There were no antidotes in those days, and it was necessary to go over pet animals night and morning in case a tick had lodged. They go for soft parts: behind the ears, inside the jaws and in the armpits. That my little dog was ill with tick poisoning was disquieting news, but I hoped for the best, knowing that my mother would do everything possible.

The next day, finals day and an edgy one in any case, I was given a message in the lunch hour to the effect that my boat *Alawa* had broken loose from its mooring at Palm Beach during the gale the previous night, and had been found on the other side of Pittwater, smashed on the rocks at West Head and completely wrecked.

Odette won the State title, and when the match was over I had a telephone message from my mother to say that despite her devoted care my dog had died, so one way and another that memorable day was one of sad losses. As I am an inveterate animal lover I need hardly say which one affected me the most.

Opera seasons in Australia were few and far between at that time, so the announcement in 1932 of a forthcoming season by the Williamson Imperial Grand Opera Company was something of an event. Italian principals were to be imported, and local auditions would be held to find the singers for the minor roles, the chorus and the opera ballet. You may think that the word "ballet" has slipped in by mistake, but in the final touring chorus some of us who could dance, but had not had ballet experience, were coached and used to bolster up the main ballet brought in at each city. In opera such as *Faust* we were on our own, without extras.

The auditions for singers were three in number, on a system of elimination. Six hundred applicants entered their names for them, and I was one of the thirty chosen as a permanent member of the Company.

Days of agony and suspense followed each audition. The final choice of names was eventually put on the notice board backstage. I shall never forget going to the theatre for the first "call". Several of the singers who had been rejected had gathered round the stage door, presumably to give vent to their disappointment by making disparaging remarks to the lucky ones: "Fancy choosing her—she can't even sing a top B!" "What does *she* want a job for? She's got a husband and money." Another one: "Just look at her figure! She'll ruin the show!" I simply could not understand this attitude. I felt very sorry for those who had not been chosen, but it was my first introduction to this seamy side of stage life, and I lost some sleep over it.

At the first full-dress rehearsal on stage, everyone was positively bursting their lungs to outdo the next one, and hoping the Maestro would see how well they knew the music. The Maestro could speak no English, which was just as well. He shouted his instructions to the producer, who translated: "Watch him! And put some life into it—don't stand there like dummies! I know you don't savvy what you're singing about, but do try to *look* as if you do!" We were very inexperienced and kept our eyes glued to the conductor. Another instruction: "Can't you boys and girls sing *piano* when the Maestro indicates it? And when he says *forte*, he means FORTE!"

Aïda was one of the operas performed, and there was a call for us to present ourselves to be fitted with costumes. It was a misnomer to say that we would be "fitted", for the only way to acquire a presentable looking costume was to make a dive for it as soon as you saw it. The resulting scrum was rather worse than the opening hours of a sale in a large departmental store, or feeding time at the zoo. The life of the chorus singers is very different today, when all costumes are fitted and everything is conducted in a most orderly way.

The small touring company was moderately well-behaved, but in *Aïda*, when many extras had to be brought in, it became an all-in fight. The make-up changed some characters to such an extent that they appeared to have donned war-paint. In the Triumphal Scene, for instance, everyone seemed bent on getting as near to the footlights as possible, in order that their friends could see them. Among these additional singers were six rather buxom sopranos who usually swept to the front of the stage and stayed there, as immovable as the Pyramids. We called them Footlight Fannies. At rehearsals the shorter singers had been placed at the front, and we were neither used to such tactics nor did we approve of them. We took an effective revenge.

In *I Pagliacci*, where there is an opera within the action of the opera, the villagers rush onstage and sit on benches as an audience.

Of course the Footlight Fannies rushed to the front as usual, and sat on the ends of the benches nearest to the actual audience, leaving the rest of us to find places where we could. At a pre-arranged signal we would contrive to stand up, or ease our weight from the seats. The benches would tip up, leaving the Footlight Fannies either to slide ungracefully into the footlights they loved so much, or to stand up as quickly as they could. The public thought this was all a part of the show, and the newspaper critics said how well produced it was. It must have looked most realistic, for hats were knocked askew or off altogether, and there was a good deal of anguished chatter.

The Company provided a good training ground, and competition was very keen. One night in *Aïda* four of the soldiers escorting the tenor, Radames, offstage, forgot to lower their spears when passing under the tent flaps. This nearly brought the entire scenery down. "Fire them!" shouted the stage director, and they were fired. They could be replaced so easily.

I did not actually endanger the scenery at any time, but I had a small mishap in the first act of *Madam Butterfly*. It was after the beautiful opening chorus and we, Butterfly's relatives, were all fluttering and twittering about under the cherry blossom trees. I felt a chilling draught around my head. "Your wig!" hissed one of my stage relatives, and I turned to see it suspended on a twig which had gone clean through the bun on top. Summoning up all the Japanese art I could muster, I bowed to my "relatives", fanned myself madly and shuffled into the wings. The stage manager was there and had witnessed the whole episode. I expected instant dismissal, but all he said was: "Gor Blimey, Hammond, can't you keep your ruddy roof on?" He said it so loudly I was afraid the audience would hear.

I began to develop a love for the atmosphere of backstage theatre. To hear the orchestra tuning up was the most thrilling sound, and I enjoyed hearing the small call-boy—no Tannoy system in those days—calling for beginners, and tearing about with such an air of command. "Half an hour, ladies, please!" And the final call: "On stage, ladies, please!" His dignity sagged a bit as curtain time grew closer and closer, and it would be: "Hurry up, girls! No loitering there! Lift those skirts!" The love of the theatre was entering my bloodstream.

At home things were not so happy. The financial clouds, which had been drawing imperceptibly closer, now deluged us with their full fury. We were engulfed in the Big Depression. "Walbrook" had to be sold, that beautiful house where we had had such a carefree childhood. It was bought by William (Billy) Morris Hughes, a former Prime Minister of Australia, and we moved into a small flat at Kirribilli, an area which clusters round the northern end of Sydney Harbour Bridge. It seemed terribly cramped and small after the spaciousness of "Walbrook".

I was earning a salary of £3 per week from the Williamson Opera Company, and of this my father insisted that I pay thirty shillings into the running expenses of the flat. I was chosen to go with the opera tour to Melbourne, and I had to send home the extra ten shillings I was paid for being on tour. I had never lived in digs before and I greatly missed the home cooking and comforts I had always known, especially in the sort of digs I could afford out of a salary of £3 weekly. But I was glad to have been chosen to go on the opera tour, and a small part which had been allotted to me gave me confidence. The part was Giovanna in *Rigoletto*, seven bars in all. Giovanna is the handmaid-cum-guardian to the heroine Gilda, and it was difficult to make me look old enough for the part. My Gilda was Lina Paliughi. She had a glorious liquid voice to which I listened with joy, and I could hardly have had a more charming person with whom to sing my few bars. I remember keeping my eyes glued on the conductor for cues, as this part of my musical training had been firmly inculcated into me. Later I learned to watch without appearing to do so.

I had been a member of the Royal Sydney Golf Club since 1931, and I represented that Club right up until my departure from Australia. Before being elected to go on the opera tour I had entered my name for the New South Wales Golf Championship. When I was told I was to go with the opera tour to Melbourne I wrote at once to the Ladies' Golf Union, notifying them that I must withdraw my entry.

Miss Una Clift, who was then President of the L.G.U., knew

of course that I had twice won the junior State championship, and that in the previous year I had been runner-up in the senior event. Miss Clift was a great personality, and without further ado, she approached Mr E. J. Tait, who was himself a keen golfer as well as being the owner, with two brothers, of the J. C. Williamson Company. Mr Tait had never realised that the Joan Hammond doing chorus work and singing a small role in his opera company was the person whose name was cropping up so frequently in the world of golf. He granted me leave of absence so that I could compete.

This marvellous stroke of luck must have inspired me to feel that I should reward his kindness in releasing me to play in the event. I played some of my best golf ever, beating my friend Odette in the semi-finals, and going on to win the title from another friend, Miss Vedas Ebert.

The event had been played over the Royal Sydney Golf Club course, and when the final was over I went up the long flight of stone steps leading from the last hole to the clubhouse at this beautiful course. Lady Hore-Ruthven, later known as Lady Gowrie, then wife of the Governor of New South Wales (later the Governor-General of Australia), was waiting to present me with the Cup. She made the usual short speech, shook my hand and made the presentation. Neither of us realised that that first brief encounter was the beginning of a close friendship which was to span thirty-four years.

There was another presentation connected with that event. The Members and Associates of the Avondale Golf Club, where I had played my first serious golf and of which I was still an Associate Member, gave me a set of stainless-steel shafted clubs. I had represented the club in many inter-club matches and until that time I had played with the old hickory-shafted clubs belonging to my father. Except for the three woods, I have the Avondale clubs with me to this day, and I often use them, as they are lighter than my current set. I was overwhelmed with gratitude.

I returned to Melbourne and my work with the opera company. When I arrived at Spencer Street station I was met by the entire company and the number one conductor, Maestro Emilio Rossi, from La Scala, Milan. As I alighted from the train they greeted me with a magnificent rendering of "For She's a Jolly Good Fellow", and never have I heard it sung better!

In writing of the State Championship Final the golf reporter of the *Sydney Mail* made the comment that "Miss Hammond has conquered some of her shyness, no doubt through being accustomed to facing crowds across the footlights with the opera company". This was very shrewd of him. My shyness has been and still is a source of great embarrassment, often causing me to behave in a way I feel is quite foreign to my nature. To enter a room and hear myself announced by a Master of Ceremonies or uniformed servant is to make me feel that some vital garment has fallen off, or a zip fastner come undone. I break into a massive perspiration on face and neck, and then I am in agony lest it should show through my dress as a result of running down my spine. No matter how I try to talk myself into remaining calm and composed, it is of no avail.

One could hope that having gone through the agony of arrival and then mixing with the guests, one would be over the hurdle. But no. Leave-taking is just as bad. The absolute dread of disengaging myself from a group, seeking out host and hostess, saying goodbye to them and expressing thanks, has caused me to outstay my welcome in order to put off the ordeal as long as possible. This all seems to be due to an over-sensitiveness which has nothing to do with the type of "nerves" one feels on stage or concert platform.

After I had won the State Championship, the golfing fraternity expressed the hope that I would represent my State in the Australian National Championship which was to be played in Adelaide. This was a problem, for I had been engaged to continue with the Williamson Opera tour, and we were to go to New Zealand. I did not hesitate for long. Singing was my first love and I wanted to stay with the opera.

By this time we had become a very happy and united Company, but the tour was nearing its end. We were all sad when the final night came and we had to disband.

I did not leave New Zealand with the rest of the company. I

C

had been invited by the management of the new Civic Cinema in Auckland to sing twice daily there for three weeks. I accepted, and sang two songs and the aria, "One Fine Day", as prescribed. I was glad to have this extra time in New Zealand, for I was coming to like the country very much.

On my return to Sydney I found I had plenty of golf dates but few singing engagements. Anything that came along I snapped up quickly. It is interesting to look back and see the sums I earned from singing in those days. In spite of my loathing of figures I kept neat account-books in which I wrote everything down. Music Clubs paid me two guineas, for which I would sing two groups. At one time I was engaged by Grace Bros., a large departmental store in Sydney. Every afternoon for a week they had a special dress display, and while the public drank their tea and ate their sandwiches, I sang songs appropriate to the dresses being shown. While bridal gowns were on parade I sang "Because", and so on. For this week's work I received four guineas.

At home things were very tight financially and the money I earned, little as it was, was useful. In 1933 I had a stroke of good luck. As State Champion golfer, the *Observer* offered me a job as their golf reporter. This was my introduction to journalism, a phase of my life that I greatly enjoyed and would not have missed. Within that year I went from the *Observer* to the *Mail*, and from the *Mail* to the *Telegraph*, with which paper I stayed for the rest of my time in Australia. The only proviso was that I could not write about myself, as to do so would have jeopardised my amateur status.

My salary on the *Telegraph* was £5. 5s. per week, but it usually rose above this by reason of payment for special articles. The giddiest financial height I reached was £7. 3s. 1d. for a special article.

In that year I won the Australian Foursomes title with Odette Lefebvre, and I was playing golf in a great number of competitions, inter-club matches and other events, as well as representing the Royal Sydney Golf Club. I succeeded in establishing some course "records" and in clocking up the wins I needed to stay at the top of the golf world, that essential status which assured my journalistic position.

During this time, life was full to overflowing. I was attending harmony and theory classes at the Conservatorium of Music, as well as my singing lessons. I was playing a great deal of golf and these were my best years in the game. Every evening I went to the offices of the *Daily Telegraph* to collect by telephone all the Associate Club competition scores, and write comments on them. I was often sent to cover other sporting events, and these I enjoyed. The assignments I hated being asked to do were concerts and fashion parades. As far as concerts were concerned, I felt I had not sufficient musical knowledge to turn in a fair report. To be sure I was studying theory and harmony, but I knew that a little learning was a dangerous thing. Once I persuaded a fellow journalist to cover a concert for me, though he knew nothing whatsoever of classical music. He produced an excellent criticism the next day, and I asked him how he had done it. He laughed.

"Oh, I just checked up that the programme had been performed as announced, and then I mugged it all up out of books on music, the sort that gives details of the composers and how their works should be played, and what the movements mean, and all that. The rest was easy." He made no pretence about having any musical knowledge, but he was an excellent journalist. I thought, "Good for him".

By 1934 my brother Noel and I were supporting the flat at Kirribilli as well as ourselves. From singing I earned £33. 5s. that year which helped to augment my salary from the *Telegraph*, and life was very full if somewhat exhausting. Playing golf was an essential part of my job, and I was very persevering in an attempt to reduce my handicap from four to the elusive two. Often I worked at my desk at the *Telegraph* until late at night. Sometimes I had to go long hours without eating, and this worried my mother greatly. She would keep a dinner hot for me until I got home, often after 10.30 at night. I felt I was doing a useful job in life and I was happy. The days were constructive and full of purpose.

Certainly my golf did not suffer as a result of these activities. I won the State title again that year, managing in the final to win eleven holes in a row. The papers said that I had played flawless golf on that occasion, as a winning sequence of eleven consecutive holes in an important match was probably without precedent in women's golf.

Remembering that my first senior State Championship had been won when I was on a hurried leave from the Williamson opera company, I began to wonder if rather hectic conditions suited my game better than a more peaceful preamble. In October that year I was to play in the Champion of Champions Annual Scratch Competition at Manly. Just before that competition I was in New Zealand, representing Australia in the Tasman Cup. It was the first time that a team had left Australia, and the first Tasman Cup match to be played. I was the baby of the team.

I arrived from New Zealand by boat on the morning of the event at Manly, and I hurried there quickly in order not to be scratched from the competition by reason of being late. I made it in time, but only just. I won the event at great speed, taking three and a half hours to complete the thirty-six holes, with a rest of only ten minutes between the first and second rounds. Later that year I made a really determined effort to reduce my handicap from four to the desired two, and at the very last minute I did it, playing the scratch score of seventy-five at the Lakes course. It was almost the last available hour of the Sydney handicapping season. In the opinion of the press not enough young players at that time bothered to visit courses other than their own in order to reduce their handicaps.

Life seemed to be speeding along at an even faster pace with the coming of 1935. Sir Benjamin Fuller's presentation of Grand Opera came to Sydney, and there were some very distinguished names in the casts. They included Muriel Brunskill, Florence Austral, Walter Widdop, Norman Allin and Ben Williams. The singer engaged to sing Venus in *Tannhäuser* dropped out very unexpectedly, and Sir Benjamin Fuller approached the Conservatorium of Music to see if a replacement could be found at such short notice. My name was put forward, and I had twenty-four hours in which to learn the part. Thea Phillips was singing

Elizabeth in the opera, and although the part of Venus was not one I particularly wanted to sing, it was good experience. As a result of this I was also asked to sing the part of Helmwige in *Die Walküre*.

The papers were saying that I had set a standard in Australian golf, and this placed me under a responsibility not to relax my efforts. In some form or other, I had been press material ever since I won my first junior golf championship in 1929, and the more that was expected of me the more I tried to give. I did my best to maintain a high standard in order to justify the confidence placed in me.

Then my big break came.

I had been booked by the Queen Victoria Club in Sydney, to sing a group of songs during a reception to be held in honour of Lady Hore-Ruthven (Lady Gowrie). Lute Drummond, who knew a member of the committee in charge of the arrangements, had put my name forward as a young singer who should be given a chance. There was strong opposition to this. Other members of the committee and some of the artists booked to appear felt that I was too young, too inexperienced to sing on such an occasion. I should let the Club's function down, they said. But Lute's friend on the committee said she would guarantee the result and so won her point. Grudgingly it was agreed that I should sing.

The reception was held in Sydney at the Australia Hotel. I was gauche, I knew that my clothes were inadequate, and of course I was quite unused to singing before the King's Representative. In the small room allotted to the artists, four of the other performers (who were well established) left me in no doubt as to what they thought of my being there. I was completely cold-shouldered, so I sat quite still in miserable silence, wishing that I could be on a golf course instead.

My small contribution was placed in the second half of the programme to give the established ones time to prepare thoroughly for their most impressive pieces which were still to come. Then: "Go on. It's your turn now, but mind you make it short."

I went out and sang. I have not the least idea how much applause I earned, but I know I took several bows. I was too scared to sing an encore, as I had been told so definitely by the experienced artists that I must make my appearance brief.

The next artist was singing her second group and I was scrambling into my coat, anxious to be gone. A committee member came into the room.

"Her Excellency wishes to hear Joan Hammond sing again, so you will all have to wait. She wants you to sing 'The Green Hills o' Somerset' again," she added to me, "and any other song you like to sing."

I need hardly dwell on the frigid reception this request was given by the other artists.

Soon afterwards I received an invitation to go to Government House. I was shy and nervous as usual, but the easy manner and charm of Lady Gowrie soon put me at my ease. This wonderful lady asked me about my singing and about my work, and I was able to remind her that she had presented me with my first senior State golf trophy. She then admitted to me that on that hot afternoon at the Queen Victoria Club reception, the heat had made her drowsy and she had been half asleep through most of the programme. Suddenly she found she was wide awake, and listening to a "peerless young voice", as she called it, and she wanted to hear more.

Once Lady Gowrie learned from me that I had no financial backing, and that I was in fact supporting my family, she decided, with characteristic determination, that I should go abroad to receive further training, which might lead to a world career. Thus Lady Gowrie became a close and lasting friend, as well as a fairy godmother to me. Throughout my career she shared my joys and sadnesses—a friend to whom I could turn at any time for any reason. She was warmhearted and witty, kind and wise, and she was never too busy to concern herself with the troubles of others. She had a deep understanding and love of classical music. I am grateful to have known her and to have been honoured by her affection, and her many devoted, selfless deeds on my behalf.

Through Lady Gowrie and her relative and aide, Ivie Price, a "Joan Hammond Fund" was opened. Miss Price knew the friends upon whom she could rely, and set the fund in motion with a meeting and two large dinner parties at Government House, after which I sang so that the guests could hear the voice they were backing. Miss Price became a staunch friend, and she has remained so ever since.

The next step was to find an organiser, the right sort of person to manage the fund and organise the money-raising functions. I suggested Leonora Wray. She knew me and all the golfing fraternity well, and with her charm and administrative abilities I thought she would be the ideal person for the job. Miss Wray dedicates herself to any job she tackles; and she was a tireless factor in encouraging and helping young golfers. Deservedly she was awarded an M.B.E. for her services to golf, for both she and Miss Clift did more for golf in New South Wales than anyone else.

I was overwhelmed by this sudden change of fortune, by this bright new dawn which promised soon to break. But most of all, I was filled with gratitude and humility that these good people should trust me, and have faith in me to make the best use of the wonderful opportunity they were giving me. The Director of the Vienna Boys' Choir, Rector Schnitt, had heard me sing while he was in Sydney, and he suggested that I should study in Vienna and live at the Schloss Wilhelminenberg which was where the famous Vienna Boys themselves lived. The Schloss had been the hunting lodge of the Archduke Rudolph.

My mother was rather quiet about it all. With her fiercely independent spirit she resented the fact that my family could not give me this opportunity themselves, though she realised that, owing to the Depression, such expenditure was out of the question.

The fund was set at £A1,250, which was equivalent to rather less than £1,000 sterling at that time. Miss Wray, with Kate Egan as joint secretary, lost no time in getting things moving. Many personal friends of the Gowrie family contributed large sums, and if I single out two names now it is because those two people helped me when I was in desperate need in London. I was literally penniless when Andrew Reid came to my assistance most generously. Another time I was down to my last few coins because a cheque in payment for two concerts was overdue. Mrs Fred Payne saw me through that crisis.

The fund was completed in a little less than a year. I owe the organisers so very much, and if this tribute is tardy it is none the less sincere and deeply felt.

From June 1935 to 6 April 1936 when I left Australia in the Norwegian freighter *Dagfred*, chartered by an Italian line during the Abyssinian War, I was still keeping abreast of all my usual activities. I was playing golf, and represented Australia against the visiting British team.

It was during this season that Odette and I went to Melbourne for the Australian Title and Interstate matches which were being played at the Royal Melbourne Golf Club. We arrived at Sandringham station only to find we had just missed the last cab to the course, and there was no chance of getting another. We were due to hit off from the first tee in twenty minutes.

No player likes to be late on the tee, particularly for the Championship. Moreover, we were members of the New South Wales State Team and our behaviour reflected on our State. I felt the usual trickle beginning to form on my face and neck.

"We shall have to walk, so let's start," said the practical Odette. She picked up her gear.

"We'll never make it." I gathered up my own heavy case and clubs.

At that moment a battered dirty-looking old truck loaded with empty crates came towards us. Simultaneously we held up our hands to thumb a lift, and to our great relief the truck stopped. We explained our plight. "Hop in," said the driver.

He insisted on driving us right to the front of the Clubhouse. What a royal arrival for the impeccably dressed Odette (always the smartest golfer), and me! But we were on the first tee in time, and that was all we cared about.

Fossicking through my account books I see that I won £25. 15s. in golfing money-orders that year. These enabled me to have my various cups engraved, and I see that I also bought a vase, though I cannot now think why. For the rest I bought an evening bag, a powder compact and a mirror, which doubtless I needed for the large number of concerts at which I was singing to help the fund. At last people were becoming aware of me as a singer as well as a golfer. I worked at my job on the *Daily Telegraph* right up until the day before my departure, and though my golf suffered during those last few months, I think I was able to do my job well enough to earn my pay packet.

I had been so happy in my newspaper work. The late Eric Baume, the journalist, often came to talk to me and ask about my singing, and Paul Brickhill, who was later to write that famous book *The Dambusters*, was another who often paused at my little desk for a chat. He was such a bright-faced youngster, rushing hither and thither with copy. He wrote a résumé of my activities up to that time, and it was published in the *Sun Junior*, our house journal.

My biggest journalistic scoop had come about when I wangled a lift in the pilot boat which was going out to escort a liner into Sydney Harbour. The New Zealand players Oliver Kay and Bessie Gaisford were coming for the Australian Championship Meeting, and they were passengers on this liner. I scrambled aboard her by shinning up the rope ladder flung over the side, found the girls, interviewed them, and went ashore again before the liner docked. My article was printed in the first editions of the *Telegraph* while the other press representatives were still greeting the players. These happy days were nearly over, and I did not realise how much I was going to miss them.

The year passed in a whirl. My mind was a kaleidoscope of hopes and dreams through which ran an unwavering streak of determination that come what may, I would justify the confidence which had been placed in me.

The newspapers said that while no one would grudge me my chances abroad, my departure was "the worst thing that could happen to Australian golf". I had "set a standard", and in always trying to improve my game I had given a good example which "should encourage other young players to do the same". I was the "only stroke maker in the State", they said. It was very gratifying.

I shall never forget the final concert, which took place on the eve of my departure. Sydney Town Hall was crowded with friends, supporters and well-wishers. I sang songs and arias, so many of which Lute Drummond had taught me, and she was my accompanist. At the end, amid all the bouquets and baskets of flowers, I could only say: "Thank you very much for all your wonderful kindness. I will do my best." A small inadequate speech, so desperately meant.

There had never been any real difficulty in choosing between singing and golf. My golf handicap when I left was two, the lowest of any woman player in Australia, but singing was my whole world, and I stood at its threshold.

The next day when I boarded the *Dagfred*, there were more friends, flowers and presents. I particularly remember Miss Wray's parting gift. It was a box containing every imaginable sort of first-aid equipment, something to which I had never given a thought. The most valuable item was a bottle of Condy's crystals, which I used for gargling and putting in questionable water for teeth cleaning and general sterilisation. I still have some of those same crystals. I carry the bottle in my make-up case, and I would not be without it.

When the *Dagfred* reached Melbourne, Lolita Marriott was on the pier to meet me. I had spent so many happy holidays with her family at Toorak, and we had become close friends. Now she was the last to say goodbye.

"How do you feel about it?" she asked.

"Like the weather," I answered glumly. It was grey and cold and cheerless—an exact summing up of my frame of mind. The passage to Adelaide was rough and stormy, but I am never a victim of seasickness and I was able to go to meals with the Captain and First Officer during the whole voyage. All the other passengers, and even the Italian representative, succumbed.

Finally we left Australia from Fremantle on 16 April. I felt miserable. I was very naïve and innocent, unable to understand smutty stories, innuendoes and suchlike. I used to laugh in what I hoped were the right places, but I had no idea what I was laughing about.

The first real jolt to my innocent outlook on life and people came as suddenly and unexpectedly as a star falling from the heavens.

PART II

Threshold

THERE WAS ONLY ONE other woman passenger aboard the *Dagfred* beside myself. She was a middle-aged French Moroccan lady, and we shared a large, comfortable cabin. The poor woman was very seasick all the way to Melbourne, and only a little better between Melbourne and Adelaide, but she seemed quite friendly. After leaving Fremantle she was very much in evidence.

There were two Italian men passengers and the Italian Line representative. We five, plus the Captain and First Officer, dined in a small "dining-cum-sitting" saloon—when my fellow passengers had all recovered from their seasickness.

Because I played games, including bridge, I was popular with everyone and was able to join in any of the entertainments arranged for us on such a small ship, though they were few enough.

Soon after we left Fremantle "Madam", as the French Moroccan lady became known, recovered from her seasickness. With it she seemed to shed her outer skin of niceness to reveal a sour and embittered interior. She began by making insinuating remarks about me playing games all the time with the men, and my protests that there was no one else with whom to play did not seem to penetrate. She accused me of making use of the early part of the voyage, when she was sick, to gain their friendship and to estrange them from her. Things became very unpleasant. Whenever the rest of us played deck games or bridge she would sit and watch us with a venomous stare. She made dreadful remarks in French, and although I did not understand them the men told me their purport.

The Norwegian Captain, who was very charming, had accepted responsibility for me until we reached Genoa, when he was to put me on the train to Vienna.

"Have you noticed anything odd about 'Madam', Joan?" he asked casually.

"Well, yes. She's unfriendly, and she looks at me in a most peculiar way. I'm quite scared of her."

"Hm'm. Well, let me know straight away if you're worried too much, will you?"

I agreed, thinking this was not a very promising start to my new life.

Quite by chance one of the men discovered that "Madam" was writing slanderous letters about us all. The Captain acted promptly. He moved the Italian representative into the hospital, and put me into the cabin thus vacated. This was a great relief, as I was becoming really afraid of "Madam" and it seemed possible she would do something rash. On the more positive side, I was delighted with the move because I felt part of the ship. The small single-berth cabin I now occupied was on the lower bridge, and as I was being given lessons in navigation by the stars, an exercise hitherto unknown to me, it was an ideal position. Up until that time I had only understood coastal navigation, and the celestial variety was very interesting.

Every day "Madam" was caught spying, either on her fellow passengers or the crew, and the Captain would deal with her personally. The weather was very hot and it seemed to me at times the ship was not moving at all. I was very anxious to get to the end of the journey, and I could only thank heaven that my interest in the workings of a ship kept my mind occupied. I was allowed to spend a lot of time in the chart room, where I followed the ship's course and learned how to use a Morse light.

The *Dagfred* docked at Colombo and the Captain took me ashore. This was my first taste of foreign life. We visited a Buddhist temple, and I had a ride in a rickshaw. I found the temple most unusual and interesting, but the sight of the emaciated coolie pulling the rickshaw upset me very much, and I vowed I would never ride in one again—a vow I have kept. We visited the native quarter and then went to the zoo, which was most depressing. It was a badly run zoo. Both surroundings and animals looked lifeless and uncared for.

On 3 May I noted that I had seen for the first time the Great Bear and Polar Star. This was a tremendous thrill for me. My beloved Southern Cross was still visible, so I had not quite lost touch with my homeland. The heat was increasing daily, and although I felt in the middle of a furnace bodily, my spirit was almost foundering in the icy atmosphere of intrigue and conspiracy. It was all so strange to me.

Often I sat on deck just watching the sea, a vast expanse of ocean with this small vessel in the middle. I thought of those scurrilous letters "Madam" had written, and in contrast my mind turned to the warm memory of a letter I had received on the day when I was to play in a state golf championship final. There had been two letters that day, and one was for me. When I turned it over to slit the envelope I read on the back in large writing: "Good luck for today!" Signed "Postie". The thought behind this simple action had touched me deeply, and I am sure it inspired me to play better golf and win. It is these small things in life, the finding of sudden kindness and generosity, that help to prepare us and build us a saner outlook for the future.

Nevertheless, the episode of the French Moroccan lady left a scar on me. From that time until now I have been very wary of strangers and slow to make friends. I became sceptical, doubting rather than trusting, and my subsequent life in Vienna did nothing to change this outlook.

I thought too of *Alawa*, my boat at Palm Beach, and the many happy hours I had had in her. All manner of past events flooded my memory, making all the more painful the return to the present and the doubts of the future. I was still amazed that I was on this small ship going further and further from home. Out there in the unknown lay my destiny and the answer to the question—should I make good?

By now "Madam" had become so peculiar that she would not eat meals with us, and insisted on having her food taken to her cabin. She had announced her intention of posting the letters at Suez, and it was suggested that the Italian representative should try to gain her confidence and see if she would reveal her plans to him. Eventually she told him that she had a number of urgent and important letters to post at Suez, and that she did not wish them to go with the ship's bag. He promised to go ashore with her when the ship docked, and see that the letters were correctly stamped and posted. He got possession of the letters and took them to the Captain, who thought it possible that "Madam" had seen through the Italian representative's friendliness, and had another batch of letters, other than the ones she had given him.

The Captain decided to take no risks. From Suez he sent a cable to Miss Wray: PASSENGER ABOARD INTENTIONALLY TRIED TO HARM MISS HAMMOND THROUGH MALICIOUS LETTERS TO TRUTH AND SMITH'S WEEKLY WHICH ARE GROUNDLESS CALUMNIES MY DUTY ASK YOU EXPLAIN EDITORS STOP FORWARDING LETTER TODAY. It was signed CAPTAIN DAGFRED. He also wrote a letter "To Whom it may concern", and this letter was signed by the First Officer, the Italian representative, and the two Italian men passengers.

The Captain took me ashore at Suez and at Port Said, where we went to see a mosque and again, the native quarters. I found this experience saddening and depressing. Such poverty was stark and tragic, and at that time, unknown and incomprehensible to me. It shocked me forcibly and stirred feelings of pity and helplessness. To be a witness to the plight of others and not be able to help was wounding to the soul. This other side of life had, until then, been hidden in a tangled mass of ignorance and youthful belief that all in the world was good and beautiful; sin and ugliness existed outside my world and were therefore unrelated to me.

While we were in the Suez Canal area I had to listen to a speech by Mussolini, which we received on the radio and which the Italians interpreted for me. I was not particularly interested until one of the Italians became heated over the political situation and began to criticise Britain. I knew by this time that the two Italians were Fascists and were getting home while they could. Being politically ignorant at that stage I was not a very good adversary, but I argued as best I could and I managed to put in a few broadsides, culled from conversations I had heard at home and in the *Daily Telegraph* offices. They never spoke about Britain again in my hearing, so perhaps my efforts were not in vain.

The next stop was Malta, where I had a complete tour of the island. It was fascinating to see the goats being milked in the streets of Valetta and people buying the milk on the spot. I thought it a very quaint island—I should have been thrilled if I had known that I should later return there on a recital tour! In the meantime to visit places which existed in the year 3000 B.C. was almost too much for me to comprehend. It was all so different, the culture and the whole way of life. I was a tiny atom from a young new world.

Since leaving Fremantle "Madam" had disembarked only at Suez. When the *Dagfred* reached Naples she made her final disembarkation, and she was met by the police. I was never able to discover her history, but I wondered greatly what had happened in her life to make her so bitter and so intent upon minding other people's business instead of her own. I knew nothing about the menopause, but on mature reflection I think this may have had something to do with her behaviour, as she was man-crazy and therefore jealous of any woman younger than herself.

We arrived at Genoa on 16 May. The Captain took me ashore and showed me some parts of the city. The next morning I had to go through Customs, and then buy my rail ticket to Vienna. The Captain was rather worried about my making the remainder of the journey alone, and I was sorry to say goodbye to him as he had been such a good friend. That evening he gave me a dinner, and saw me on to the 9.20 p.m. train for Vienna. I had not booked a sleeper as I did not want to spend the money, so I sat up all night. I eventually reached Vienna at 9.45 p.m. the next night, 18 May 1936, and Rector Schnitt met me.

The first part of my travels was over. I felt tired and lonely.

Rector Schnitt took me straight to the Schloss Wilhelminenberg, a large castle on the edge of the Vienna Woods overlooking the city. When daylight came I discovered that the surroundings were very beautiful, and as the castle was on such a high elevation the clear clean air and the panoramic views of the countryside were a source of delight.

I was taken down a long, wide corridor on the first floor. It was rather like a gallery, glassed in on one side, so that one could see into the courtyard below. The very high ceilings gave an added

D

look of spaciousness to the rooms, and the huge tall doors and double windows were curiosities to me. The Rector had arranged for me to have a sizeable sitting-room with a small bedroom adjacent. There was also a washroom which at first I thought contained a shower, but to my dismay it had only a toilet and a washbasin.

On the first night in my new quarters, I was unhappy, restless and sleepless. I am never happy sleeping in strange beds at the best of times, and this was one of my worst experiences as I was in a foreign land and in an odd type of castle which I felt sure housed many ghosts.

I awoke late the next morning, and after washing my face and cleaning my teeth I went in search of a bathroom. I wandered about for some time, fruitlessly opening doors, until it became clear that I should have to go to the centre wing of the Schloss and find the Rector.

I met him in the hallway between the ballroom and the suite formerly occupied by the Crown Prince Rudolf.

"Good morning, Rector," I said brightly. "Could you please tell me where there's a bathroom?" I was clad in dressing gown, with a towel over my shoulder and a sponge bag in my hand. He looked somewhat astonished.

"A bathroom?" he repeated incredulously. His speech was quick and nervous when he was ill at ease. "I'm not quite sure what you mean. You wish to bath now?"

It was my turn to look astonished.

"I like to have a bath or a shower every day, but I can't find a bathroom," I said firmly.

His face became apoplectic. "In that case," he said, "I shall have to ask the Countess." He turned away and disappeared through a nearby door.

Ask the Countess? What could he mean? Did one really have to obtain the permission of the aristocracy before having a bath in Austria? What an extraordinary custom!

He came back with a look of great relief on his face. "It's all right," he told me. "The Countess says you may use her bathroom every morning between 7.0 and 7.30." He added confidentially:

"You see, there's only one bathroom. Everybody else . . . well, they manage in the wash basins."

I realised that a signal honour had been given me. The bathroom was very large and ornate with beautiful fittings. The Crown Prince and his illustrious guests must have enjoyed wallowing in the bath as much as I did.

Later that morning I was introduced to the elderly Countess Kinsky. We took to each other immediately, and I learned that she had been a famous opera singer, Carmen having been her finest role. Although in her seventies she was still a very attractive woman.

The next shock was the food. It was poor in every sense of the word. My stomach rejected it. There were seldom any green vegetables or fresh fruit. The meat was sometimes deer, which I could not digest, or hunks of meat cooked up to look like goulash but in no other way resembling it. I rarely knew the origin of any of the meats served, and I ate for the most part black bread and jam. There was no butter, but a substitute which I imagine was a kind of margarine. The seating arrangements in the dining hall reminded me of boarding school—except that I now sat with the masters.

There were a number of older ex-choir boys who acted as prefects over the present-day young choristers. Their one topic of conversation was politics. They pestered me with questions about Australia, and even asked what language was our mother tongue. My small pocket English-German dictionary became thumbed and battered, as well as inadequate. I heard the word "Nazi" for the first time, and Hitler's name was often mentioned. I wished I could have followed every word, but I knew too little of the language at that time.

The Rector had asked me to pay him monthly in advance for my board and lodging. This was a financial shock, especially as Herr Gomboz, the chief conductor of the choir, wished to be paid in the same way for coaching me. His fee was 237 Austrian schillings per month, while singing lessons cost 200 schillings for the same period. The Rector had arranged for me to go to a singing teacher in Vienna. Her name was Frau Eibenschütz. She had an apartment in the second district, which I learnt from the older boys at the Schloss was the predominantly Jewish quarter of the city.

An entirely new existence began for me. On most Sundays I was taken to the Burgkapelle to hear the boys sing Mass. I used to sit upstairs in a private box which in former times had been used by members of the Royal Family and their guests. One could sit and listen without taking part. Masses by Haydn, Mozart and Beethoven were most beautiful.

From Mondays to Fridays inclusive I left the Schloss at 9 a.m. to go for my singing lesson. The walk down to the tram took twenty minutes, and it was another half-hour before I reached the city, where at the Opera I had to catch a bus to the second district. In fine weather I walked this part of the journey, traversing the length of the Kärntnerstrasse and crossing the canal. I returned to the Schloss for lunch, and then I would sit and learn by heart until about 4 p.m., when Herr Gomboz would coach me. He was an excellent repetiteur as well as being such a good conductor. After the evening meal, which was a sort of high tea, I would read or talk with the senior boys, and finally go to bed at 9 p.m.

My days were very full, but there were two other things I added voluntarily to my curriculum. One was skipping. I had left Sydney with a skipping rope in my luggage, and I had skipped every day on board the *Dagfred*. When the sea was rough the exercise had been quite comical. The second self-imposed task was the keeping of a diary. Mrs Cecil Lloyd, the mother of two of my schoolfriends, had given me a five-year diary when I left Sydney, and for this I owe her many thanks. I kept on with a series of five, or four-year, diaries throughout my career until 12 November 1964, when I stopped recording my activities except for spasmodic entries.

Whenever the choir gave a concert at the Schloss the Rector asked me to sing. This was good practice as I sang everything in German, and there were always interesting people present.

Elisabeth Schumann and the Director of the State Opera were among the guests on one occasion.

The first momentous theatrical experience I had was when I went to hear Goethe's *Faust* performed at the Burgtheater. I had never attended such a long performance in my life. It started at 7 p.m. and did not finish until 11.45 p.m., but I enjoyed every moment of it and came away feeling exhilarated.

I soon realised that I would have to move into the city in order to go to the opera as often as possible. I could only go from the Schloss if one of the older boys accompanied me, or if the Rector happened to be going himself, as he did occasionally. I then met him after the performance and drove back with him. He had a car and chauffeur at his disposal.

It was a very interesting experience to see how this famous choir lived and worked. The entire organisation was wonderful in conception. The boys all came from poor families, and their schooling was free during the time they were members of the choir. They travelled throughout the world, and the money they earned during these tours obviously went into the expense of maintaining, feeding, and clothing them. Two choirs were kept busy in this way, and part of their obligation to the Government was to sing the Sunday Mass at the Burgkapelle. They were fully occupied attending school, rehearsing and travelling.

I became very involved with their activities as the Rector invited me to go with them when they had to participate in festivals, such as the Liszt festival at Eisenstadt. It was an education for me. I saw a great deal of the country and learnt the language at the same time, as the boys always spoke to me in German. We used to travel in a bus, and being the only female I was an object of great curiosity.

There was a delightful occasion when the young choir boys had their "Confirmation Day". After the ceremony we were all taken to the Prater, a great park which comprises much of the artificial island between the Danube and the Vienna Canal. There were many amusements, including a Big Wheel from which little cabins were suspended. The Wheel revolved slowly, and as each cabin reached the top of its circle the occupants had a breath-taking view of the city and the surrounding countryside. When we returned to the Schloss the boys were presented with watches. I thought the whole idea quite charming.

I had by this time become very friendly with Emmerich Eber, one of the older boys. He had been asked by the Rector to accompany me to the city when there was a particular opera or play I wished to see. I resented this, as it meant I had to pay for two instead of for one; and this was another reason which made me decide I must eventually go and live in the city.

Emmerich was called "Eber" by everyone, and that is how I addressed him. I thought it was his Christian name, and it was many months before I learnt that it was in fact his surname. But he was and always has been "Eber" to me.

Eber was the saxophonist in a jazz band I heard playing at the Schloss one evening. It was quite a shock to hear such a band in this stronghold of classical music, and I went to investigate. I was told that it was a band formed by the older boys in preparation for the summer weeks which were to be spent in the Tirol, where the choir ran a pension at a small mountain village called Hinterbichl. This was another interesting facet of their lives. The Rector had told me about it, and also that I should be going there with the boys for two months, as the Schloss would be closed and the teaching staff on holiday. Certainly there was no lack of variety in the boys' lives.

Soon after my arrival in Vienna I received an invitation to have tea at the British Legation with Lady Selby, wife of Sir Walford, who was the British Envoy Extraordinary and Minister Plenipotentiary in Vienna from 1933 to 1937. This invitation was a direct result of Lady Gowrie's activities on my behalf, and it was a very happy introduction. Lady Selby became very interested in my voice, and after hearing me she followed my career through to the end. She gave me every opportunity to be heard and seen as much as possible by the musical hierarchy of the city, and I found her to be a most gracious, kind and sympathetic person in whom I felt an immediate trust. Her friendship meant a great deal to me, and I never cease to remember her generosity. My clothes must have been an eyesore to someone who dressed with such elegance, but this did not deter her from inviting me to dinners, teas and large affairs such as the celebration of King Edward VIII's birthday.

Two exceedingly friendly people I met on these occasions were Mr and Mrs Mack, now Sir Henry and Lady Bradshaw Mack. Sir Henry was at that time First Secretary at the British Legation with Sir Walford Selby. It was at a party given by the Macks that I sang "Danny Boy". Strangely enough I sang this lovely, haunting traditional air only twice more, both times in recitals. One of these was in Johannesburg, and the other in Folkestone, Kent, the county known as the Garden of England. The melody appealed to me greatly, but the tessitura was better suited for the tenor voice, and no matter whether I tried it in a high, medium or low key register, I never felt vocally suited to it.

Sir Henry and Lady Bradshaw Mack included me in several parties at their apartment, and I nearly always sang for them. They must have wondered about my appetite, for though my stomach had shrunk in size, I was able to fill it well on these occasions. To eat food I liked and to which I was accustomed, in such good company, temporarily improved my outlook on life in Vienna.

On the evening of 2 July 1936 I had my trunk open and I had begun to pack in readiness for the journey to Hinterbichl. As I was doing so I remembered that I wanted to practise part of a Strauss song that had not been going too well. I went to the ballroom, where I did all my rehearsing, and I decided to do some scales too. Suddenly I had an uncanny feeling that someone was in my bedroom. Still singing I opened one half of the huge doors and ran along the corridor. As I turned the corner I saw a boy rush from my room down the staircase that led below. I pursued the boy hotly, but when he reached the ground floor he went on down to the basement, knowing that I could not follow him, as the basement was for the boys only. Nevertheless I started down after him, but when I heard the sound of boys washing I returned to my room, feeling defeated.

I went through my belongings and found that the only two

pieces of jewellery I possessed and thirty Austrian schillings had been stolen. The jewellery consisted of a single-stone diamond ring given to me by my parents for my twenty-first birthday, and a gold expanding bracelet.

This incident shocked and enraged me. It was so blatant, and it was made worse by the fact that I knew who the thief was. I could not go to Rector Schnitt as he had left the previous night for Hinterbichl. The Herr Engineer, who was next in charge, spoke very little English, but I had to do something, so armed with my dictionary I found him and told him exactly what had taken place. He seemed to get the general picture, and he said he would do as I asked and advise the police of the theft. But the following day, he was nowhere to be found, and the day after that I had to leave for Hinterbichl. It was clear that nothing would be done until I told Rector Schnitt.

We left Vienna at 9 p.m. by train, and I was in a carriage with two small boys and two of the servants. It was one of the worst journeys I have ever had, for I did not sleep a wink sitting up in that uncomfortable third class carriage. I was tired out when we left the train at Lienz the next morning to travel for a further two hours by coach to Hinterbichel.

At the first opportunity I told the Rector about the theft, and he assured me that he would report it, but I felt that he spoke without conviction. He went on to say that the boy in question was one of their best singers, and that the whole incident would have an unfortunate reflection upon the choir. This I realised, but I found the entire situation very unsatisfactory. Thirty schillings was a lot of money to me, and the two pieces of jewellery were not only of sentimental value, but were my only possessions of any worth. It was perhaps fortunate that the boy had not come to Hinterbichel as he was spending the holiday break with his mother. He was a very handsome lad, and a great favourite with the Rector. There was no more I could do, so I resigned myself to waiting until the Rector had had time to act and obtain results.

I was in bath trouble again. Despite the fact that I was paying a good sum for my board and lodging, I was housed in a small attic bedroom such as the staff used. I had to obtain a key to a funny little bathroom on the floor below. Having bathed, for there was no such thing as a shower, I arrived at breakfast with a good clean face, only to be told that the bath would cost me an extra schilling per day. I thought about this added expense, and then told the Rector that I would forsake the hot bath and have a cold one instead. He was not very happy about this, as he knew that I had already had two bad colds, and he did not wish to have a corpse on his hands as a result of my bathing in the icy mountain water.

I assured him it would be all right. The next morning I got the key from the maid and filled the bath. Feeling very brave and righteous I plunged in with great abandon, but the shock took my breath away. I have never got out of a bath so quickly.

It was after this experience I resolved that while in Europe I would do as the Europeans do, and wash myself from the hand basin and bidet—I now knew what these strange contraptions in a bathroom were used for. I realised then that European countries, and Austria in particular, could not afford to heat water indiscriminately. The longer I lived there the better I understood that it was an expensive item. The extreme cold of the winter months made it a struggle for the poorer people to warm enough water for general use, let alone for baths. If I had lived in a country area in Australia I should have learnt this lesson sooner; there, during a drought every drop of water has to be conserved.

The pension was run entirely by the boys of the choir and their prefects. They waited at table and did just about everything but go into the guests' bedrooms to make the beds and clean the rooms.

The village was at the head of one of the many valleys with towering mountains rising steeply on either side. It was very, very beautiful, but the rarefied air and the feeling of being hemmed in depressed me. The only other mountains I knew at that time were the Blue Mountains near Sydney, which are nothing like the formidable, gigantic mass of the Austrian part of the Alps. I thought the Gross Glockner glacier a really remarkable sight.

My first and last adventure as a mountaineer was disastrous. Eber had talked me into climbing the Grosse Venediger, one of the highest peaks seen from the front of the pension. Someone lent me a pair of thick, heavy boots, a very warm jacket, and an alpenstock. I was told to take only the barest necessities, and this was good advice indeed. I took my toothbrush, a hairbrush, some handkerchiefs, a small piece of soap and a flannel. They went into Eber's knapsack. He was our guide and an excellent one, for he knew the area well, and had done a lot of mountain climbing. Two Yugoslav boys made up the quartet.

It took us two hours to reach the first hut. We did not rest there very long, but pressed on for another two and a half hours which brought us to the Defreggerhaus, where we were to spend the night. By this time I would have thrown the boots away gladly, and walked barefooted. My feet ached terribly, and I had a large blister on my right heel. After a very solid meal one went and found a spare bunk, which was a very hard pallet, dumped one's belongings underneath, removed one's boots, and that was it. One simply remained in one's clothes and placed the rough blankets over the lot, hoping that fatigue would do the rest. Fatigue was no help to me, and I lay there for hours unable to entice the angels to put me to sleep. I could still feel the boots on my feet, and the weight of them dragging round my ankles. The bunk got harder and harder. We were 8880 feet—or 2960 metres—high that night, and I would not have cared if I never saw a mountain or glacier again.

We were awakened at 4 a.m., and after two rolls apiece and some brown tack called coffee, we set off to see the sunrise. It was snowing heavily and there was a strong wind blowing. The temperature was four degrees below zero—I froze! We climbed the Venediger, and I have to confess to being speechless at the wonder of it as the sun came up. There we were, minute specks on this vast expanse of packed snow, high above the world, seeing something so breathtakingly beautiful. It was certainly worth the effort, but that is not to say I would ever do it again. When I saw some of the gaping chasms I was glad we were all roped together, though I felt that even this amount of security was too small.

My feet still felt as if leaden weights had been attached to them, though I had covered the blister as best I could with a handkerchief; but it was a case of anguish and enchantment, and the thought of having to traverse the distance to Hinterbichl sickened me.

We went back to the Defreggerhaus for morning coffee and more rolls, and we packed some sandwiches for the return hike. Eber took us down by another route, one far more dangerous than the ascent. It would not have been quite so frightening if the two Yugoslavs had not wanted so desperately to take back some edelweiss, that lovely, rare mountain flower. It meant leaving the track and going along perilous ledges. My feet had been dragging since we left the top, but I could not be a spoil-sport and refuse to join the hunt. As a reward for my suffering I was the one to spot the first cluster of the delicate blooms.

The descent was difficult and at times even the Yugoslavs quailed and wished that they had never heard of edelweiss. But it was a matter of no retreat, for Eber had told us that once we started the downward journey there could be no going back, and how right he was!

By the time we reached Hinterbichl I had four more big blisters on my feet. Eber teased me, as it meant that I could hardly walk, let alone dance in the evenings when the dining-room tables were pushed back and the floor was cleared. I loved dancing.

It was difficult for me to study at Hinterbichl as the only piano at the pension was in the dining room. I would pick my moments so that I did not disturb the guests. Herr Gomboz was also there, and he usually coached me late in the afternoons.

On Sundays the jazz band became a small orchestra which accompanied the Mass in the lovely old village church. I was asked to assist by playing the violin, as only one member of the band could play this instrument, which caused the overall sound to be rather thin. We rehearsed on Saturdays, and always with an audience, as the guests wandered in to listen. The first Mass was by Schubert, and it was one with which at that time I was unacquainted. I thought it most beautiful; in fact the Masses were the best part of my sojourn in the mountains.

I was very amused and interested to see the local peasantry

dressed in their native costumes for the Tyrolean Festival. The mens' hats and lederhosen, and the full, colourful dirndl skirts of the girls were most attractive as they swished and swirled on the village square. The bands and dances as well as the different customs were strange for me to accept.

While in Hinterbichl I learnt the role of the Countess in *The Marriage of Figaro*, and also Micaela in *Carmen*. The next one was Elisabeth from *Tannhäuser*, in which opera I had already sung Venus in Sydney. Then came Elsa, a *Lohengrin* role, followed by Agathe (*Der Freischütz*), and Pamina from *The Magic Flute*, so no time was lost.

The weather depressed me. It rained nearly every day, and the wind rushed up the valley. I prefer the ocean, the bush, wide open spaces and, of course, a good measure of sunshine. I felt oppressed and hemmed in. This sensation of being a prisoner was persistently with me during my whole stay in Vienna. Nevertheless, I was glad when the time came for us to return there from Hinterbichl.

The first thing I did was to report the loss of my ring and bracelet to the police. After such a lapse of time they were unable to do anything about it, and I knew the Rector wanted to let the whole episode pass into oblivion. The boy in question had not returned to the choir, though he went back after I had left the Schloss.

I had made up my mind to move and I discussed it with the Rector. He fully agreed, especially as winter was coming. I had felt the cold up in the mountains, and now the cool autumn winds were blowing through my scant apparel. The food was worse than ever and I had lost a stone and a half in weight.

I went to live as paying guest with a kind, elderly couple who lived in the Neustiftgasse. The food was a great improvement, though there were never any second helpings, and the first was too small for a hungry singer! On Sundays when their daughter and son-in-law came for lunch, the daughter would comment on the small helpings: "Give 'the Joan' more than that!" she would say indignantly.

The bath situation was worse than it had been at the Schloss.

The bath itself was swaddled in a dust-sheeet, and one had to indulge in an unveiling ceremony before having a tub. I was allowed two free baths a month; more than that cost extra money.

As I lived in the city I was able to go to the opera, ballet or drama almost every night. I heard Lotte Lehmann, Kirsten Flagstad and Elisabeth Schumann, and I went to an unforgettable performance of *Fidelio* conducted by Toscanini. In a single week I heard *Götterdammerung, Tannhäuser, Elektra, Der Rosenkavalier,* and *Don Giovanni* with Richard Tauber. I went twice to the ballet that week, and I also saw G. B. Shaw's *St. Joan.* It was a cultural orgy.

I used to sit either in the third or fourth gallery, where there were ledges for scores. Many a budding young conductor gave himself an evening's hard work "conducting" a whole opera without once looking at the stage. The admission price for the galleries was one schilling to sit and fifty groschen to stand. I stood for most performances, but I paid my schilling for the Wagner operas. I had learnt the hard way. One evening I stood throughout *Götterdammerung* and the next day I was too tired to walk to my lesson. The money saved the night before was spent on the tram fare.

Paying for everything in advance had its drawbacks. I was now being coached by one of the opera house repetiteurs, and when I caught a bad chest cold and had to miss some lessons, he refused to make them up, despite the fact that they were already paid for. In common with many Viennese, he thought every Australian or American must be wealthy. I found another, and far superior, repetiteur, whereupon the first one offered to make up the lessons. He was the only unpleasant person with whom I had dealings there. He found his way to Australia, and I saw quite a lot of him when working with the Elizabethan Theatre Trust.

At this time I had some trouble with my teeth, and the dentist to whom I went was Dr Alfred Komma. He soon became a great friend. He took me to many of the places of interest in Vienna, and these included the renowned "Heurigers" beergardens. Here, sitting under the stars, the patrons drank beer or the wine of the district and listened to the music of accordions, or small threepiece bands. If they wished, they could bring their own food, and the atmosphere got more and more lively as the night progressed.

It was Alfred who introduced me to a delicious type of savoury which I have enjoyed ever since: a fresh pear with gorgonzola cheese. I developed a taste for cheese only after I went to Vienna. In Australia I could not take to it.

Through Eber and Alfred I learnt to use the familiar form of speech "du". I had been taught never to use it except by mutual consent, as people did not like anyone, especially a foreigner, to use the familiar form loosely. This I respected, for the use of it was then a mark of special friendship.

Every Sunday I visited some place of interest, and I often went up to the Schloss to see the Rector, and the Countess Kinsky, who had been so benevolent about the use of her bathroom. The day nearly always ended by my going to the opera or a theatre.

Through Lady Gowrie's friend, Mrs Fred Payne, I met Grace Palotta. She was a retired Viennese actress who had been very popular in Australia when she played the leading role in *Floradora* at the beginning of the century. She was still very beautiful, straight-backed and graceful, with a warm personality. She took me to theatres and always gave me a good meal at a restaurant or at the excellent pension in which she lived. The meals were much appreciated by my unhappy stomach, but apart from these material gains, I greatly valued Miss Palotta's friendship, for I was still very lonely. The day came when I was completely broke— not a groschen to bless myself with. I turned to Miss Palotta, and she came to my rescue with nineteen schillings, the price of a cable to Miss Wray in Sydney. My monthly money came a week later. I knew my landlady, singing teacher, and music coach would all be wanting their money, and being unable to meet my commitments was a situation I found intolerable. No one seemed to have trust.

The inquisitiveness of the Viennese people was a severe trial to me. They wanted to know everything about you—your pedigree, your father's occupation and earning power. Personal questions always embarrass me, though in this case I think the interest of the Viennese was probably genuine. They were so animated and pleasure loving, and such good mixers. Above all they loved music and art, and were only too happy to help all students. Doctors and dentists charged only a nominal fee once they knew you were a student, and one dentist refused payment altogether for a small filling he had done for me.

Shopping in Vienna was never a happy experience. Just as I found it difficult to say "No" to a party invitation which I did not want to accept, so did I find myself in a quandary as to how to retreat from a shop. I knew what I wanted, liked or disliked, but I resented being pressed to buy something I knew I should never like or wear. The shop assistants followed one to the door trying to make a sale, pestering one to buy. Bargaining in the markets was a different matter. This was expected; in fact to force the price down a little gave the customer prestige.

Walking on the cobblestones wore my shoes out quicker than anything else. My feet had never troubled me until I went to Vienna. After walking mile upon mile round golf courses back home in Australia, it seemed silly that a few weeks of pavements and cobblestones could cause my feet to be so troublesome. I had always been taught to buy good shoes and to go to good dentists. Neither of these admirable tenets could I follow at that time. I knew that every penny had been donated for my study. I see by my monthly statements, which I wrote out meticulously and sent back to Sydney to Miss Wray, that shoes were the most recurring item. They seemed to fall to pieces after a few weeks.

My feet always became icy cold when I sat to learn by heart. A Norwegian student who admired my last remaining pair of flat-heeled shoes that I had brought from Sydney, asked me if I would like to swap them for her footwarmers. I had never heard of such things before, but the idea of having warm feet appealed to me enormously, and I agreed to the swap. To put both feet into the extraordinary article, and to feel the warmth generating, was sheer luxury, though the appearance of the thing was unfortunate. It looked like a lovely tabby cat, but the Norwegian student assured me it was the pelt of some animal the name of which I did not know. After that I felt happier about using it.

Talking of pelts, Miss Palotta advised me to buy a cheap fur coat. I felt the cold terribly, and I had suffered several bad colds. I really needed something to keep me warm in the chill winds of the long winter months. I wrote to Miss Wray accordingly. The reaction in Australia was not favourable, as the word fur meant mink, sable, or ermine.

Miss Palotta took me to a furrier who kept a very prosaic stock. He found a very cheap fur coat which fitted me, but heaven alone knows what the skins were! It served a very useful purpose, even though it fell to pieces, bit by bit, after three years.

My overall view of Vienna was one of sadness. I found the baroque architecture fussy and overdone, and the Viennese people, despite their exterior brightness, were really living a life of which they were ashamed. After the 1914–1918 War, they had been forced to abandon their former splendour and elegance, and to adopt a much lower standard of living. There were beggars everywhere, and they would follow you and cling to you because they knew you were foreign.

The lustre of former royalty was now tarnished. The city reposed like an old, stately lady, living on the dreams of a past glorious world. She was trying to reorientate herself to the humdrum, workaday situation in which she now found herself.

It depressed me. I was never happy in Vienna. I felt encircled, locked in, oppressed by the ghosts of the past. The theatre and my work kept me from dwelling on the miseries confronting me daily.

The music was a constant source of joy and wonder, a veritable treasure-chest the discovery of which helped me to keep a balanced outlook. It was filled with music I had never heard, operas I had never seen, and which were now unfolding as I pulled them out of the chest and examined them as if they were rare gems. Someone said to me at that time: "Your bones must be satiated with music of every kind!" It was true.

A concert agent, to whom I had given an audition, became very interested in my voice. He was honest enough to say that he could not do anything for me at that stage, but he very decently sent me free tickets for orchestral concerts and recitals. After my day's work, I lived in another world from the moment the curtain went

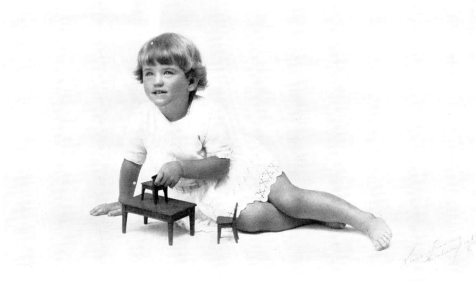

Above: The author,
aged 2½ years

Left: The author in 1959

On the verandah of the Royal Sydney Golf Club after winning N.S.W. State
Junior Championship, 1930

Following the first London recital at the Aeolian Hall, 16 November 1938

Going on Ambulance Duty during the war with Pippo in bicycle basket

Above: In the Artists' Room at the Royal Albert Hall, 1954. *Left to right:* Sander Gorlinsky, Dame Alicia Markova, Beniamino Gigli and the author

Below: The author with her parents and Walter Süsskind (*left*)

Above: Acknowledging the thanks of Miss Leonora Wray following four recitals given in Sydney and Melbourne to raise funds to send a team of young golfers overseas, 1949

Below: The author singing at a Sydney Town Hall meeting to open a fund for the Opera House. Geoffrey Parsons at the piano. *Seated l. to r.:* Joern Utzon (whose design was chosen), S. Haviland (Chairman of Opera House Appeal Committee and Under Secretary for Local Government), Sir Richard Boyer (Chairman, Australian Broadcasting Commission), J. J. Cahill (Premier), H. Jensen (Lord Mayor), P. Morton (Leader, State Opposition), Professor S. H. Roberts (Vice Chancellor, Sydney University), Mr Andersson (joint architect), 1957

With Eugene Ormandy at Carnegie Hall, New York, following a concert with
the Philadelphia Orchestra

The author, 1956

up or the concert began. My taste changed as time passed, but I count myself lucky indeed that I was able to hear the best.

In November Sir Walford Selby arranged for Bruno Walter to hear me. The great conductor could not have been nicer.

"You have an unusual voice of great attraction," he said. "Get in touch with me next season." I regret to say I did not do so.

I saw snow falling for the first time. The trees looked unbelievably beautiful, and the branches were weighed down almost to the point of snapping off. I watched the sun's rays glistening so brightly on the pure white of the snow, and I had a mad desire to dive into it. But when I saw some boys playing snowballs and having a rough and tumble, I thought better of it.

My first Christmas away from home was sad and strange. I had been asked to help the small English choir at the Church near the British Embassy, as a big effort was being made for Christmas Day because the Duke of Windsor was to be present. We rehearsed on Christmas Eve, and everything went according to plan on the 25th. Sir Walford Selby read the first Lesson, and the Duke read the second. The choir managed to keep together in between.

Lady Selby took me back to the Legation. She gave me a lovely handbag for Christmas, and I had a little talk with the Duke. He had a natural easy manner, which made you feel that he really enjoyed talking to you.

Miss Palotta had invited me to dinner. There was a gale blowing and it was snowing heavily, but luckily the trams were still running, so I was able to catch one back to within a short walk of my digs. So Christmas had come and gone, and I had felt a great nostalgia for my homeland, family and friends.

I saw the New Year in with the son and daughter of my singing teacher. I had an uneasy feeling that I was not making any progress and that I should soon have to make a change, but of course this was not the time to mention it.

The next big event was being taken by Lady Selby to Vienna's most exclusive couturier. She realised that I had no suitable evening dress to wear when I was to sing at a large party at the

E

British Legation for the Duke of Windsor. She swept aside my protests and there was I, a raw poor Australian, transplanted into the world of High Society. I was intimidated by the owner of the salon and by the models, and I would have liked to say "yes" to the first gown offered and make my escape. But Lady Selby insisted on the colour I liked, which was powder blue, and she was adamant that the style should be simple, with a slight train. The ultimate dress was one of the loveliest I have ever had. It was a beautiful blue material, with a shimmering silver effect.

It was also my luck that a delightful New Zealand lady, Mrs Allan, was visiting Vienna at that time. Miss Palotta brought her to hear me sing while I was having a lesson. When Mrs Allan heard about the concert for the Duke of Windsor, and the dress Lady Selby had given me, she insisted on presenting me with shoes to match the dress. Accepting charity was not easy for me, but both these kind, diplomatic ladies made me feel that they were only giving me what was due.

The event was a happy one for me. It was my first solo concert; almost a recital. The Embassy was packed with people who had come to meet the Duke of Windsor. The programme I had prepared was mixed and suitable for all tastes, but designed to please the Duke: the most popular of my group of English songs was Eric Coates' "The Green Hills o' Somerset". The evening went off splendidly, and people commented that my dress looked elegant and becoming. I felt a million dollars in it, and it gave me added courage.

I had a long talk with the Duke when the concert was over. He asked a lot about Lord and Lady Gowrie, and he spoke of Sydney, which of course pleased me greatly.

I was having another worrying moneyless patch. The monthly amount had not arrived from Sydney, and the day after the concert at the British Legation, where I had looked and felt so grand, I had exactly two schillings in my pocket.

It was such a relief when the money came, after a week of anxious waiting. I have always detested owing money, and even today I pay accounts too quickly without stopping to check them, with the result that I have on occasion paid them twice.

I found through the student grapevine that I was paying too much for my digs. The cost of them was 240 Austrian schillings a month, with an additional 8 schillings to the maid, which my friends said was unheard of. Miss Palotta came to the rescue.

"You must go and live with my friend the Baroness, Joan. She has a good apartment in the Theresianumgasse. There are other paying guests there, and you will have a nice room," she said.

"Is there a bathroom?"

"Of course."

The Baroness's daughter V. lived with her, and sometimes I was invited to their small sitting-room at the back. Their rooms could be shut off from the dining-room and guest rooms. I met several young Hungarians, Yugoslavs and Greeks in that small sitting-room. They talked of politics, and seemed to be very anti-Hitler. I thought at the time that perhaps they did "protest too much", but it was very interesting.

All the time it was becoming more and more obvious to me that I should have to make a change of singing teacher. I remember queuing for a seat at a Furtwängler concert (under whose baton I was eventually to sing), and then being taken by Lady Selby to the opera especially to hear Richard Tauber in *Giuditta* (little did I know that within two years I would be singing with him); during the interval I felt I must discuss my doubts about my singing teacher with Lady Selby, and she agreed that I must make a change.

My teacher had been kind, but she was also very shrewd, and I knew that she was hoping to obtain publicity through my increasing activities and the interest of Lady Selby. She also had the sense to recognise the great potentiality of my voice. She was not one of the best known teachers by any means, but doubtless Rector Schnitt had sent me to her for good reasons.

I knew that the extensions of my voice were not developing as they should, and I could see no point in spending money to remain vocally static. It was a "tearful break-away", but it had to be done.

For a time I went to nobody, but listened and asked questions of other students when we met at the opera.

I gave an audition to the Vienna radio, and to my surprise they booked me for two performances. Both were during the off-peak listening time, but it meant that I was given a hearing, and I received encouraging results. I also gave an audition to Starka, an agent who placed me on his books. The desire to earn money was uppermost in my mind.

I had an enthralling new musical experience at this time. It was a performance of *Parsifal*. I queued for hours to get into either the third or fourth galleries, and I was lucky to get a seat in the back row of the fourth gallery. No opera had moved me as much as this one. I quote from my diary: "I felt as though I were in a church. The tenor was dreadful, but even he could not detract from the wonderful orchestration. It is like one glorious extended symphony." I still prefer to hear the music of *Parsifal* without the voices.

I finally chose a Polish singing teacher of great repute who had allegedly taught Lotte Lehmann. She was enthusiastic about my voice, and said she could make me a world-beater. In her time she must have been a great voice moulder, and she struck immediately upon my weakness—a lack of agility. If she had kept her appointments she would have been ideal, but she kept her pupils waiting for anything up to an hour and a half for a lesson, after which one was liable to be told that she was too tired to teach any more. I stuck this for a while and then gave up, as money and time were so important.

The hand of Fate was moving again. News came to me that Lady Gowrie wished me to go to London for the Coronation of George VI. In the meantime my agent got me an audition for the Director of the Aussig Opera House, and I was signed up on the spot. This was marvellous; on my return from London I would begin to earn my living at last.

On 9 May I left for London by train, travelling third class in uncomfortable, overcrowded conditions, but this mattered far less than the fact that my luggage cost as much as I did! I had with me my golf clubs, a violin, a portable typewriter, a gramophone and several records, and I would not be parted from any of them.

The thrill of arriving in London for the first time was again dampened by the lack of money. My fund must have been getting very low, for no cheque had arrived before I left Vienna.

Lady Gowrie had arranged for the Victoria League in London to give me a ticket for the Coronation, and this was awaiting me at the bank. She had also arranged for me to stay with a family in Chelsea until I could find suitable accommodation, which I set about doing immediately.

Some people in Australia may still remember a Scottish tenor, Robert Scott, who had been doing quite well in Sydney until he decided to try his luck in London. We had kept in touch, and I now asked him to help me find some digs. He fixed for me to see a room in Earl's Court the day after I arrived. The terraced houses looked pretty grim to me, but Bob assured me it was a nice district and that the prices were reasonable, especially in view of the fact that there was a big demand for accommodation because of the Coronation.

He was right. Mrs Jones, the jovial landlady, showed me a front room with an old upright piano, very out of tune and said I could sing and practise if I wished. My bed and breakfast would cost me seventeen shillings and sixpence a week. I moved in that day, and I found Mr and Mrs Jones to be the friendliest people I had as yet met on my travels. Their warmth of character offset the drabness of the surroundings, and theirs was the only house in which I was ever allowed to practise.

I was struck by the difference between these homes and those in Vienna, where even in the poorer districts the apartment houses had parquet flooring and a heavier type of furniture. Cheap carpets and linoleum, and flimsy furniture seemed to be the London equivalent. I had been intrigued by the double doors and windows in the continental houses and I missed them, even though the British winters were rarely as cold as those of the majority of European countries. Central heating was not at all general in England at that time, and one felt the cold much more than on the continent.

Mrs Jones called me at 3.30 the next morning as I had to be in my seat in the Mall by 6 a.m. for the Coronation procession. She had packed some sandwiches for me, and her husband George very kindly drove me to the nearest point and showed me where to go from there. I had a long, long wait, but when the procession eventually passed by I was speechless with admiration at the splendour of the pageantry in all its rich colours. It was a very exciting occasion for me.

I went to bed early that night, and the next morning, as usual— bath trouble! The bath was in the kitchen, and it was covered by a board which served as an additional table top! I had to wait until the kitchen was vacated and the board removed and placed outside in a small backyard. There was no room for it inside. I had a fit of giggles as I sat in the bath, for there was no lock on the kitchen door, and George could easily have come in, having forgotten that the P.G. was in residence. This bathroom was the highlight of them all.

My fairy godmother, Lady Gowrie, had arranged for me to meet Mrs Fred Payne and Ivie Price. This link with Sydney and my fund was a happy one. I went to lunch or dinner with both ladies on several occasions.

I had been invited to play in a big golf event at Beaconsfield Golf Club in Buckinghamshire. All the members of the British team who had visited Australia in 1935 were there. It was grand to see their Captain-Manager the late Mrs Hodson, known to us all as "Hoddie", and Mrs J. B. (Pat) Walker, a most vivacious and lovable person. Pam Barton was playing great golf and attracting large galleries, and Isabel Greenlees and Phil Wade were as impeccably dressed as always. Finally "Wee Jessie" Anderson, now Mrs George Valentine, completed the reunion.

I won a prize that day. It was a most useful leather bag for taking a change of clothes and shoes to golf. I used it for many years.

For a week I was a typical tourist in and around London. Armed with bus and underground maps I found my way about and went to see as many places of interest as possible. The Maze at Hampton Court intrigued me, the Tower of London saddened me, but Kew Gardens in its glorious spring colours was pure joy.

I queued at the Royal Albert Hall in order to hear Gigli. This was an expense I could ill afford—I missed the courtesy of the free seats I had had in Vienna. How encouraging it would have been if I had known that later in my career I myself should sing with Gigli in that same hall, and how intimately I should come to know the backstage regions through the many performances I gave there. As it was, I marvelled at the tiers of boxes and the dark red plush, and I did wonder, just vaguely, if I should ever sing there.

So many generous friends of Lady Gowrie's entertained me. Her sister, Mrs Fleischmann, had me to lunch at her London home, and offered me the use of her large, beautifully furnished drawing room and concert grand piano. The Dowager Viscountess Hambledon and her music-loving son, the Hon. James Smith, were wonderful to me. Mrs Payne took me to the Derby, where I won a much needed £2. I was taken to Covent Garden Opera House to see *Tosca* with Lawrence Tibbett as Scarpia, and through Australia House I was given an invitation to a Garden Party at Runnymede.

Clothes played a minor role at that stage in my career, and I often wonder how I looked when going to luncheons and dinners! I needed all my money for lessons and buying music, which was quite a large expense. Soon enough my musical appreciation would be severely curtailed in London. The price of seats for opera and concerts was far beyond my means, even the cheapest seats. Mrs Payne had taken me to Glyndebourne, and when I heard two friends discussing the cost, I realised it was no place for young students.

My financial position was very delicate again. I had to find new digs, as Vi and George Jones had only let their front room because of the shortage of accommodation in London during the Coronation festivities.

It was a relief to pay at the end of the week instead of monthly in advance. Nevertheless, I had not received an allowance from Sydney, and I was sick with worry. I remembered that Andrew Reid had said that if I found myself really short during the duration of the fund, I could go to his bank in the City of London and money would be advanced to me.

The day came when I had only sixpence left, and this I used for my fare to the City and Mr Reid's bank. They handed me ten pounds without question. I paid my rent and found another room in the Old Brompton Road. This was a better address than my former one. It was a properly run establishment with several rooms and, thank goodness, adequate bathrooms. The cost was thirty shillings per week for bed and breakfast.

Relations of Lady Gowrie's, the Scotts, invited me to spend a weekend with them. Mrs Scott sent me a return ticket from Paddington, a courtesy which impressed me greatly. Their large house, rather like an old castle, nestled in a fold of the Cotswolds, and was built of the local stone.

I was intrigued to find upon arrival that my bag and its meagre contents were wafted away, and later when I was taken to my room, everything had been unpacked and put away.

The following morning the youngest daughter, Barbara, who is still one of my dearest friends, took me to play golf. After lunch we all went to the Duke of Beaufort's magnificent home to watch a rehearsal for one of the forthcoming pageants which were so popular in those days. That night my one and only evening dress had been placed on the bed for me to wear. I bathed and then looked at it for some time. I thought I might look overdressed, so I wore my best short day frock. When I arrived downstairs I found that my host and two friends were in dinner jackets, and Mrs Scott and her daughters in long dresses. They quickly put me at ease by drawing me into the conversation, and the evening passed swiftly and pleasantly.

The next day we played tennis; it was my first game in two years and I loved it. Later we went to visit the stud and parts of the large estate. That evening when going to my bedroom I noticed that my short dress had been placed on the bed. I never saw the maid. I decided to go against her again—I wore my long dress. Of course I arrived downstairs to find the men in tweeds and the ladies in short frocks: if only someone had told me, "Do

put on whatever the maid leaves out for you, because she *knows*!"
The next morning I travelled back to London a wiser woman.

An important meeting took place on that Monday. Mrs Payne introduced me to Dino Borgioli and his wife. Dino, as he insisted on being called, was a famous tenor, and after he heard me sing, he became very enthusiastic about my voice, and said he would like to teach me. I discussed it with Mrs Payne. I knew that Mrs Borgioli handled all Dino's affairs, and Mrs Payne undertook to tell her about my meagre finances. A sum was agreed upon which seemed very high to me, but I wrote to Miss Wray in Sydney telling her what had been fixed. I began lessons immediately and a few days later my allowance arrived, so I felt easier about the situation.

My social life was still flourishing, as so many friends of Lady Gowrie's invited me for meals, or to the opera at Covent Garden. Barbara Scott took me to the tennis at Wimbledon, and the golfer, Enid Wilson, whom I had recently met, took me to play golf at Sandy Lodge. She is a fine conversationalist—a very erudite person. My health greatly improved with all this exercise and good food such as I had always been used to.

It is poetic justice to record at this point that when Ivie Price invited me for a long weekend at her family home in Bucks, I wore whatever the maid put out for me!

I was having four singing lessons a week from Dino. After a few weeks I began to have doubts about his teaching, as my throat muscles tired easily. This worried Dino, but the trouble soon passed and the voice began to develop.

Mrs Payne arranged for me to audition for the impresario, Harold Holt. He explained that he normally engaged only established artists, but that he would like to have me on his books for the future. He introduced me to several musicians, and gave me tickets for any concerts he was promoting.

Lady Hambledon arranged for me to give an audition at the Old Vic. She thoughtfully sent her car and chauffeur to take me there, and Joan Singleton, who usually accompanied Lady Hambledon's son, the Hon. James Smith, played for me.

The highlight of the Old Vic audition was meeting the dynamic Lilian Baylis. She offered me a contract.

"I should like to have you here, dear," she said to me. "You have just the sort of voice I need. I can't pay very much, but it would be good experience for you."

"I should love to work here, Miss Baylis. But you see, I'm under contract in Vienna. I could only be here for short periods."

Miss Baylis was very understanding. "Oh well, it can't be helped, dear. Never mind. Just let me know if you change your plans. I should love to have you." She died that same year, so I never saw her again.

Three days later I sang for Sir Thomas Beecham. I always loathed giving auditions, and on this occasion I felt very conscious of my inexperience. Sir Thomas said very little and I felt very little, but he made a note about me.

I had taken out a British driving licence, which I still retain in its original red folder. The Borgiolis asked me if I would help them by sharing the driving of their car to Salzburg, where Dino was to sing in *Falstaff*. Pat used to get tired, and both she and Dino thought it a good idea for me to come along and help, so that I could also continue my lessons. I was all for it, as it meant a free journey, and a reduction in fees for my lessons. It was an interesting journey through Rheims to Strasbourg, through the Black Forest to Ulm, then via München to Salzburg.

Toscanini was conducting *Falstaff*, in which Dino was singing, and I was able to attend all the rehearsals and every performance. It was an electrifying experience and I met the great conductor many times, though I never actually sang for him. Bruno Walter was there too, conducting *Don Giovanni*.

I was lucky enough to work with Maestro Alberto Erede for two weeks. He put me through the role of Violetta in *La Traviata*. He was meticulous over the smallest details, and he was no clock-watcher either. He went on and on—time was of no account; only the music. A session with him was most stimulating. I also worked with another great coach, Erich Leinsdorf. Both he and

Erede became famous conductors, and I learnt more in half an hour with either of them than I did in months with former coaches. Thus, attending performances and rehearsals at the Festspielhaus, and with singing lessons and daily coaching, I found this a golden opportunity to pack in a tremendous amount of musical knowledge.

Falstaff was one of the highlights of the entire season for me. Stabile sang the name part, and John Brownlee, the renowned Australian baritone, was also in the cast. It was a great pleasure for me to meet him. Many years later he and his charming wife entertained me in New York, and John attended my recitals.

I was very much on the side lines, but after I had met Percy Hemming, who was such a power at the Royal Opera House, Covent Garden, I was highly tickled to see how various singers fluttered round the great one, in the hope of being engaged by him. In fact I saw much that amused and astonished me—such jealousies and bitterness among the artists.

Acting again as chauffeur, I drove the Borgiolis to Venice. We passed through the Dolomites which I thought were beautiful, and which I longed to sit and paint. In Venice I had my first ride in a gondola, but we did not stay long there as our ultimate destination was Florence. It had been quite a long journey from Salzburg, and I realised that I was a great help to Pat Borgioli in relieving her of the driving. She had plenty to do without the extra fatigue of sitting for hours at the wheel.

I was housed in a small room in a pension run by Dino's family. It was cheap after London—all meals were inclusive for the equivalent of £2 per week. I began to work straight away with a Maestro Cortini. When the Borgiolis wished to go anywhere I accompanied them as driver, so once again I was lucky enough to see a lot of the surrounding countryside. We went to Via Reggio to visit Puccini's home on Torre del Lago.

Dino was singing Alfredo in *La Traviata* during the Florence Festival, so my lessons were somewhat spasmodic. The funny thing was that Pat, when we were in London, had made me promise that I would never tell anyone that he was teaching me. It had seemed very odd to me, but I had given my word.

Meanwhile I was learning Italian, and relearning Italian operas in their original language instead of in German.

When I had been in Florence for two weeks my agent in Vienna wrote telling me that I must report to Aussig by a certain date. I told Dino . . . He flew into a Latin rage, and said it would be quite impossible. I had never been spoken to in such a way, neither did I think he had the right to impose his will on me. I was furious.

I went down with a severe chill. The doctor put me on a diet of dry biscuits and rice, and though I survived the ordeal, my voice was very sick for at least three weeks. Once again I was having great doubts about Dino as a teacher. Despite my recent illness, I knew my voice was not as it should be. I have always known instinctively that nature is the surest, safest guide to voice training. If the cords become inflamed or the muscles tire easily, the voice is not being correctly produced. I had reached a critical moment.

Pat then announced that she had decided to leave the car in Florence and return to London with Dino by train. I had a long discussion with Dino, who said that I must also return to London, where he would continue with my lessons. I knew that I should return to Vienna, where I was due to begin my professional career, and where I should be earning money instead of spending it from the fund. There was my luggage, too. I had left a lot of it with Alfred Komma.

The decision came from London. I was informed by Mrs Payne that I must return there, and that was that.

I had loved the Art Galleries of Florence and much that I had heard and seen there, but I was surprised by the behaviour at the opera performances. The audience would clap, shout and boo until they had brought the opera to a standstill. For at least ten minutes after the tenor had entered, the conductor and orchestra had to wait until the uproar had subsided. I had felt embarrassed for Dino and the other singers, but their conduct taught me a lot and prepared me for what I saw later in Naples and the southern opera houses. There they had extra tenors and sopranos waiting already made up in case the public did not like the advertised cast!

If they liked the singers they were generous in their approval, and shouts of "Bravo!" "Bene!" or "Simpatico!" would fill the theatre. The audiences were musically educated, and any unnecessary display of vocal gymnastics displeased them. "That's enough —now come off it!" was shouted to a soprano who held a note too long in *Rigoletto*. A tenor with an unfortunate top register called forth a candid comment: "Stop him! He croaks!" Clearly the artists had to do well or give up.

I travelled third class back to London. Evidently Dino had stipulated that I should not return to Vienna. It was all very difficult, as I had contracts to fulfil. I met Lady Selby again and told her of my plans to return to Vienna, but, much to my surprise and dismay, I was now told that I must return to Florence. I knew that the Borgiolis had requested this, and that they had once again gone over my head in the matter of my career and the way it should be run. Mrs Payne, who was one of the first contributors to my fund in Sydney, and who had been so helpful to me in London, felt that Dino was the best judge as to where I should go. I was sad at the thought of leaving England and my friends. I loved the country, as I still do.

So once again I was on my travels, going back to Florence by the cheap route via Dieppe. I had a little time in Paris on the way, where I walked about and saw as much as I could, wearing out my shoes as usual in the process. Back in Florence it was cold and my arm ached. I wrote in my diary that I should like to stay in bed all the time, as the weather was too cold for me!

I went again to study with Maestro Cortini, and I took up my Italian lessons once more. Christmas came—a strange one, but at least they served "plum pud" at the pension. I had to wait until midday for a bath, as the water was never hot earlier than that. Maestro Cortini fell ill and was unable to work for two weeks, which was a terrible waste of my last bit of money. It was a confused time in which I felt I was being pushed hither and thither, often to no point and without any consideration for what I myself wanted. Then, early in February, a contract came for me to sing at Glyndebourne. It had come through Harold Holt.

This contract did not state any conditions at all. I wrote to the management at once, asking whether I was to be given small parts or whether I should be understudying, and saying that I should like a specified outline of what would be required of me. I also wrote to Harold Holt telling him of my reaction to the contract.

Next was a letter from Pat Borgioli, telling me to accept the Glyndebourne contract. I did not reply to her until I had heard from Glyndebourne. The letter soon came, and it informed me that I should be understudying the roles of Donna Elvira in *Don Giovanni*, and possibly Pamina in *The Magic Flute*. Apart from that, my permanent position would be in the chorus.

Despite the Borgiolis, and their possible influence with the Glyndebourne Opera, I refused outright. In Vienna my voice was ranked as worthy of main roles in small theatres, graduating to the prominent opera houses. This I believed to be the only sane procedure. I felt that if I had gone into the chorus at Glyndebourne I should almost certainly have been a chorister for ever.

This disagreement with the Borgiolis caused an irreparable breach between us. Dino was a great singer and musician. He played the piano entirely "by ear" and it was a pleasure to hear him strumming arias and songs. In common with many artists, he had little knowledge of finance, so it was left to his wife to manage his affairs. I often wondered if he knew what fees were charged for lessons; in fact, I am sure he was ignorant about this subject. It would be fair to say that I learnt a tremendous amount about voices, singers, and life in general through the Borgiolis.

I made up my mind and returned to Vienna. I signed on for two years at the Vienna Volksoper, and started work immediately. One very satisfactory clause in my contract was that I could have permission to go to London to sing if I received any offers I wanted to take up. The only conditions were that I should not be away longer than three weeks, and that I should give adequate notice of my departure. This I thought was very fair.

I have never rehearsed as hard anywhere as I did in Vienna. Our pay was very little, but we were learning our art, so it did not matter. We began at 9 a.m. and worked through, with only a coffee break, until 2.15 p.m. Then we were free until 5 p.m., when we started again and worked until 7.15, or longer. The rehearsals were divided between music and production, and would be either in rehearsal room or on stage. After rehearsing, we would snatch a sandwich, and then slip into the artists' box and watch a performance. On Sundays, if I were not scheduled for a performance, I would go out with Alfred Komma.

My operatic debut was as Nedda in *I Pagliacci*. The critics were enthusiastic, and most constructive. This made me aware, for the first time, of the difference between a knowledgeable critic and the poseur, who becomes carried away by his own eloquence and writes flowing, meaningless phrases to show a mastery of the pen rather than a knowledge of music.

After Nedda came Martha, in the opera of that name by Flotow. I loved the music of this delightful light opera, especially as I was able to sing "'Tis the last Rose of Summer". It was a snag to have to sing it in German. Constanze in Mozart's *Die Entführung* followed. I never liked this role. It was vocally unsuited to me, and the plot did not appeal.

A political cloud developed during this period. Hitler and his hordes invaded Austria in a bloodless coup. The first important change in our lives was that on reaching the stage door, instead of the usual greeting "Grüss Gott" flung gaily to the stage door keeper, we now had to say "Heil Hitler" and raise our right hands accordingly. We all found it hard to remember.

Then an order was issued for all Jews to put boards outside their shops, stating that they were Jewish owned. Most of the shops in the Kärntnerstrasse seemed to have these gruesome boards on display. Streets that had been normal and attractive became strange and ugly.

I was overjoyed when Lady Gowrie wrote telling me she was going to London. The fund had almost dwindled away, and she was worried about it. I could exist on my opera salary, but that was all. I got permission to go to London at the end of May.

Lord and Lady Gowrie were staying with relations at 29,

Berkeley Square, a gracious, elegant house which has since been demolished. It was lovely to see them and tell them all I had done since I left Australia.

Lady Gowrie knew my financial position, and she was so concerned that she rallied all her Australian friends in London and invited them to a party at "29", at which I sang, and gathered in more credit to the fund. Miss Wray was also busy at the other end of the world keeping up interest. I made some records and sent them out to her, and they were played to supporters of the fund. My friends Mr Reid and Mrs Payne were also present at the party at "29".

Dino Borgioli was in London, and pressure from him as well as from my friends caused me to agree to take some more lessons. I begrudged the money, as it was so hard to get and seemed to disappear so quickly, but I did not want to go against the people helping me, for they were also keen supporters of Dino's. Maestro Erede was conducting at Glyndebourne, and I was lucky to have him coach me during this short visit. He took me through The Countess in *Figaro* and Donna Elvira in *Don Giovanni*.

I was very sad when Lord and Lady Gowrie left to return to Australia. I felt I had lost my anchorage, but I soon went back to Vienna and continued my operatic work. I had now graduated to the State Opera.

I had not been back there long when I received a cable from Harold Holt asking me to return to London, so once more I made the journey to England. When I arrived, I found that I was to give an audition at Covent Garden. I was not very pleased about it as I felt sure it was a waste of time, but I gave the audition and prepared for my return to Europe. Then I was told that an audition had been arranged with Stanford Robinson, a young and highly capable conductor on the staff of the B.B.C. Ivor Newton accompanied me. The introduction to "Robbie", as he was called, proved to be one of the most fruitful of my career. As a result of the audition, I received a contract from the B.B.C. to sing two operatic arias with orchestra. I began rehearsing with Ivor at once.

Then came a contract to sing in *Messiah* at the Queen's Hall
with Sir Thomas Beecham. So he had not forgotten! It was a
pleasant surprise.

During this early part of September 1938, the threat of war was
gathering fast. All my friends advised me to stay in London until
the situation resolved itself one way or the other. On 28 September it was announced that Neville Chamberlain was to have a
meeting with Hitler, Mussolini and Daladier the next day. That
night London was given an anti-aircraft and searchlight display.

I was astonished that the situation was so serious. The Austrian
newspapers had certainly given little indication of what was going
on outside the Nazi-controlled areas, and I was so busy with my
work that it was hard to realise that the political situation could
upset my plans. September 30 and all was well. Neville Chamberlain made his famous remark: "Peace in our time." Ignorant
though I was of world affairs, I wrote in my diary: "I wonder! I
feel that Britain is showing a weak front, and we have not been
told all that Germany is getting from this agreement."

I soon forgot the war clouds. A telegram came from Vienna
reminding me of my date for return, and I replied that I had extra
engagements to fulfil. The day came for my B.B.C. performance,
and again I wrote in my diary: "It evidently went well, and
Stanford Robinson very delighted."

I was surprised at the amount of fan mail and the number of
congratulatory telephone calls I received (and a sweet telegram
from Margaret Bannerman) as a result of the broadcast. I took
myself to hear the Busch Ensemble play a Brandenburg concerto
at the Queen's Hall. It was my way of celebrating my first B.B.C.
appearance.

After the broadcast Hughie Green offered me a music hall tour.
I liked him very much and I needed the money, but nothing
would make me accept this kind of engagement.

A memorable meeting at this time was with Mr Tillett, of the
agents Ibbs and Tillett. I was asked to give an audition for him at
the Wigmore Hall, and this I did. He was very kind and charming,
and although he knew I was under contract to Harold Holt he

F

said that his agency could get me work which he would put through the Holt Agency, and they would split the commission. His advice was invaluable at that time, and it also served me well in the years to come.

Things happened very rapidly, and my agreement with the Vienna Staatsoper was being stretched to its limits. Lady Hambledon said that she would back me in a recital if Harold Holt would put it on. He agreed, and the recital was planned very quickly. My choice of accompanist was Ivor Newton, but I was disappointed to learn that he was not available. The services of Gerald Moore were booked, in which I was very lucky. Both Gerald and Ivor were so easy to work with. Gerald was absolutely imperturbable, no matter what happened. His sense of humour stayed uppermost even when the water pipes burst in his Marylebone flat, which impressed me greatly. His wife Enid had the same tolerant attitude to life, and I liked them both enormously. I met Gerald for the first time in a bad fog, my second experience of a pea-souper. We both agreed that we looked better in a fog!

The recital took place at the Aeolian Hall in Bond Street, which is now used by the B.B.C. as a studio. It was my first real test. Harold Holt came into the artists' room just before I was due to go on. He was smoking, which was no help in that small, airless room.

"I don't like your hair, Joan," he said. "You should have it frizzed up a bit, or something. And that dress—it doesn't do anything for you."

I looked at him and I looked at my dress, which was pale blue and bought off the peg in a large department store.

"Thank you very much," I said. "You're really most encouraging."

He realised that he had not been very tactful.

"I'm sorry," he said penitently. "I'm over-anxious, maybe. It's just that I want you to make a big hit. I suppose you haven't got a bit of jewellery you could wear, have you?"

"I'm afraid not." I thought of the ring and bracelet which had been stolen from me in Vienna. "I haven't got anything real, and I don't like imitation."

"A bit of paste wouldn't have come amiss," said Harold. "But you'll do."

With this I went out to give my first London recital, hoping that I should be judged on my performance rather than on my appearance. The hall was full. Ivie Price was there, and several friend's of Lady Gowrie's. Gerald Moore was a pillar of strength and encouragement. I am sure I sang in a daze and I know I was very glad when it was over.

The critics were very kind. At last I could begin to feel that I was making progress, for a contract came from the B.B.C. to sing Nedda—*I Pagliacci* again!—but in English. Robbie, bless him, had been true to his word and had proved that he really did like my voice. Rehearsals began immediately, and it was no trouble to learn the part in English after having sung it in German. Harold got me what he called a "fill-up" engagement to help pay the rent, as he said. It was at a Press and Advertising Dinner at the Connaught Rooms, and my fellow artists were Paul Robeson and the duo pianists, Vronsky and Babin. Two days later was the first performance of *I Pagliacci*, so my days were full. There was another live broadcast of the opera two days later again.

My success was almost too much for me to comprehend. Another B.B.C. contract followed, for excerpts from *Francesca da Rimini*.

During my spare time Molly, Lady Sanderson, took me to hear a recital given by Elena Gerhardt, and to a performance of *Messiah* at the Kingsway Hall. This was of great interest to me, as my debut with Sir Thomas Beecham in *Messiah* was only a short time away. Through Sir Thomas I met the delightful singer Lisa Perli—Dora Labette. She had a soprano voice of beautiful lyric quality, and she very generously took time out of her busy life to show me how Sir Thomas liked the soprano part sung.

I had a piano rehearsal with him, and the orchestral rehearsal was held on the Friday evening before the Saturday matinée. My fellow artists were all well-established in the profession. They were Muriel Brunskill, Webster Booth, and Norman Walker.

The rehearsal began on time, but after about half an hour I was fascinated to see that the hall was filling with people, who all seemed to have tickets. I thought that maybe Sir Thomas permitted rehearsal tickets to be distributed. Then I noticed that his secretary, standing down there at auditorium level, was trying to attract the great man's attention. At last she succeeded. He looked down at her witheringly.

"I have told you on *no* account am I to be disturbed during a rehearsal."

Undaunted the secretary pressed on. "But Sir Thomas, something dreadful's happened! There's been a double booking and the hall's been hired out for a concert. These people are the audience!"

Sir Thomas's beard twitched as he looked at his unhappy secretary. He spoke calmly and deliberately. "This hall has been booked for my rehearsal of 'The Messiah' every Friday evening for the past hundred years," he said. He cast a quelling eye at the rapidly filling hall, put down his baton and turned to us.

"There will be no performance of 'The Messiah' tomorrow," he said, and strode majestically off the podium. For all his regal progress his beard was twitching madly.

The quartet of soloists followed him off the stage to our dressing room. To me it seemed quite unbelievable—a nightmare situation in which I was just a small entity. Sir Thomas's secretary came in.

"Sir Thomas says he's sorry the performance has to be cancelled," she said apologetically. "I suppose you might as well go home," she added tamely.

I had not even opened my mouth at that dramatic rehearsal, and it was to be one of my most important engagements to date! I was a very depressed young soprano.

The next morning, the secretary telephoned to say that the performance was to go ahead as if nothing had happened, and I was to be at the Queen's Hall at 1 p.m. There would be a one hour rehearsal, and then a break of one hour before the performance.

The most important thing about it all from my point of view was that Sir Thomas realised my dilemma—having to sing this work twice within a short space of time with scarcely a break and no previous orchestral rehearsal. He announced that he would rehearse the soprano items first, as this was my initial performance of the work. Everyone was sympathetic, and my fellow artists did not mind at all that the one hour rehearsal was mainly for me.

With all the confusion it was difficult for me to gauge my own performance, but Sir Thomas was very kind and the press notices were good. Quite a few contracts came in as a result, and I sent a telegram to Vienna explaining that this further spate of work would keep me in England for a little while longer.

All through that busy time, pressure had been put on me to continue my lessons with Dino Borgioli. I had steadfastly refused. His fees were high and I wanted to save as much as I could from my small earnings. Besides, I did not agree with him on the question of breathing. Pat asked me to act as chauffeur for them again, but there was no mention of reduced singing fees. I felt it would be a complete waste of time. I had set myself a daily target of work and I was sticking to it. I explained this to the Borgiolis, and they agreed.

I then discovered that my fund organisers in Australia had heard, through the Borgiolis, that I was not having lessons. That was quite a shock, but there was worse to come. First, I was accused of not telling the world that Dino was my teacher, and second, I was told that as a sufferer from hay fever and sometimes asthma, I could never succeed.

I reminded Pat that she had extracted from me a promise that I would never tell anyone that Dino was teaching me. I really think she had forgotten every word about it—anyway I hope so. Now she wished the world to know. It was a complete volte-face. Dino was no longer young, and Pat was probably thinking of the future when he would need to teach in order to live.

Wherever I went after this, I was asked about Dino as a teacher. As I had never told anybody that I had studied under him, I wondered how I was supposed to know about his teaching qualities, and I could only guess that it was now common news in England that I had, in fact, been his pupil. But I was wrong: the news had come from Australia. It had been reported in most of the Australian papers that the world famous tenor, Dino Borgioli, was now teaching the young golfing singer who had gone to Europe to study!

Ivor Newton invited me to join him for his Christmas dinner party in London. After all the confusion and upsets of the previous few weeks the invitation was particularly welcome, and I have never forgotten his gesture in thinking of me and saving me from a lonely Christmas. Instead, it was a most happy and memorable one. He also arranged a concert party for his friends, Lord and Lady Howard de Walden, to be held in the village hall at Chirk. The party consisted of Keith Falkner (now Sir Keith), Jan Smeterlin and his wife, Ivor and me.

Chirk is in North Wales, and we travelled there by train in bitterly cold weather. It was my first long train journey in the British Isles, and Chirk Castle, the home of the Howard de Waldens, was like a dream to me. I have a passion for old castles and this one was particularly fascinating, though I should hate to live in one unless it had central heating. Imagine the cost!

I was given a bedroom in one of the large turrets. A fire was burning brightly in the grate. On the bedside table was a decanter of Scotch, and another of brandy, with a siphon of soda water between them. Never before had I seen hospitality extended to this level.

After the concert on the Saturday night, which had been in aid of the Chirk and District Cottage Hospital, we were given a sumptuous party.

The next day Keith and I played six holes of golf in the snow, using red balls. Our feet and hands were frozen. The snow was crisp and hard underfoot, and there were patches of green under the trees. The greens had been swept clear for us. The Welsh countryside was beautiful, even in winter, but it was too cold to play golf, so Keith and I went back to the castle and played squash.

There was a dinner party that night, and I saw for the first time "Snap the Dragon". This is an old Welsh custom to usher in the New Year. Dishes of raisins with brandy poured over them are ignited, and you must eat one that is burning. It was great fun.

Two choirs came to the castle and entertained us with carols. I watched their faces as they sang, and I realised what joy it gave them. You could almost see their troubles dropping off them one by one, like berries off a tree. Singing was their outlet, their relaxation and safety valve, their escape to another realm. Some of us escape by going to a cinema, theatre or concert, but the Welsh in those small villages escape through the glory of their own voices. No wonder Wales is the land of choirs.

I started the New Year by studying with Ivor. The day was too cold and windy for walking or sight-seeing.

The next day, 2 January, we all returned to London. It had been a wonderful New Year for me, and I shall never forget the warmth and magnitude of that delightful family's hospitality. I often visited them in their Belgrave Square home, and enjoyed making music with them.

On my return to London I gave an audition for the H.M.V. recording company, and my choice of a ballad was "The Green Hills o' Somerset". Walter Legge, who later married the contralto Nancy Evans, and subsequently the German soprano Elisabeth Schwarzkopf, was the representative who heard me. He turned me down. This did not surprise me.

I had another B.B.C. booking to sing two arias, of which "Casta Diva" was one, and a duet with a tenor in a programme of operatic excerpts with Robbie. My fees were small, but I was able to save a little.

Once again Dino got in touch with me and said he wanted to hear me. I was not keen to have lessons again as I did not want to break into my savings. But Dino was very insistent, and said that Mrs Payne had told him he was to continue giving me lessons. I managed to hedge until my second recital, but this was not easy, for when Dino heard my voice he was much struck by the improvement.

Encouraged by the success of my first recital, Harold Holt had decided to put on a second, also to be given at the Aeolian Hall, but this time with Ivor Newton as accompanist.

I had chosen the programme and began rehearsing with Ivor. On one freezing day on which there were heavy falls of snow, I took a taxi to my rehearsal—an unheard of luxury for me. When I joined Ivor I found I had no music—I had left my music case in the taxi! I was in a terrible state about it, as the entire programme was in the case. Ivor smoothed me down, and suggested that I contact the B.B.C. library. This I did immediately, and to my relief I found they had copies of all items and were willing to lend them to me. Eventually I recovered my own music from the Lost Property Office at Lambeth Bridge. I was happy again.

Whether it was the luxury of a taxi ride or the panic over my lost music I do not know, but I fell ill. I had an extremely sore throat and I was running a high temperature. My recital had to be postponed. It was a bitter disappointment. Meanwhile, luckily for me, my agent in Vienna was very patient and understanding about the long delay in returning there.

I eventually gave the recital on 22 February. The critics were unanimous in their praise, and more important, Harold Holt was receiving enquiries for my services at concerts. My English backers were pleased with my success, and felt that their confidence had not been misplaced.

Two days later I returned to Vienna, as usual by the cheapest route, and went to live in my old digs with the Baroness. I noticed a great change in the city. The beggars had completely disappeared, the streets were clean, and the coffee-houses were empty. The German take-over lords were beginning to kick the easy-going Austrian serfs into shape. Nothing seemed the same, but it was grand to see Alfred Komma again, and he had taken good care of my surplus luggage.

The director of the Staatsoper, had scheduled me to sing Mimi in *La Bohème* and Violetta in *La Traviata*. Rehearsals and performances began straight away, and I plunged into work. I had still to complete my number of Neddas in *I Pagliacci*, the Marthas and the Constanzes at the Volksoper.

I felt my first stage fear during *I Pagliacci*. A Greek tenor was singing Canio. He was short and stout and by no means handsome, but he had a magnificent voice of wonderful quality and volume at rehearsal. On stage for the performance he became a different person. His voice became almost strangulated through nerves and muscular tension. His eyes bulged, and he really seemed to feel he was Canio. In the opera it was necessary for him to come at me, his Nedda, with a knife, and so deeply did he feel the role that he was really dangerous. More than once two members of the chorus had to keep him from wounding me. I was terrified, and so was the baritone who sang Silvio, who was the cause of Canio's jealousy in the opera. The producer padded the blade of Canio's knife as much as he dared in case there was a real mishap, but we were all relieved when there was a change of tenor. Especially me.

For Aussig I was scheduled to sing Micaela in *Carmen*, Mimi again, and Mignon, which was an unsuitable role for me. I was also to do Amelia in *Simone Boccanegra*. For the Staatsoper I was told to prepare Elisabeth in *Tannhäuser* and Donna Elvira in *Don Giovanni*.

I was at the beginning of a new phase in my life. A wonderful operatic career was opening up before me in Europe, and there would be visits to Britain for concerts and B.B.C. engagements. The future was full of promise.

One day the Intendant sent for me and told me I must produce my birth certificate, and those of my parents and grandparents, in order to prove I was Aryan. It all seemed rather silly to me, but I wrote off to Somerset House for the necessary documents for my forebears, and home to Sydney for my own. This was my first experience of the Hitler boot.

On 28 April the entire staff of the Opera House was ordered to attend a speech by Hitler, which would be on the radio. It was put on the notice board as a general rehearsal for foreigners and natives alike—no one was exempt.

As the stentorian voice of the strutting, bombastic little man filled the room, I felt everyone was looking at me. Their God, their Hitler, ranted and raved against Britain, and my reactions were carefully noticed. When it was over one brilliant young conductor, who had sat as one mesmerised all through, came back to reality with a sigh of pure joy.

"It was like listening to a new and glorious symphony by

Beethoven," he said ecstatically. And he seemed such a sane, intellectual type of man.

I was still being invited at odd times into the Baroness's back room for the sweet thick Turkish coffee that I had come to like very much. I was meeting counts, and a prince from Hungary, and one from Yugoslavia. There was also a young man they called "Yasha". They seemed to make too much of a point of saying how anti-Hitler they were, and Yasha often boasted of writing anti-German slogans on walls, and of helping old Jewish people to get out of the country. Many of the things they said did not quite ring true; it was most intriguing. I knew the penalty for going against the regime.

I visited my old teacher, Frau Eibenschütz, in the Jewish district, and found that her son Karl was now in uniform, and speaking fiercely against the Jews. This puzzled me as I knew he was what we called a "mischling"—that is half Christian and half Jewish.

Harold Holt sent me a contract for 12 August, which was to be the opening night of the Promenade Concert Season at the Queen's Hall, under Sir Henry Wood. There was also another contract for me if I could go to London immediately. It was to sing with Richard Tauber and the Boyd Neel Orchestra, also at the Queen's Hall, in what was to be known as a Georgian Music Festival to mark the bicentenary of Queen Charlotte's Maternity Hospital. There was yet a third engagement, a recital sponsored by the Hon. Mrs Coke.

I was hesitant about accepting these dates, as the fare to London and back would just about eat up the fees, but Harold said it was important.

I went to buy my ticket at the American Express as I knew one of the boys there. He told me I should have to pay for the ticket in foreign currency, as it was forbidden for the new German money to be used. This was rather a blow, as I had hoped to use my savings, which had mounted up a bit, for my fares. But my friend managed to fiddle something for me, and though I was concerned for him, he assured me that no one would be any the wiser as to how I had paid.

I went to London on the 16 June. Three days later I sang at Mrs Coke's, and the Georgian concert at the Queen's Hall was on the 21st. I sang the recitative and aria, "Mi tradi quell' alma ingrata", from *Don Giovanni* with orchestra, and a group of songs by Haydn and Gluck with piano. As a finale I sang a duet with Richard Tauber: "Welch' ein Geschick" from *Die Entführung*. Tauber was a great artist and an excellent musician. This concert was in Georgian period costume and I enjoyed it greatly—after I had recovered from my initial nervousness. When these two engagements were over I went straight back to Vienna.

Each time I returned there I found that Vienna had changed a little more. So many friends had left or were about to leave. People were not so friendly; they seemed almost afraid to speak. The one great blessing about being in Vienna was that I was on my own and could make my own decisions. In London there were so many people telling me what to do, where to go, and what to sing. They had the best of intentions, of course, and that made it all the more difficult to ignore their well meant advice. Often it was conflicting. I felt like the bone between several dogs.

Soon I was receiving letters advising me to get out of Vienna, but I could see no reason for panic. I read only Austrian papers and I had no idea of the general world situation.

Meanwhile a most interesting young woman had come to live at the Baroness's apartment. Her name was Maidi and she spoke seven languages fluently. She was very attractive, and appeared to have private means as well as a job that kept her on the move. She came and went without giving any intimation as to what her work was.

Maidi was at all the backroom gatherings—far more often than I was, so I imagined she must be a close friend of the family, perhaps a one-time colleague of the Baroness's daughter V. Maidi often questioned me about Australia, but as she had such an enquiring mind it seemed quite natural. She had an intimate knowledge of all the capital cities of the world, and she was a brilliant conversationalist. Politics were never discussed at meals with the other paying guests, but in the back room they were the main topic of conversation. I could never quite pinpoint their particular beliefs, except that they seemed to be ferociously anti-Nazi.

My pal Alfred Komma once more agreed to care for my surplus luggage while I was away in London, where I had to go for the opening Promenade Concert, and my friend at the American Express again wangled the ticket money for me. If he had not done this I could not have left Vienna.

A Jewish opera-coach who knew I was about to go to London asked me to take his watch and chain to an address in Hampstead. He told me it was of great sentimental value and he would never be allowed to leave the country with it, even if he could obtain a pass. Looking back, I think it was rather rash to agree to carry out this mission, but it would have been hard to refuse. So the day after my arrival I sought out the Hampstead address he had given me. An elderly man opened the door just wide enough to see who was outside. He seemed to expect the watch, perhaps it contained a message. As I was sure I was at the right address I handed it over. I never got further than the doorstep.

I could feel that London was preparing for another Hitler shock. At last my eyes were opened to what was happening in the world. I was reading English newspapers and seeing things through British eyes instead of German.

One day as I got off a bus at Hyde Park Corner I saw the Baroness's daughter V. crossing the road. I could not understand it, for I knew there was a ban on leaving Vienna for holders of Austrian passports. But there she was, dressed as I had so often seen her, unmistakably V.

I hurried after her and called her name as I got close. She gave me a fleeting glance and leaped on to a moving bus. She gave no sign of recognition. It was a shock. Why had she not told me she was coming to London at almost the same time as myself? And why did she not want to know me? This enigma was to be solved later.

The price of digs had risen considerably since my last visit and I was soon worrying about my finances. If only I could have brought my Vienna savings with me all would have been well. Everything cost more, especially clothes.

On 12 August I had the one and only orchestral rehearsal in the morning for the opening Promenade Concert that night. Sir Henry Wood was a most sympathetic and workmanlike conductor. He knew exactly what effect he wanted from the orchestra, and he wasted neither time nor words about getting it.

My fellow artists were Frank Titterton, and the pianist Benno Moisewitsch. It was a stimulating and interesting concert, but I knew that I sang badly. Sir Henry did not agree, neither did my fans, but I was not deceived. I have always known my vocal failures and successes and I could not deceive myself.

The next day I had very favourable press notices, and a pleasant surprise from the agent, Mr Tillett. He had an important booking for me to appear at the Norfolk and Norwich Thirty-fifth Triennial Musical Festival. The conductor was to be Sir Thomas Beecham. I was to sing in the Kodaly *Te Deum*, *Messiah*, and Berlioz' *Faust*. This was an exciting prospect.

I had planned to return to Vienna on the 15th, but Harold Holt was dead against it. I had my return ticket and I did not want to change my plans, mainly because of money. My small reserve was at an end, and I hated not having the next week's rent in my pocket.

On the 14th the news in the papers was really alarming. I certainly had no desire to be caught in Vienna, but what could I do? My money was there. But I cancelled my return ticket, and said I would advise the American Express about my return date later.

Three days later I found myself at Andrew Reid's bank in the City. I was completely broke. Once again I was helped out.

I was too independent to ask for immediate payment after the Prom Concert. The cheque took some time to reach me, as it went through Harold's office, and by the time ten per cent was deducted it seemed a mere drop in a very large ocean of increasing expenses. Five guineas, three guineas and two guineas were the extent of my early fees. Deduct ten per cent, and the answer is microscopic.

On the 21 August I received a reply-paid cable from Vienna, ordering me back. This seemed to suggest that war was far away, yet according to the London press it was imminent. My dilemma was serious. I cabled back saying I had caught a chill and was confined to bed.

On 1 September I felt my white lie was justified. Germany attacked Poland, and war became inevitable.

London had a black-out that night, and so did the mind, body and soul of Joan Hammond. My future was about to crumble beneath this looming catastrophe. Ahead was an impenetrable void. All my hopes and ambitions could be bowled over like ninepins.

This was the blackout within me.

PART III

Shadows

To witness a great nation rising slowly and shaking itself, like some huge monster from the deep, was an unforgettable experience. During the first few weeks, after the Declaration of War, all cinemas, theatres and places of public entertainment were closed. The air raid sirens shrilled and wailed on occasions, and the initial sensation of fear of the unknown gripped most people.

I had finished preparing the Kodaly *Te Deum* and Berlioz' *Faust*, and had polished up the soprano part in *Messiah*, which I was to sing for Sir Thomas Beecham at the Norfolk and Norwich Festival. I found these works musically satisfying, and I was looking forward eagerly to the rehearsals and the ultimate performances.

I received a severe jolt. The Festival was cancelled, and it was my one and only booking for September.

This is one of Britain's most important Festivals, and the engagement would have been a most prestigious one. But the preliminary announcement of works to be performed had been made, and the soloists' names had been published, and because of this my agent received tentative bookings for me in spite of the cancellation.

I had put my name down for the W.A.A.F. soon after the declaration of war. When I received notification to go and be interviewed and have a medical examination, I was elated. The thought of rejection never entered my mind. I had been feeling rather lost and rudderless in the early sea of unreality and uncertainty.

I duly presented myself at the stated time, and I was dismissed so rapidly I hardly had time to realise what had happened. I was unfit for service with the W.A.A.F. because of my arm, which ranked as a disability. So that was that.

The next thing was to see Harold Holt to discuss future prospects, if any. I asked about concert work.

"Joan," he said, "classical music is out. No one will want to listen to operatic arias or serious songs until the War is over. Take my advice and learn 'Roll out the Barrel' and 'Hang out the Washing on the Siegfried Line'".

My incredulity amused him. He sat back in his chair and went through his characteristic routine. He pulled out a cigarette, pushed the pack away, drew out a beautifully made gold lighter, and after a second or two, inhaled deeply on his cigarette. Watching the smoke spiral upwards he went on: "This is bad luck for you, Joan, just when you are on the threshold of a career. But we don't know which way things'll go, and the lads'll want light stuff."

"I'm worried about my minute bank savings."

"Just send a cable to Australia and ask for more."

"I can't do that. The fund must be at an end."

"Funds are never at an end," he said. This he really believed, and I could not convince him that my fund was not a limitless pot of gold.

Harold was a jovial, kindly man with no great love of the classics, but with an intensely perceptive ear and eye for classical artists. He followed in their wake and blossomed as a personality in presenting them and directing them. He was in the business for money, although he had private means. I believe his predecessor, Lionel Powell, was just the opposite, inasmuch as he was a great lover of classical music. He loved his artists, and found it difficult to refuse them when it came to demands for higher fees.

By the end of September permission was given for cinemas to open again. Harold had given my name to the quickly formed honorary organisation for troop concerts, and soon I was singing, naturally for no remuneration but free transport, at camp concerts in and around London. My first war concert was at Chelsea Barracks.

Concerts were not really appreciated at this stage. The men were anxious to be active, and one sensed their restlessness as day after day passed with nothing happening. These early concerts were at Pirbright Camp, Croydon Air Force Base, Wellington Barracks, and hospitals at Epsom, Mill Hill, West London and Hammersmith, as well as big air raid shelters such as the one at Dolphin Square.

Classical music was suffered but not enjoyed. I could not adjust myself to singing popular songs. I preferred to take on any job rather than try to entertain with material unsuited and distasteful to me. One had to put up with thick clouds of smoke and general noise during concerts. It was sickening at first. Reeking pipe tobacco, cigarette and cigar smoke blended into nauseating throat irritants which distressed many an artist.

Harold received an offer for me to go to Australia for the Australian Broadcasting Commission. The terms were such that I refused outright. I was not ready for such a tour, and the A.B.C. were justified in not making it an attractive offer. Pressure was put on from the Australian end by my Fund committee, but I knew that a tour under such conditions would be disastrous for me. I needed the work, but I had made up my mind that, if I possibly could, I would hold out and refuse work which I considered would not advance my status. That was my policy.

My Fund committee were very angry at my refusal of the A.B.C. offer. Their concern for me was sincere, and they had been using their influence with the A.B.C. I had acted contrary to their wishes, but I had no idea at that time that they were behind the offer. I thought I was dealing with my agent in London and with the A.B.C. representative, William James, whom I had met on two occasions with Harold.

I must admit to suffering many qualms about this decision, as only two paid engagements had come in, but just as the cupboard became bare once again, two B.B.C. contracts arrived.

I shall be indebted forever to two conductors for engaging me when the future was at its blackest, and I was living as though on a razor edge. These two men, Sir Thomas Beecham and Stanford Robinson, were aiming in the same direction in their different spheres: Sir Thomas in the concert world and Robbie via the B.B.C. Wartime restriction hampered their initial efforts, but somehow concerts began again at the Queen's Hall and the Royal

Albert Hall. Robbie and his orchestra were installed at Wood-norton, a beautiful old house situated near Evesham.

Events soon proved that I had made the right decision in not returning to Australia. If I had gone there, I should have had to stay there for the duration of the War. As it was, my career leapt ahead in the British Isles.

In January 1940 I received a contract for three performances at La Scala, Milan. It was for two *Bohèmes* and one *Traviata*. This contract came through the Italian agent who had heard me at Salzburg. He kept his word when he assured me that he could get me work in Italy.

The contract also included performances in Madrid and Barcelona with an Italian company. The operas were to be Rossini's *William Tell*, two by Verdi: *La Traviata* and *La Forza del Destino*, Donizetti's *L'Elisire d'Amore*, and *The Magic Flute* by Mozart. The whole engagement to last a month, with rehearsals to take place in Milan. This was the most exciting prospect of my career.

I haunted the Passport Office. I had to produce a letter from the agent, the contract, and eventually a cable, before finally achieving a permit to travel. All passports were invalid for the duration of the war.

Before leaving for Milan I went with a concert party, arranged by Sir Seymour Hicks, to Tenby, South Wales. The concert was given in a vast hangar at Pembroke Docks, R.A.F. It was freezing and there was no heating. The audience and artists all wore top coats. My vocal cords felt like icicles, and how any sounds came from them is more than I can think. The scenery around Tenby was beautiful, but the most enjoyable part of this engagement was meeting Sir Seymour Hicks and Richard Llewellyn, author of *How Green was my Valley*. The long train journey passed most happily in their company. The conversation was lively, witty and most entertaining.

Needless to say I caught a bad cold which nearly put an end to Milan, but not quite.

I went to catch the 7.35 p.m. train to Folkestone but it was packed. I managed to squeeze on to the 9.15 p.m., and as a result I fell asleep and got carried on to Dover. There was no train back to

Folkestone until the next morning, but some soldiers offered to take my baggage and see if there was any other form of transport available, but the roads were thick with snow and nothing could get through. So I found myself installed in the Grand Hotel for the night, determined never again to sleep past my destination.

I eventually caught the 9.30 a.m. cross-channel steamer the next day. We crossed in convoy with aeroplanes overhead and destroyers close by. It was rather frightening, and I was beginning to doubt the wisdom of accepting overseas engagements.

Worse was to come. The French authorities were grim and the atmosphere was terribly strained. Everyone seemed rude and bad tempered and on edge; they were obviously full of uncertainty and apprehension about the future. I had a day to fill out in Paris, so I took myself to Nôtre Dame and Montmartre.

Italy was only slightly better. Food was already rationed and the famous espresso coffee tasted rather like stewed, burnt rubber. There was no bacon, little sugar, and poor quality bread. A great change had come about in such a short time.

I began rehearsing immediately. I noticed after a week of working with the Italians and listening to their talk in restaurants and trattorias that there was an uneasy undercurrent and suppressed excitement. The former carefree manner had vanished and I felt an outsider. Groups of people would have their heads together talking in undertones, just as it had been in Vienna.

My agent was more than enthusiastic about my prospects, and he had received good reports of me. Nevertheless, I felt more embarrassed every day, for I sensed something unpleasant in the air, though I couldn't quite place it.

I went to the opera most nights, and I was particularly impressed by Puccini's *La Rondine*. I always sat in the gallery because of the need to conserve money, and there I found that in common with all other female galleryites, I was subjected to annoyance from the male element. The greater the crowd in the galleries, the greater their activities. There would be bottom pinching and a sudden pressure from a man directly behind you. If you looked behind and tried to evade him, he would smile and shrug his shoulders as if to say: "I can't help it! I'm being pushed against you!" He would then leave you alone until he thought you were once more absorbed in the opera, and then he would start pinching and pressing again. A mild rebuke would sometimes rid you of this nuisance, but at other times it was necessary to move away, only to receive the same treatment from the next man! I was convinced that they came to the opera with only one aim and object, which was *not* to hear the opera.

Meanwhile, the atmosphere was becoming more and more strained and oppressive, and I felt that something would have to give. Three days before my debut as Mimi in *La Bohème* I was sent for by the Director. My agent was also there, and both men were very tense. You could have struck matches on the atmosphere.

"Signorina Ammonda," said the Director, making a brave attempt at my name, "we have the unpleasant duty to inform you that the political situation in our country is about to develop into a very serious declaration. I have discussed your position with Signor B., and we feel it is imperative for you to leave here as soon as possible. Please see your Embassy officials today."

There was a long pause as the Director watched me for my reactions. I knew exactly what he was trying to tell me, and while I had no desire to be caught in Italy if they were entering the war against the Allies, it was nevertheless something of a blow to have my first chance to sing at what is possibly the most famous opera house in the world, so wantonly scattered with the senseless ashes of war. But there was nothing else for it. The crowing, immaculately clad Italian officers were already openly reviling the British, and I was well aware of the political seething and general unrest.

Within twelve hours I was once again being rattled across Italy into France. The fare was my own responsibility, and although I had received advanced rehearsal fees for living expenses in Milan, there was very little left for me to start with in London.

It was a dreadful journey. Even in the short space of time I had been in Italy, France seemed to have undergone a further change for the worse. There were troops everywhere, laden with their gear, and with women and children clinging to them as the trains drew away taking their loved ones to some unknown destiny. Faces were like masks, some staring helplessly about them with the expressionless eyes of deadened senses; others looked vital and fierce, ready to fight the enemy. The French Customs officials treated everyone coming in from Italy as a spy. I was asked endless questions, and every piece of luggage was examined minutely. The whole country seemed to be preparing itself for some indeterminate disaster.

On arrival at Calais I was told that there was no boat that night. We were herded along like cattle and I was given a small room in the hotel on the quay. My personal disaster was dwarfed in my mind by the enormity of the situation facing France. I longed to be back in England, the land of law and order.

When I eventually got back to London I left my luggage at Victoria and went to an address in Queen's Gate, where I rented a very small room on the top floor. The multifarious addresses I had in and around Queen's Gate were an immense joke with Ivor and Gerald. Ivor had actually said he would get a special address book in which every page would be H for Hammond, as no ordinary book has enough pages for H.

At one address in Queen's Gate I had a miniature room on the top floor back. The furniture consisted of a divan (I can't think how they got it in), a chair, a small shallow inset cupboard, and a tiny washbasin and mirror. No such luxury as a dressing table. But it cost only twenty-two shillings and sixpence a week for bed and breakfast, and this was so cheap I was willing to concertina myself and my possessions. The greater part of my luggage was left in the basement box-room. I had to walk up and down five long flights of stairs for nearly everything I wanted, including music. It was at this same address that the fluctuations of fortune allowed me to change, on two occasions, from "top floor back" to "second floor front". I felt a millionaire in that spacious room, but the longest period I stayed in it was two weeks! Then it was back to my miniature room, as thirty-eight shillings and sixpence was too much for me. My landlady was very forbearing, and called me her "migratory tenant with restless means"!

On that first evening back in London I immediately rang Harold to tell him what had happened. Then I went to bed and slept for hours. When I awoke I really felt that my trip to Italy had been a nightmate. I slipped back into life in London determined to work harder to redress the disappointment and the setback to my career.

Within two days I heard from a Mr Preuss of the Parlophone Record Company, which was a part of the E.M.I. group of companies just as H.M.V. and Columbia were. Mr Preuss gave me a two hours' test, a really thorough trial, quite unlike the previous cursory one given by Walter Legge for Columbia. As a result of Mr Preuss's test I was signed up by The Gramophone Company, later E.M.I., but placed under the aegis of Walter Legge on Columbia label, not Parlophone. This was wonderful, as Columbia was a more expensive label with a large classical output, whereas Parlophone was mainly serving the lighter side of music.

Concerts were starting again, and my next happy surprise was a contract to sing with Sir Thomas Beecham at an orchestral concert at the Queen's Hall on 23 March, which seemed an eternity away!

Meanwhile, the Dublin Operatic Society offered me a contract. This was a direct result of my opera broadcasts with Robbie, and my appearance with Sir Thomas. This engagement nearly fell through as I was required to sing two Paminas in *The Magic Flute* and two Mimis in *La Bohème*—four performances within six days. Much as I needed the money I refused, so they changed the booking to two performances of *The Magic Flute*, which I gladly accepted. I was to be there on 29 March.

I was in poverty street again, and was forced once more to move to cheaper digs in Courtfield Gardens. I could not confide in Harold, as he would have said in his practical way: "Hard up, are you? Then why refuse to sing four performances in six days?" I knew that four performances in six days, as well as rehearsals, would be far too strenuous for me at this stage, and would also be vocally ruinous, so I endured poverty instead.

Fortune was slowly changing. A contract came for a performance of *The Creation* in South Wales for 28 March, the day before I was to be in Dublin. Harold assured me that I could catch an early train from Swansea on the 29th which would connect with the Irish Mail train the same evening. I should be in Dublin on the morning of the 30th to begin rehearsing. I was not altogether happy about it, but I agreed.

At the Queen's Hall concert I sang the little-known aria from Handel's *Alcina*—"Mi restano le lagrime". Sir Thomas had been very keen for me to do it, and as it is such a lovely aria I was glad to agree. The concert was a sell-out, as all Beecham concerts were, and I enjoyed a modicum of success. It was a very busy time, as I was learning opera in English, and also studying *The Creation, Elijah, Hiawatha*, Beethoven's Ninth Symphony, which has such a demanding soprano part, and Sullivan's *Golden Legend*.

My lessons with Dino had virtually stopped as they were beyond my means, and in any case breathing was still a bone of contention between us. I was still convinced that abdominal breathing was the best, whereas Dino liked, not clavicular breathing, but a sort of relation of it which kept the breath high. After three or four lessons I felt my throat muscles tensing, and my voice tired quickly as a result of keeping the breath too high.

I eventually arrived in Dublin on schedule, and my first taste of opera in English was really funny. I hadn't a notion about the Irish and their happy-go-lucky approach to life, which is especially noticeable when things become difficult. This was an abrupt switch from my rigid German training, and at first I felt like open revolt, for a full dress rehearsal was the first call I had! The other members of the cast did not even know their roles. The producer, Charles Moore, had spent many years producing opera in Germany, and at Covent Garden, and he was at a loss to know where to begin. The members of the chorus were amateur, which did not help, and absolute chaos reigned at that full dress rehearsal. There were four different operas to be rehearsed and staged within the space of five days. It was a glorious muddle, which was thoroughly enjoyed by the Irish. You just cannot be angry with them for long. My two performances came and went, heaven alone knows how, but the audience and the company were completely happy.

My Irish tenor was a charming chap, but musically insecure. As Pamina I had to rush downstairs towards my beloved, overjoyed to see him, but he should remain sad and withdrawn. Pamina sings to him: "But you are sad—have you no word for your Pamina?" The tenor is supposed to sigh and wave his Pamina away. She tries again: "What, am I to avoid you? Then you love me no more." He then repulses her completely.

But my tenor simply beamed at me as soon as I appeared, and was obviously delighted to have me on stage with him. The text of the opera did not matter to him at all. My efforts to counter this happy reception were of no avail. He was so relieved to have me there to help him with his words and cues that he just couldn't bring himself to rebuff me, no matter what the text of the opera demanded. It was both moving and comical, entirely out of character as far as the opera was concerned, but completely in line with what I knew of the Irish.

An unforgettable night for me was when I was asked by the theatre management to attend a performance of *Rigoletto* as a member of the audience. I agreed most willingly as I had two free days between my own appearances.

I heard something unique and spontaneous that night. It happened during the second interval. There was a slight altercation going on in the gallery, and then a moderately good tenor voice began to sing "La donna è mobile". Gradually the theatre became silent and everyone listened. Some of us moved down to the orchestra pit to get a better view. There he was standing in an aisle, bursting his lungs with the sheer joy of vocal expression, and gesticulating to suit the mood of the aria. When he finished everyone laughed and applauded. One of his friends shouted: "Come on, Sean, give us another! You're better than the tenor on stage tonight." Sean needed little encouragement; he let go with less control and more noise into "Lovely Maid in the Moonlight," from *La Bohème*.

I wouldn't have missed this rare experience. These young

Irishmen are so natural and uninhibited. It was a delightful interlude, marred only by the fact that he didn't know when to stop. I
don't know how they eventually managed to quieten him, but
the opera was delayed for a time while the gallery settled. I was
told that it was by no means an isolated incident. If they take a
dislike to a singer, an amateur enthusiast makes the most of the
chance to show his own worth.

It was in Dublin that I met Ian Blacker, a nephew of Lady
Gowrie. I had been invited to stay with the Blackers at Castle
Martin in the Curragh, the magnificent stretch of downland
famous for horse breeding. Ian took me about and showed me as
much of Eire as was possible in the four days I was staying there.
He came to my final performance as Pamina and we set off in his
jalopy for Castle Martin, but it was four hours and two burst
tyres later when we arrived. This casualness I found typical of my
delightful friend and his carefree countrymen. My introduction to
Ireland and the Irish had been most rewarding and unforgettable.
Friendship with Ian grew into a very happy relationship which
ended abruptly and tragically. He joined the famous Black Watch
Regiment, and I last saw him in London in 1942 when he passed
through on his way to the Middle East. Soon afterwards I heard
that he had been killed in action. His cousin Patrick, only son of
Lord and Lady Gowrie, also joined that gigantic, ghoulish grave
of young men who died for King and Country in North Africa.

The conductor for *The Magic Flute* had been my namesake,
Arthur Hammond. He was an upright, dedicated and wholly
sincere musician. As with so many other British conductors, his
chances to flower and expand were cruelly confined. So many
young, eager and talented musicians suffer the same conditions.
They never get more than a few odd bones of concerts thrown to
them which the top-notchers have not time to accept.

These top-notchers, the giants in any sphere, all have that
indefinable, unteachable quality called "personality". To be an
excellent musician is hardly enough. At a broad estimate, there
may be two dozen conductors earning enough in England to
keep themselves and their families. A handful succeed and are
accepted. But for the rest . . .

During the War, opera was non-existent until the Carl Rosa began again in 1942. Orchestral concerts were rare, so what hope was there for the young and upcoming musicians? I felt more compassion for would-be conductors than for instrumentalists.

I was soon to meet two other conductors with brilliant prospects; Leslie Heward and Harold Gray. Leslie was one of the truly great men of music. If he had cared a little more about the cut of his tails and not treading on the wrong toes (two very important facts to remember, both in the provinces and in London), he would have "arrived" and would have been duly acknowledged. My first recordings on Columbia were with Leslie and the Hallé Orchestra.

In August 1942 Leslie was again to conduct recording sessions with me at Manchester. I was recording the "Letter Scene" from *Eugène Onegin*. Leslie fell ill, and Warwick Braithwaite came to take his place. Leslie was dying from advanced tuberculosis. Within a week he seemed to fade and diminish. It shocked and horrified me. He was so bright, and took such an interest in the recording sessions. I felt sick within as I talked to him and tried to make light of a hopeless situation. He passed away two weeks later, and he was a great loss to British music.

Back in London I found a contract awaiting me to sing yet again with Richard Tauber. This was one of several. Later he conducted two concerts with me as soloist. Musicianship of his order is a rare quality in a singer.

In May 1940 Germany invaded Holland, Belgium and Luxemburg, and a month after that Italy entered the war and became our enemy. Dino was arrested as an enemy alien and interned. It was a necessary move, but it was always a shock when one's friends became pawns in the political war game.

I did my first gramophone recording session on 14 June 1940. It was an exciting day for me. Gerald Moore accompanied me, and my old friend Alfredo Campoli played the violin obbligato in the Bach-Gounod "Ave Maria" and "On Wings of Song" by Mendelssohn.

The entire procedure was of the utmost fascination. To realise

that the music we were producing in the studio through microphones was being transmitted and cut into a wax disc seemed
incredible. With wax the sound was cut into it as opposed to
being transmitted onto it. I soon learnt that the slightest studio
noise or "frog" in the voice would be recorded, and this meant
starting all over again. We would have to wait for some time
while the wax disc was changed. It was quite a business, and that
is why, on occasions, so little was done during a three hour
session.

How revolutionary is tape! One can start and stop immediately
and re-do sections without wasting time. But every new inven-
tion has initial snags. The feed-back on loud notes used to mar the
perfect product, as it was a sound spread onto the flat surface of a
tape. This has been overcome now. It also takes much longer to
listen to the recordings and decide which is the best, as many
more are completed during sessions, and there are always sections
which have been re-done and which must be heard and selected
for the complete whole. In other words, on the old wax disc you
heard an uninterrupted, unbroken performance, as in a concert
hall or opera house. Today you are hearing a doctored version,
added to which are numerous technical gimmicks for producing
special sound effects which are normally lost in a "live" performance.

I was very thrilled to have made these recordings, and waited
eagerly for the first pressings to appear on the market.

France surrendered on 17 June 1940, and things became grim
again on the Hammond front! My affairs had begun to look
hopeful, but by the end of June my impecunious state was such
that I could not afford an accompanist. Thanks to Lady Gowrie's
sister, Mrs Fleischmann, I was at least able to rehearse. I used to
walk daily to her London house in Bryanston Square from my
various addresses in the Kensington area.

Just when I was seriously considering applying for the dole,
three of Dino's pupils asked me to carry on and teach them during
his absence. This helped considerably, but it was a mere drop in
the ocean. I went to see Lady Cholmondely at the Admiralty in

the hope of joining the W.R.N.S., but she strongly advised me to hang on, as she felt sure the music world would revive, and I should be of greater value as a singer than as a "Wren".

A lucky break came. A great friend of mine was getting married and moving out of London, and she offered me her Mews Cottage. This was really manna from heaven, especially as there was a minipiano in the cottage which she later gave me, and which served my purpose throughout the War years and up to 1950. My friend also wanted me to take over one of her French poodle's puppies. His name was Pippo. As I could hardly feed myself, I refused to be tempted by this adorable wee bundle of fluff.

At the wedding, at the beginning of August, I sang "Panis Angelicus", and before departing on their honeymoon, my friends insisted that Pippo should be part of the Mews Cottage ménage. Although many of my friends called in at times, it was often lonely, and Pippo was certainly good company.

In July that year the late Dame Myra Hess made her famous contribution to a City's needs by starting lunch hour concerts at the National Gallery. These concerts were a musical oasis, as the programmes were of the highest quality. I sang at one of them, and found the audience most appreciative—the concerts became a boon to London's music-starved public. It filled a large gap. No tribute can be too great to pay to Dame Myra for her work in organising the concerts.

At the beginning of August I sang at a benefit concert with Richard Tauber and the London Philharmonic Orchestra. I received a fee of two guineas for expenses, and that is what it cost me for attending rehearsals. I mention this concert because the next day no paper recorded that I sang, and poor Harold Holt was hoping to glean a small complimentary criticism to place in his concert advertisements. He accrued plenty later, but, as it was, neither of us got much out of that particular engagement.

August 23 was the beginning of the real War in London. The first air-raid warning was at 3.45 a.m., and by nightfall the next day we had had six warnings, and had heard aircraft and gunfire for the first time. I was fascinated by the searchlights. It seemed like a festive display as the beams chased each other across the sky. I heard bombs fall, also for the first time, on the night of 29 August.

Sepember brought with it tragedy and fear. On the night of the 8th all London seemed ablaze. The noise of screaming people, as bombs and incendiaries hurtled from the sky in the biggest raid yet, was terrifying. A large piece of shrapnel came through the skylight of the Mews Cottage, and landed in the bath. I had to circumnavigate that large chip in the enamel for many weeks. My most difficult job was trying to cover the hole made by the shrapnel.

Two days later Walter Legge telephoned to tell me that the "master tape" made at my recording session with Gerald and Alfredo had been damaged during the raid. This was bad news and very disappointing, for not only had the "master" been damaged, but so had the second one as well, which the record companies make in case the first one is damaged.

The 13th was a very unlucky day for me. Four bombs dropped in Eaton Mews, where the cottage was situated, and one of them was a time bomb. Soldiers billeted nearby came and ordered us out, telling us to make it snappy if we valued our lives. The cottage had rocked and jerked with each explosion, and I had thought that my chips were already up, and Pippo's too, but as we were still alive I put Pippo on his lead, grabbed my toothbrush and golf clubs, and made for the Army air raid shelter with the other Mews dwellers. When we had settled ourselves I took stock of my possessions, and I had a fit of giggles as I realised that I had brought toothbrush and golf clubs, but left my handbag to the mercy of the time bomb!

It was eerie going back to a windowless abode. Our Mews was in the news again two days later, for a German airman landed among us, attached to a parachute.

The month of October was ushered in with a short-notice contract to sing with Robbie and the B.B.C. orchestra in a broadcast of *Young England*. The raids were increasing in severity and length, and people were again rushing to leave the metropolis. I had to travel from Paddington to Evesham, and I would not have thought it possible to survive in such a seething mass of humanity. It was chaotic, for in addition to civilians there were soldiers, sailors and air force men all laden with kit. I managed to get on to the train, but I had to stand all the way. Many such nightmare journeys followed this one.

The B.B.C. followed this contract with two more. The most comforting thing about dear Auntie B.B.C. was that she paid, which was more than many other organisations did. During those War years many mushroom concerts sprang up and were advertised as being in aid of some charity or other, but the unknown agent or organisation benefited first. If the tag "charity" could be used, the organisers were relieved of the necessity to pay entertainment tax.

I was in Evesham for four days. On my return I learnt that my pupil, Norman Wright, a very promising tenor, had been killed during an air raid the night before. His entire family had been killed outright when their home received a direct hit. Two nights later another family I used to visit were killed in a raid. They had been friends of my mother.

These were my first experiences of death from bombs, and they affected me greatly.

My next B.B.C. broadcast was actually from a theatre at Stratford-on-Avon, but the rehearsals were at Evesham and we were driven across by bus. When I got back to London another shock awaited me. This time it was a summons for showing a light during the hours of black-out. This had apparently come from my windowless bathroom, but I was at a loss to know how, as I had turned off the main switch before leaving London, because of the electric water-heating system.

I duly appeared in Court at Gerald Row. It was my first brush with British Police and they couldn't have been nicer, but I was very nervous. I had heard of previous black-out offenders (all male) and that they had all received different fines, which I found puzzling. A middle-aged man's case was heard before mine, and it was his third offence. He was fined £5. When I took the oath and stood in that funny little box my legs felt like jelly. My offence was read out and I was asked whether I was guilty or not guilty. In quavering tones I replied: "Not guilty." I was about to qualify this, when the irritable magistrate (for he was that all right, probably tired from sleepless nights of raids, as were we all) said: "A fine of £10, to be paid within two months, or seven days' imprisonment."

I almost swooned with shock and began to say something, but a voice said: "Step down, please."

I had no chance of paying the £10 fine, so I elected to go to jail. A very kindly man urged me to think about it and report back to the Gerald Row Police Station within two hours. I told him I had no choice. I could have wept with relief at his reply:

"The law is truly an ass at times. Borrow the money. Jail is not for you."

I then realised that he was an officer of the Court responsible for seeing the sentence carried out. To have received such a severe fine for a first offence seemed so unfair and biased. Perhaps that magistrate was a misogynist!

I did borrow the fine money, and was relieved to repay it.

My first miscellaneous concert in Wales was with three well established artists: Mary Jarred, Trevor Jones and Roy Henderson. They were a delightful, amusing trio, especially Mary. I was naturally shy and gauche.

Accommodation had been offered and I was only too glad to accept it. We were met at the station by the organisers of the concert, and Mary and I were left at one address while Trevor and Roy were taken elsewhere. Our very cosy Welsh hostess led us up a narrow staircase into a small room with a three-quarter size bed. I lagged behind, thinking that the choicest room would be for Mary, but to our mutual astonishment the lady said: "We've put you both in here, loves. You'll keep each other warm and comfy." She had gone before we recovered from the shock.

Mary sat down on the bed and pushed her hat back on her head. She said in that delightful broad North Country accent of hers: "I don't know about you, love, but there is one thing certain —we can't share this bed. Let's toss a coin and see which of us has a cold and has to go to an hotel."

H

Mary was amply supplied with nature's largesse of figure. To me at that moment she looked an extra, extra O.S. She was big, and I did look short and small beside her.

She tossed a coin. "You call," she said.

"Heads." Heads it was.

"Right, ducks." Mary gathered up her things. "Now I'm suffering from a bad cold, and it would be unfair of me to pass it on to you, so I must go to an hotel and get a single room."

"But it's not fair . . ." I began, but Mary went on. "We have no choice, and don't think I mind," she said. "No one could sleep a wink sharing a bed with me. If I got into this"—she prodded the uncomfortable looking bed—"you'd be on the floor in no time. A person of my size needs room."

"At least let's split the cost of the hotel room," I said. Mary wouldn't hear of it. "Rubbish! I lost the toss and I pay."

She went downstairs and explained our predicament. I heard her blowing her nose and talking in an adenoidal way, as if she were really afflicted with a terrible head cold. Later when I met up with them all at the concert hall, I learned that Roy and Trevor had been in precisely the same quandary. Roy had lost the toss, and he and Mary had ended up in the same hotel, which was a disastrous one. That was why accommodation was included in our contracts.

This was the first of many, many concerts in all parts of Wales. Until I was financially secure, I had to agree to accept accommodation if it were offered. My main reason for not liking this arrangement was that it entailed sitting with the family and joining in family discussions. This I found very tiring before singing.

The Welsh are the most hospitable people, and kind beyond all expectation. I enjoyed their sing-song voices, but most of all I admired their complete absorption in and wholehearted propensity for vocal display. They really loved singing, whether solo or *en masse*, and what glorious voices Wales has produced! Especially male.

I soon became very wary of local accompanists who possessed music degrees which were proudly placed after their names on the programmes, but some of whom could not even manage the most simple accompaniment.

Once, when I was a member of a quartet appearing at a mining town up one of the valleys from Swansea, we all arrived on the same train and we were met by the local organiser.

"Hope you're in good voice for tonight. That last lot they sent us"—and he listed some well known names—"were dreadful. We expect the best, you know, and if you go down in our valley you'll go down anywhere."

What a greeting! He was quite sincere and honest in what he said.

I am thankful to say that our solos, duets, trios and quartets were all rapturously received, and the organiser came to our one and only dressing room after the concert.

"I told them in London not to send us a band of croaky has-beens, and they've taken my advice. You were good."

While he hurried out to control the crowd of autograph hunters we slapped each other's backs. "Thank goodness we've gone down in this valley! There's hope for the future."

These concerts were very exhausting at times, for the Welsh liked the evening to go on interminably, and any concert finishing under three hours was a disappointment to them. Often speeches were made during the interval, and to the artists the concerts seemed never ending.

At another one we sang *The Creation* in the first half, and miscellaneous items in the second! The hotels in many of the mining towns were poorly equipped for travellers spending the night. Once I fell into bed in one of these drab, freezing rooms, and within an hour I awoke feeling wet and clammy. I switched on the light and looked under the bed-clothes. Steam from a hot body and damp sheets. I leapt out of bed and got fully dressed, and then lay on top of the bed ticking off the hours until the night porter called me at 5.30 a.m. I had to catch the first train down the valley in order to connect with the London train.

Three days later I fell ill with mild pneumonia. It cost me four engagements which I could ill afford to lose, and it taught me a lesson. Thereafter I always placed a mirror between the sheets to test the water content in any hotel bed. In fact, if I am in doubt anywhere at any time, I use a mirror for this admirable purpose.

Apart from the appalling journeys when trains were jam-packed and there were long delays caused by wrecked carriages and rails, music-making during the war was a pleasure. One of the most acceptable and amusing gestures of appreciation was the type of after-concert tribute which came in the form of a flower-decked box containing delectable scarcities, caused by severe food-rationing, such as butter, eggs, sugar, jam, ham, tinned meat, cheese and chocolates. I was always told not to open such boxes until I was back in London. I did as I was told, and it was as good as opening a treasure-chest. I had heard many stories of the black marketeers of the valleys of Wales, but I never connected them with my own hard-earned "bouquets".

Of the thirty-odd concerts booked for me in Wales, five had to be cancelled as I was unable to get on a train at Paddington. Most journeys I had to stand. When there was a lull in the air raids and people were back in London, I occasionally managed to get a seat, but as soon as the raids began again the stations were chaotic and the usual pandemonium broke out. I can only describe these times as sheer hell. One could get caught up in the mael-strom of mass movement, and it was terrifying. Troops had passes, and stations were littered with kitbags, rifles, gas-mask holders and other equipment, not to mention tired, bewildered children who had been brought back to London only to be removed again, bemused elderly couples, and extraneous travellers such as I. Evacuated families were repeatedly asked to remain in their temporary homes, but they flocked back to their beloved London in their hundreds as soon as the raids let up a little. This complicated matters for the W.V.S. and other wonderful services, for people panicked after a bad raid and wanted to be evacuated all over again! Many business people shut up their London homes and rented places out of the Greater London area They commuted daily rather than spend their nights in a possible inferno.

At the end of 1940, I began singing under the auspices of ENSA (and later of CEMA), and continued throughout the war.

An important engagement in December of this vital year was to sing in the *Messiah* at Bradford with Dr Malcolm Sargent. Travel-wise it was disastrous, as the line was bombed just outside London and the carriages were in complete darkness for three hours before we crawled slowly into Peterborough. Thereafter some speed was achieved, but we arrived at Bradford $6\frac{1}{2}$ hours late. Everyone accepted it cheerfully, but that darkened train, crammed to capacity, I found very disquieting. It was a cold, damp night and the windows were closed. I was fighting claustrophobia while we were stationary for twenty minutes in a tunnel just out of King's Cross. I was saved by sudden laughter and a raw Cockney voice. I couldn't see the owner of it, but I heard his reply when somebody asked him why he, a Southerner, was heading back to the Green Howards in Catterick Camp. "Some bloody fool made a mistake," he said, typically.

Dr Sargent knew of our tiring train journey and he made the rehearsal as easy as possible. The tenor and I had not previously worked with him, so we had a piano call before the orchestral rehearsal. This meeting with Dr Sargent was to be the beginning of a long and wonderful musical association. He was always meticulous, punctilious to a degree (he would ask you to be at a rehearsal at a certain time and he was ready for you within minutes—unique among conductors) and he was sympathetic. His consideration for his artists was most noticeable.

This was the turning point in my career. The B.B.C. sent me four bookings, and many concert engagements came in at the end of 1940. I sang in *Bethlehem* with Robbie and that splendid soprano Lisa Perli (Dora Labette) at Stratford-on-Avon on Christmas Eve. It was a great climax to a year of doubt, indecision and financial worry. My path had now been set, and my career was beginning again.

In London I had to attend lectures on fire fighting and first aid. The latter was still fairly fresh in my memory after the Life Saving examinations for the Bronze, Silver and Gold Medals in Sydney.

All civilian men were being trained and one episode remains with me still. I was walking Pippo in the large gardens running down the centre of Eaton Square. There were shrubs of all kinds, some very dense and suitable for a game of hide-and-seek. On this summer evening I came around a blind bend and encountered a well-dressed man, complete with rolled umbrella and bowler hat. On seeing me he levelled his umbrella at me like a rifle, and shouted: "Boom! Boom! Boom!" I stood stock still, not wishing to spoil his fun.

"I'm dead," I answered. He raised his hat.

"I beg your pardon, Madam, but there is a Home Guard exercise here this evening, and I thought you were one of the enemy." He lowered his umbrella and went on his way somewhat sheepishly.

I was delighted with this bit of whimsy as there was an air raid in progress at the time, and here we were preparing for the invasion of Eaton Square, bowler hats and all.

During the nights I'll admit to feeling afraid. Although some horrifying raids occurred in daylight, the night raids filled me with terror.

1941 began with an ENSA concert at Bangor in North Wales. I had the usual dreadful journey, with changes at Crewe and Chester. In London I travelled by tube, as it was the quickest way of getting about. The tube stations during the War were surely a unique sight. As they were far underground they were comparatively safe from bombs, and every night the platforms were lined with people sleeping, and at some select stations, on two-tier bunks provided. There was just enough room to step in and out of the trains. At times the stench was nauseating. Entire families lived in this way from dusk to dawn. They brought their bedding, and small stoves for making tea. Some clutched hot water bottles. Many families claimed their own "pitch" and they occupied the same spot every night, while strangers to the scene were regarded with suspicion. As it was after midnight when the trains stopped running, and about five o'clock in the morning when they started again, there were not many hours of silence during which these poor people could sleep in peace. It was an education to see them.

Contracts began to flow in nicely. Two complete performances of *La Traviata* for the B.B.C. with Robbie came my way, and an abbreviated version for Latin America that was transmitted live at two o'clock in the morning.

I sang at the old, acoustically excellent Colston Hall in Bristol with Sir Adrian Boult. I sang with him on several occasions during my career, and he was a gentleman in the best sense of the word, completely lacking artificiality or pose. Nothing appeared to ruffle him, and with his quiet authoritative manner he had absolute control of the orchestra.

The Colston Hall was popular with all musicians. It had such atmosphere. When it was destroyed by enemy action there was a feeling of losing a friend, somehow—a friend in the sense of a building containing the memories of so many great moments. Old theatres and halls all possess certain indefinable characteristics which became indelibly imprinted on the minds of sensitive artists. One looks forward to returning to some of them as soon as the contracts arrive—the Colston Hall, London's Royal Albert Hall, and the St Andrew's Hall in Glasgow (now burned down), the Usher Hall, Edinburgh, all come to mind as places to which I loved to return.

On 13 February 1941, in the Birmingham Town Hall, I recorded "One Fine Day" and "They call me Mimi" with Leslie Heward and the City of Birmingham Symphony Orchestra. This disc was the first of mine to be issued, and it made its appearance on 11 April of that year. There was a government ban on recording in any language other than English at the time, though this was lifted soon after the end of the war.

We had a piano rehearsal on the previous night, in a suite in the Queen's Hotel, and a three-hour session in the morning with orchestra. We would rehearse the aria first and then go for a "take". One could sing the same aria anything from six to ten times. Even the dropping of a cellist's bow, or the touching of a conductor's baton against the stand, not to mention the artist's dissatisfaction with some note or phrase, would cause another "take". I very soon learnt that recording sessions were the most testing, tiring and unsatisfactory forms of art. One never knew what the end result would sound like until several weeks had elapsed. I was lucky to have E.M.I.'s head technician, Arthur

Clark, in charge of all my early recordings. He was thorough and painstaking, and to watch him handle wax discs was like watching an antique dealer handling some enormously valuable piece of china. If Arthur said that he had a good "master" you could be content.

I was keeping my fingers crossed that this time the "master" would not be destroyed by enemy action. On 7 April I recorded "The Green Hills o' Somerset" and "Waters of Minnetonka", with Gerald as my accompanist. This was to be the second record of mine to be issued.

It was in September that I completed the most fruitful session; four arias "in the bag", as Arthur would say. Raids had begun on Birmingham, so we were transferred to Manchester. Again I had the pleasure of recording with Leslie Heward. No time was wasted at a session with him—he knew what he wanted and the Hallé Orchestra obeyed him promptly, beautifully. This orchestra always produced some of the finest playing to be heard from any orchestra in Britain.

Two discs were the result of that three-hour session. They were "O My Beloved Father" from *Gianni Schicchi*, and "Love and Music" from *Tosca*, both by Puccini, and "May Laurels Crown thy Brow" ("Ritorna Vincitor") from Verdi's *Aïda*, with Mimi's Farewell from *La Bohème*—Puccini again.

As far as I was concerned, that recording session was epoch making. When discussing with Walter Legge what arias I should sing, we happily agreed upon those from *Tosca*, *La Bohème* and *Aïda*, but we could not agree over the fourth side. We wanted an equally short aria to be coupled with what Walter Legge thought would be the attraction: "Love and Music". As I was not especially well known, he wanted a fairly popular aria for the "flip" side.

I had learnt the role of Lauretta in *Gianni Schicchi* while in Florence, and this brief, poignant aria appealed to me enormously. In the opera itself it sometimes passes with hardly any recognition if the singer fails to interpret it well. As a vignette taken from a large portrait and made into an important whole, this recording has become popular beyond my maddest dreams. Walter did not know the aria, and, acting as he thought in the best interests of the Company, he did not agree to its inclusion. For weeks before the session, we had spasmodic discussions. He made several suggestions, but I clung to "O My Beloved Father" with a tenacity which surprised me; the hand of Fate was obviously guiding me round the corner! I was obdurate as time grew shorter. Once Walter agreed, not another word was said.

There were many musical queries which arose during recording sessions over which I remained adamant. I firmly believed in following my individual sense of interpretation. I refused to interpret in some particular way because the great soprano So-and-So did it in that way. Voice and people are individual. That is what makes them great.

I felt that certain phrases needed expanding and certain words accentuating in order to paint the story in vocal colour. To count 1.2.3.4. in a bar is not making music, but to make a rallentando of 3 and 4 and still maintain good rhythm is making the music say something to the listener. How deadly are the musicians who play and sing with technical perfection and in strict time, with no musical *rubati* or the caressing of a note or phrase!

I believe it was Von Bülow who told the story of the famous old violinist who was reputed to have said: "It took me one half of my life to learn to play in time, and the other half to learn how to play out of time."

To be able to toy with rhythm without losing control of it is one of the attributes of great aristry. So many promising musicians fail because of this inability to play with a phrase. With some, especially singers, a sense of rhythm is inherent. They may never learn to read music, but they are born with an ability to handle rhythm which enables them to juggle with words and phrases in a way which makes a delightful whole. But I would never advise aspiring young singers to rely on the assumption that voice and rhythm are enough. One is fully aware that accompanists, who also coach, will drum the notes into unmusical singers, and many such singers have become famous without being able to read a note of music. But one cannot get far today without a certain degree of musical ability.

A well equipped singer is to be relied upon, and conductors would choose the musician rather than a voice.

There is so much enjoyment to be had from music if you sing and play an instrument. You learn quickly, and you have the immeasurable pleasure of participating in chamber music, which is immense fun, while you learn. I used to look forward rapturously to meeting once a week with three other students to play quartets, or trios if one could not attend. If I were able to play the violin now with any degree of competence, then this form of relaxation, as I would call it, would be a joy. There is, of course, the problem of finding others who share this view!

At the beginning of February 1941 I obtained a gas mask for Pippo. This side of the British people is a remarkable and wonderful one. The cause for the preservation of domestic and wild animals is great indeed. Quickly expanding populations and densely inhabited cities can cause ruthless and unnecessary suffering in the lives of the dwellers. There is no time left for thought for animals. It is quite enough to keep going in the rat race and keeping up with the Joneses. God's dumb creatures tend to be crowded out. But the fact remains, gas masks were issued for dogs in Britain, and I wonder where else in the world this would happen? The United States of America, perhaps.

Early in March a contract came for opera in Dublin, but the Government refused all exit permits, so I was unable to go. I was most disappointed as I had so greatly enjoyed my first visit to Ireland, but when this particular door slammed in my face, several more opened in the way of work. Many B.B.C. engagements were booked, and concerts came in in various parts of the country.

I had always been a hayfever sufferer, although but mildly in Australia. In Britain it seemed to get worse every year. The dust of bomb rubble and the stuffiness of London aggravated it greatly. By mid-June I was experiencing severe asthma, which kept me awake at night. This was the beginning of yearly tests and potions. Inevitably sufferers from nervous allergies spend a great deal of money in search of relief, and I was no exception.

Whenever possible I would darken my bedroom and keep cold packs across my eyes.

When the cooler air of September arrived I used to feel that the wretched ailment would never assail me again, but this was a pipe dream. In winter, if I went from a warm house out into the cold air, I would have an attack of asthma immediately.

The reason I mention this particular unpleasant ailment is the flower-bedecked platforms on which I so often sang. At first I was too embarrassed to ask for the flowers, which were sometimes right under my nose, so to speak, to be removed. But on one occasion I turned and nodded to my accompanist to begin, and a fit of sneezing came on. I decided they would have to be moved. I laughed it off between sneezes, and said to the audience: "Bear with me—achoo—hayfever—achoo—flowers—achoo." The audience laughed while an usher materialised from somewhere and began removing the flowers, while I continued my unrehearsed item. When it subsided, I dried my eyes and nose with my accompanist's handkerchief, and we got on with the performance. Thereafter, I always asked concert organisers in advance to see that there were no fresh flowers on stage. Any that were used must be well away from me.

Organisers were doing the right thing in dressing the platforms so beautifully, and I felt worm-like, but I knew that, as the concert progressed, the heat of a full hall and stage lighting would cause the flower perfume to become stronger. On one occasion I arrived at a hall to give a recital, I went to look at the stage before changing. I saw a complete drawing room set—carpet, chairs, chaise-longue, escritoire, back-cloths depicting a fireplace and window with garden scene beyond, and a boudoir grand! I had the carpet removed, as it had a few visible rents from age and over-use. I had thoughts of making my usual quick entry and landing flat on my nose.

When living in London between engagements, I became quite expert at scrubbing floors and doing general housework at the Mews Cottage. I cannot work amid untidiness, and as a consequence I tend to overdo cleanliness. I became a hard taskmaster in later years when I could afford to get help, and when I was lucky enough to find someone. To this day I am unable to sit at my desk if my room is untidy.

I cooked the first meal of my life in that year of 1941. It took me precisely four hours to cook it, eat it, and clean up. It was a simple meal of sprouts, potatoes, and stewed apples. My culinary efforts have never got beyond grills, and as I am not over-fond of chops and steaks I concentrated on vegetables. Food rationing simplified the meat question, and in any case the steak was very inferior, and only fit to stew.

Early in February 1942 I met H. B. Phillips, who was about to put his opera company, the Carl Rosa, on the road again. At a time of unrest and general insecurity, this must have been a big decision; but he was a man of enterprise and foresight. He was to be the sole means of giving the British people opera during the early war years. He was a gentleman in the best sense of the word, and I personally found him to be a man of his word. I enjoyed a friendship that lasted until the end of his life, and I learnt a great deal from this fine old man of the theatre.

My debut with the Carl Rosa was in *Madam Butterfly* at Glasgow on 16 March 1942. I had no stage rehearsal, as the Theatre Royal had some other show in progress while we were preparing to occupy the theatre for a three-week season. This was the usual procedure. No entrepreneur could afford to book a theatre for a rehearsing period. Some of the soloists used to meet, at various London addresses, and do the greater part of the rehearsals. We all met in Glasgow for the first time four days before the opening night.

That first *Madam Butterfly* left a lot to be desired. Many of the props were missing, as the scenery and such things had been in store in London and the storehouse received a direct hit which did much damage to scenery and props. It must have been a colossal job assembling everything miles away in Glasgow. The scenery looked a little worn and tired for this historic season, but it would have been folly to do anything about it at that juncture. H.B., as he was called, could have had no idea as to the ultimate success of opera in the provinces during wartime. He was courageous to put an opera company on the road at all.

My feelings after this, my first *Madam Butterfly*, were of shame and sickness in the solar plexus. I wanted to hide, vanish and never be seen again. My performance was below the standard I had set for myself. I felt it lacked so much. But one becomes numb on such occasions. There were three performances close together, on 16, 18 and 19 March. After the third one the audience gave me the most exciting reception. I could hardly believe all that clapping and shouting of "Bravo" was for me as I took a solo curtain. I tried to make the great artist, Gladys Parr, who subsequently sang the majority of Suzukis with me, come and share the acclaim, but she said, "Go on, it's you they want," and she gently pushed me forward.

How lucky I was to have had the honour of working with Gladys. I learnt such a great deal from her. She will always be the most perfect Suzuki as far as I am concerned. I used to watch her in *Il Trovatore* as Azucena, and as Prince Orlofski in *Die Fledermaus*. No matter what the role, Gladys was the character she portrayed. Moreover, she could be relied upon to step in or switch operas at a moment's notice—no fuss, no trouble. A real trouper.

My debut in *La Traviata* followed twelve days later. By then I had got to know the members of the company, and found them a very eager, talented group of professionals. Some of them had worked for H.B. before. I was a guest artist, and remained so for the duration of a long and happy affiliation over many years. I sang *Madam Butterfly*, *La Traviata*, *Faust*, *Il Trovatore*, *La Bohème* and *Tosca* with some very fine artists; and many first-rate performances were given in this, the initial operatic venture of World War II.

Kingsley Lark produced, as well as singing minor roles, during the first season. He was a knowledgeable and very capable and gifted actor-singer. The guest artists were Lisa Perli, Edith Coates, Gwen Catley, Parry Jones, Heddle Nash, Norman Allin and Dennis Noble, as well as myself. Gladys Parr, Ruth Packer, Helen Ogilvie, Tudor Davies, Hubert Dunkerley and Appleton

Moore were regular members of the company. As the years passed by, so did many of the artists come and go.

It was an excellent company to work with, as it consisted of true professionals who knew how to make do and cover up when things went wrong. One never felt at a loss if the props were missing, or that there was a possibility of drying up during a performance. Everyone thought ahead and looked for alternatives; an artist would disappear off-stage only to return as quickly with the missing prop.

In many ways Vienna had spoilt me, as nothing there was ever left to chance or forgotten. In those Austrian opera houses they had a system which seemed infallible, but of course on occasions the method broke down owing to the human element, as it can anywhere. Besides, it is simple to have an almost foolproof system in a company which was not always touring, as was the Carl Rosa. To be constantly housed and have everything under one roof minimises the chance of error. But a company touring week after week, packing, unpacking, moving scenery, costumes and all the multifarious bits and pieces that make up an opera company, such as music, instruments and endless impedimenta, demands colossal organisation. H.B. was not the man to be defeated by the obvious difficulties of touring in wartime. Every penny was watched, and slowly the company's scenery was rebuilt. He did not attempt any lavish productions until 1944, and then only a few. Everything was too costly, or unobtainable. Producers had to keep one great factor always in view—that everything had to be continually packed and unpacked. Fussy sets were useless. Strength and simplicity were the keynotes of every production. There were few companies with which I enjoyed working more.

Rising costs kill most privately run forms of entertainment. Opera is a luxury, and governments rightly realise that to maintain a standard of culture in the arts means big subsidies. One still bemoans the change from a personally run company to a government-run one. The former was compact. There was only one boss, and that meant quick decisions and complete control over all personnel. Government-run bodies seem rudderless, inefficient at times, because of their very complex structure. The British public had men such as Sir Thomas Beecham and H. B. Phillips to thank for bringing opera to the people. H. B. went everywhere with his company, and Sir Thomas often toured with the British National Opera Company. Both were essential if opera was to survive at all.

In the years to come, I so often thought of the excellent way in which the Carl Rosa was run. Those war years were not wasted. I learnt from every performance. Once Covent Garden was reinstated as a home of opera and ballet, and Sadler's Wells reopened, many of the previously starved operaphiles drifted away from the Carl Rosa. It had served a purpose. Now opera lovers from all levels of society could mix with equal pleasure at the government subsidised opera houses.

During the war, however, the general public clamoured to get tickets for the Carl Rosa. It is impossible to say whether the days of sorrow and anguish caused people to seek the greater transcendental enjoyment to be found in opera and not in lighter music, but there were always newcomers.

H.B. told me of two comical occasions. A woman went to the box office and asked:

"What's on here tonight?"

"Opera."

"What's that?"

"It's musical."

"Would I like it?"

"I don't know."

"Well, I'll have two tickets."

The other occasion was when a young man went to the box office and said:

"Can you tell me if the opera on tonight has a tune in it that goes like this?" He whistled a few bars from the famous tenor aria "La donna è mobile". The box office attendant recognised the tune, and replied: "Yes."

"When does it come?"

"Not until the second act."

"How long'll that be?"

"Another forty minutes or so."

The young man bought a ticket. "Okay. I'll come back." And he did.

Some of the newcomers to opera become fanatical about it; others drift off to light music. The important thing is that they come, and that some gain a new and wonderful form of pleasure.

Another interesting thing that emerged from wartime opera performances was that patrons came to hear the singing, as there was no accent on production. They learned to love opera for what it is—a singer's vehicle. Without good singing the entire conception can crumble dismally and disappoint enthusiasts. Take the great, well-produced voices away, and give a lavish, brilliantly produced opera with talentless, small-voiced singers, and the result is negligible and lacking in excitement or thrill.

A combination of great singers and production is not unknown, of course, but it is rare. Minor, impecunious companies should obtain the best singers available first, and then use the remaining money for the production.

Unfortunately, engagements do not come in tidily at the rate of three a week. Sometimes four or five come in, and then there will be a slack period with nothing at all.

At a time when a lot of work was condensed into a week, I found myself obliged to catch the night train from Glasgow back to London after a performance of *Madam Butterfly*. The performances began at 7 p.m. and the last train left at 9.50 p.m., so there was no time to spare.

A taxi was held in readiness, and H. B. Phillips held the intervals to strict timing by keeping the scene shifters on the move. My outdoor clothes and make-up box were packed and put in the taxi, so that I could change on the train and thus save a few precious seconds. A sleeper had been reserved for me, and a packet of sandwiches was made up so that I needn't go hungry.

It was a terrific rush from stage to Glasgow Central Station, and I was thankful when I reached the barrier to see the train still standing in the station. The platform was crowded with passengers and the people who were farewelling them.

The ticket collector gave me an odd look, and then I realised

Above left and below: Leningrad, 1957, Tatiana in the letter scene, *Eugène Onegin.*
Above right: Barcelona, 1954–5, Fevronia in *The Invisible City of Kitesh*

Bath Festival, 1959: Dido in *Dido and Aeneas*

Desdemona in *Otello*

Elizabeth in *Don Carlos*

Sadler's Wells, 1959: Rusalka in *Rusalka*

Leonora in *Fidelio*

Salome

Tosca

Madam Butterfly

that everybody was looking at me with antagonism. I was be-wigged and gowned as a Japanese! If the platform had been better lit, the wig and heavy stage make-up would have been obvious, but as it was, I looked the real thing—a native of an enemy country. Loud comments reached me.

"How dare she wear national dress in our country!"

"Look at that yellow microbe! Go home—we don't want you!"

"Aha!" said a tipsy soldier, "the enemy is with us! Come on, chaps—let's kill the Jap."

If I'd had a free hand I would have pulled my wig off. People moved away from me as if I were a leper as I threaded my way along the platform. The sleeping car was an asylum for me, and luckily the car attendant knew me. He was most comforting. He saw my distress. "Now don't fuss yourself, Miss Joan. Just relax and I'll rustle up a cuppa for you as soon as we've moved off and I've got everybody settled."

It was one of the best cuppas I've ever had!

It was a sad day when H. B. Phillips passed away. The company gradually disintegrated, and finally became swallowed up by Sadler's Wells, first becoming number 2 company, and then losing its identity completely. It celebrated its seventieth anni-versary in 1945, having given unbroken performances throughout all that time except for the years 1940 and 1941—a great feat for private enterprise.

This was the start of my rising popularity in the British Isles. B.B.C. work became plentiful, and many miscellaneous con-certs, and oratorio also, came in. I was travelling a great deal under abnormal, trying conditions. There was no food to be had on trains and transport generally was a nightmare.

I was engaged to adjudicate for the first time at the Royal Academy. This was a most interesting experience and a reward-ing task. I later did a great deal of adjudicating, and I always found it stimulating to listen to young students and artists who had just begun a career.

Among my circle of friends were musicians, actors, medical

I

and law students. As the war increased in ferocity so did our numbers dwindle, as one by one they joined up or were called up into the Services. We used to meet regularly to go to the ballet or a play. Estrées Walker was one of the few to remain in London. She was in the London County Council Ambulance Service. She is a gifted person who does everything well. As a pianist she can sight-read any music, and she has perfect pitch. She is a superb cook, and a very rapid typist. I first met her through Australian friends who had given me an introduction to her aunt when I was in Vienna. Her aunt was very kind and sympathetic to all young students.

Estrées used to do quite a lot of playing for me during the war, but as from the end of 1945 she took on the job of typing out programme notes, words and translations of songs for programmes. This was a massive task, and tiring. She spent hours with me, at the piano, while I worked out recital programmes, a task which needed tremendous patience, as it was rather similar to working out a jigsaw puzzle. I found that the key of F major somehow kept popping up and causing programme-arrangement trouble. I would select a number of slow and quick items, and then begin to group them. Sure enough too many of them were in F Major. It was a key I liked, so maybe this was the reason.

Through ENSA concerts I met Vera Wise (Mrs Barns) who did a great amount of accompanying and coaching. She was another brilliant pianist. She could transpose even the most difficult music. I have often watched her skip from one key to another without fumbling or hesitating. She has a delightful temperament and is wonderful company. I was very fortunate in having both her and Estrées to work with throughout my career.

Out of the blue, my younger brother Tony appeared in England with the R.A.A.F. He telephoned from Bournemouth to say that he had arrived and had been given leave to come and see me in London. The next evening I went to meet him at Waterloo station. We had not seen each other for six years.

The train arrived at 6.30 p.m. and I was there to meet it. I saw hundreds of R.A.A.F. men, but not one resembled my brother. I walked up and down peering into faces—one had to peer in the gloom of the ill-lit platforms. Blackout restrictions were either a severe handicap or a blessing, according to what you wanted to do.

There was one tall lad who seemed to be in the same predicament as myself. He was going up and down and we almost collided on one occasion. Finally only a mere handful was left, and the station was becoming gloomier. I was hesitating and wondering what to do when this R.A.A.F. lad came close again, and I said, almost in desperation: "Tony." The voice of the man replied "Joan!" and that is how we eventually recognised each other—by chance. When I left Sydney, Tony was in his teens, and naturally he had filled out and grown. It was marvellous having him around whenever he was on leave throughout the war years. He was flying Lancaster bombers at that stage. He ended up as a Pathfinder pilot, and was awarded the D.F.C., and Bar.

Soon after Tony's arrival in England there was another reunion. My friend Emmerich Eber from Vienna looked me up in London. Imagine my surprise to see him in the uniform of a Major in the U.S. Army!

During this time in London we used to do all our sight-seeing on bicycles. Estrées, Tony, Eber and I would set off to theatres, the Tower of London—anywhere, in fact—on bicycles. Eber was a trifle self-conscious about it until he saw an American Lieutenant-Colonel riding about London on a bike. Thereafter I went everywhere locally by bike from July 1942 until 1946.

By the end of 1942 my popularity had increased considerably. The problem was to try to keep time free for the paid work, as I was doing so many charity and troop concerts. It was an unreal existence, in a sense. Singing at an afternoon tea party at the Mansion House, where I met Mrs Churchill, Mrs A. V. Alexander (wife of the First Lord of the Admiralty), Mrs Winant (wife of the Ambassador of the U.S.A.) and Madame Maisky (wife of the Soviet Ambassador), and in the evening a B.B.C.

programme at the Criterion Theatre with Jack Payne and his band. Off to Huddersfield the next day for a *Messiah*, returning the following day, and singing at night for the American troops at the Washington Club in London. The next night there was a *Bohème* with the Carl Rosa at Wimbledon—two nights later *La Traviata* there—this was the pattern of life until November, when I had an interview and driving test for the London County Council. I took on part-time work as an ambulance driver.

Transport, especially with a dog, was something of a problem in those days. One day, while waiting for a bus, I saw a youth whip past riding a bicycle with an outsize delivery basket in front, stacked with parcels. In other words, a grocer's errand boy, doing a delivery round.

The seed was sown, and I knew the next thing to do was to find a grocer who would tell me where I could purchase such a machine. I located the nearest one, and he soon got in touch with me to say that he had an errand boy's bicycle, going cheap. When I saw it I realised why. It looked tired and worn, but I gave it a coat of paint, two new tyres and a new saddle. I tizzied up the basket and put a padded cushion in it and lined the sides. The whole thing suddenly came to life—I had an ideal means of local travel for myself and my standard poodle, Mr Pippo. He simply loved it.

We travelled far and wide on this bicycle. Up through the West End to Clerkenwell, and later either along the Embankment or through the West End, across the City and to the East End to the Ambulance Station. We went for jaunts to Kew, Wimbledon or Hampstead Heath, where Pippo could go mad with delight. I was often saddle-sore, but happy to have a completely independent conveyance for two.

I did night shifts, which meant going on duty after performances. The shift ended at 8 a.m., after which it was often necessary for me to catch a train to the north for an engagement. It was strenuous, but I felt I was doing more for the war than just singing. I realised that entertainment and entertainers, no matter in what field, were as essential as any other tool in the war kit. One of the most tiresome chores was the getting of rations. A time-waster, but necessary. The queues for everything became worse and worse.

When coming off duty in the early morning from the Ambulance Station I usually bought a daily paper. One day I was struck by the photograph, spread across four columns, of an attractive woman. The caption read: "Hostess found shot in Paris night-club." Sleepy though I was, it penetrated to my mind that I knew that face. I looked again, and stopped dead in my tracks. The name was Maidi. There again was the elegant, expensively dressed, mysterious Maidi, looking at me from the front page of the paper. Maidi, of whom I had seen such a lot at my digs in Vienna. Maidi, the intimate friend of the Baroness and her daughter V.

I was now wide awake and reading avidly. What I read sickened me, and I realised that Maidi had had her just deserts. She had been found dead in the night club in the early hours of the morning. Shot by members of a secret organisation. She was a Nazi spy acting as hostess in one of the most popular clubs, where high ranking German officers and civilians used to while away the hours. When their tongues had loosened Maidi would gather incriminating information and pass it on to headquarters. She had been responsible for many deaths. After reading all the lurid details of a career packed with intrigue as one of the top Nazi agents working in Paris, I felt momentarily paralysed. My mind flew back to that small back room in the Baroness' apartment, to Yascha, to V., and Prince D.—were they all perhaps in the same grisly game? Now I could see it all. Those people had been just too vehemently anti-Nazi to be true. The newspaper account fitted in with the little I had known of Maidi. She had certainly been a brilliant and useful weapon for those she served.

An interesting meeting occurred during this period. H.B. had engaged the Czech-born conductor, Walter Süsskind, to conduct the *Traviata* performances at London's Winter Garden theatre. Walter was a delight to work with. He played for all the piano rehearsals, and in a short time he was able to get some excellent results from the orchestra, and splendid ensemble work from the singers. One felt so confident with him, both when he was in the orchestra pit and on the concert platform. His beat was so clear, and rhythm flowed from his finger tips. There was a limpid flexibility in his style which made the making of music a complete joy.

On 23 February 1943 the B.B.C. put on the grandest show of the War. It was a massive production called "Salute to the Red Army", and it was written by Louis MacNeice.

Basil Dean produced it, and in my opinion he did a magnificent job in handling a large cast and all the effects so well. Two special fanfares were written by William Walton. Lieut. Laurence Olivier, R.N.V.R., delivered "A Foreword for Victory" from Medieval Russia when Alexander Nevsky defeated the German invaders.

"The Nazi Threat to the Soviet Union" was another big item in which the spokesman was Lieut.-Commander Ralph Richardson, R.N.V.R., the spokeswoman Dame Sybil Thorndike, while the Nazi figure was spoken by Marius Goring. Dennis Noble and I sang in the "Ode to the Red Army", composed specially for the occasion by Alan Rawsthorne. Anthony Eden, then Foreign Secretary, delivered a speech. Arnold Bax, Master of the King's Musick, wrote a solemn Fanfare for the occasion, and the conductor was Dr. Malcolm Sargent. What a galaxy! Instrumental music was provided by the London Philharmonic Orchestra and a section of the B.B.C. Symphony Orchestra, as well as the bands of the Grenadier and Scots Guards, and trumpets and drums of the Life Guards and the Royal Horse Guards, and the Royal Air Force. There were buglers from the Royal Marines, and Arnold Grier was at the organ. The sides of the vast Albert Hall were almost bursting. It was a great tribute to the Russian forces which were then in the throes of rolling back the German invading armies.

I sang in two opera seasons in Dublin in 1943. I repeated Pamina in *The Magic Flute*, and added Mimi in *La Bohème*, the Elizabeth of *Tannhäuser*, *Madam Butterfly*, *Aïda*, and Leonora in *Il Trovatore*. To go to Dublin at this time was equivalent to visiting the

Continent. There was a breezy, happy, unhurried atmosphere, and of course an abundance of food. One had to eat with care, otherwise the sudden richness of food cooked in butter, as well as every available kind of fresh fruit, caused one's impoverished ration-bound stomach to revolt.

During this visit I gave two recitals, one in Dublin and the other in Cork. Both were sold out, which was most exhilarating. I was by now well acquainted with *Messiah*, *The Creation* and *Hiawatha*. But a new work came my way. It was Beethoven's huge Mass in D. I found it a stimulating challenge, and the preparation for it filled me with pleasure.

In October that year I sang in Trecynon, a Welsh town. It was as usual a miscellaneous concert. My fellow artists were Kathleen Ferrier, Jan van der Gucht and Robert Easton. This was the first of many concerts and broadcasts with Kathleen. I recall asking her, on the return journey to London, if she was interested in singing in opera. She replied: "Oh no! I can't imagine myself dressed up as someone else. I'd look and feel a fool!"

"Nonsense! You'd be marvellous." I meant it, for she had such a fine appearance, and I was very impressed with her voice. She sang the duet "Home to our Mountains" from *Il Trovatore* with Jan, and we ended the programme with the quartet from *Rigoletto*.

At that time, nothing would induce Kathleen to change her mind no matter how often I asked her, but many years later she did sing in opera: in Britten's *The Rape of Lucretia* and, just before her death, in Gluck's *Orfeo* at Covent Garden.

I sang a great deal with another fine contralto—Gladys Ripley. Gladys felt the same as Kathleen about opera. She was happy singing in concerts, and she told me she would feel awkward "dressed up" in costume. It was strange, because Gladys was such a gay, vivacious woman, who appeared to have no inhibitions. She died soon after Kathleen with the same tragic illness.

The Carl Rosa gave a week of opera in the open air at Brockwell Park, London. The night I sang Violetta in *La Traviata* happened to be a very hot one, and the flies, bees and midges were out in full force. The make-up was attracting them, and I was really afraid of swallowing one. It made the scene with Germont Père very realistic as he came in from the supposed garden angrily swiping at the insects! The July sun blazed on to the stage and I longed to plunge into a swimming pool.

The next day I had an unforgettable swim which was nearly my last. Estrées and I had taken my two poodles for a walk in Battersea Park. In addition to Pippo, I now had a white poodle called Jani—named after General Smuts' Oomjani—pronounced Yani. He was a standard poodle who had belonged to a South African couple. They wanted to give him away, but no one would take him, so eventually a friend of mine to whom his future welfare had been entrusted gave him to me "for a few days". He spent the rest of his life with me.

Pippo loved swimming. Jani had not learnt how at that stage, but they both chased balls, sticks or anything you would throw for them. We were close to Chelsea Bridge, and we sat on a tiny patch of sand by the water. A small boy came by, and we asked him not to throw sticks into the river, as the current was running strongly.

We had no sooner asked, than the child threw a stick well out. Pippo was after it like a shot. To my horror I saw him struggling to come back when the tide caught him and he was swept out of sight. I ripped off my shoes, dived in and had no trouble getting to him, but I found it was almost impossible to bring him back. Estrées was powerless to help us, and I shouted to her to remain at the corner of the wall. I had to force Pippo to come across the tide one way and then the other, but he was so frightened that he kept pushing away and heading for Estrées. The weight of my wet clothes was dragging me down, and in trying to contain Pippo's struggles I swallowed a few mouthfuls of Thames water. I knew I couldn't last much longer. I felt dizzy and the world seemed to be slipping away, with a quick vision of my life. I gave one final desperate push. Estrées grabbed Pippo and managed to take my hand in that terrifying moment.

When I reached safety I couldn't speak for some minutes. It

had been a very close nudge with death. Naturally there was no sign of the boy who had thrown the stick.

As we walked home a woman passed us. She said loudly: "Disgraceful! Young women brazenly walking the streets in dripping wet, dirty clothes! Disgraceful!"

We hadn't given a thought to our appearance. We must have been a sight with bedraggled hair and mud on our clothes and legs.

Just about then, I heard the news of Pam Barton's death. She was a W.A.A.F. attached to an R.A.F. station in Kent and had died in an aeroplane crash. This tragic news came as a great shock to me, for she was one of the greatest and most colourful British golfers of all time.

On 5 December I sang the Marschallin in a concert performance of *Der Rosenkavalier* at Golders Green, and this was repeated early the following year. I had been rehearsing as usual at the Fleischmanns' house in Bryanston Square. The raids were very bad again, and one day when I went there, I found that the house had been razed to the ground. I was sickened at the senselessness of it all.

The following February the raids increased in ferocity. On the night of the 17th all the windows were blasted out of the Royal Albert Hall. I was appearing at a matinée of Elgar's *The Apostles* the following day and it was freezingly cold. Nevertheless the hall was packed.

I was switched from the Clerkenwell Ambulance Station to one in Cannon Street Road, Stepney. Here I was given an insight into another side of life to which I was quite unaccustomed. I was horrified to see some of the tenement houses with one water tap on the ground floor which served five floors and innumerable people. During these nightly raids every ambulance was out. We received some civilian calls as well during the worst raids, mostly expectant mothers, but any type of case at all if it became necessary to evacuate patients from a bombed hospital. There were mornings when the streets of this drab area looked like a brilliant display of *diamanté*, when the sun came through the clouds and glittered on the glass from the previous night's devastation.

I was learning a new opera during this awful period, Cecil Gray's *The Trojan Women*. The B.B.C. put it on. The work, unfortunately, had to suffer large cuts as the time allotted to its performance proved to be too short. I felt a great sadness for Cecil. Daily one could see him shrinking further into himself as the première drew near and the opera was still running over time. It must shatter one's creative sensitivity to see a work reduced and reduced until, to the writer, a skeleton remains. When one has lived with a work, eating, drinking and sleeping with it all through the time of gestation, such slashes of the pages must break something within the soul and spirit of the composer.

In any case, Cecil was a shy, sensitive man who shrank from asserting himself and his wishes over his work. I hoped for his sake that there would be no repeat performances.

Another new and lovely work for me came soon after this. It was Elgar's *For the Fallen*. Dr Malcolm Sargent decided to place *For the Fallen* before the Verdi *Requiem* on 11 November in a concert at Liverpool and later repeated the two works at the Royal Albert Hall. On both occasions when *For the Fallen* came to a close, there was dead silence before the applause broke out. Every artist knows what this means, and it is regarded gratefully as a tribute both to the performer and the work performed.

When not working, I used to enjoy going to the Sadler's Wells ballet. My first meeting with Robert Helpmann was during one of the seasons. His artistry and versatility were a source of great interest to me, and his portrayal of Hamlet, both in the ballet and in the drama, was outstanding in the wartime productions. Donald Wolfit's Shakespeare seasons were also an oasis during those years.

Now that the raids were intensified, families were flocking once again from the capital. Stations and trains were bursting with humanity. The authorities had persistently advised people not to return, but they spoke to deaf ears. Now they were trekking off with children, pets and luggage—anywhere so long as they could escape from the bombing.

I began to wonder where my energy came from when I realised that for over a month I had not slept in a bed. At night I was either on duty at the Ambulance Station or travelling in overnight trains to and from engagements. Earache and deafness attacked me, no doubt through over-tiredness, and I was forced to cancel two engagements.

July 30 will be ingrained for ever in my memory. I was booked to sing at Sheffield. Chaos reigned on the railway platform. I was caught up in the seething mass of humanity and was pushed, fortunately, on to the right train. Corridors and compartments were jammed full. Those already in the train were pushing to try to find space, while those outside were pushing to try to board the train. I was forced into the toilet compartment with five soldiers. We yelled to everyone to stop shoving and let us out, but no one could move backwards or forwards. A feeling of nausea followed by claustrophobia engulfed me. Two of the soldiers put their fists through the small window as the train moved out of the station, so at least there was a little fresh air. The six of us were virtually imprisoned in that tiny area all the way to Sheffield—we could not sit as there was no room even to bend our knees! How I sang that night remains an enigma, but I did, and the reception given me was most warming. I had come off duty that morning and gone straight to the train in my uniform, carrying a small case with an evening dress in it, and my music case. My legs ached from standing all those long hours, and they were sore from having the cases pressed against them all the way. Those soldiers had been so considerate and helpful. The memory of their behaviour was as warming as the reception given to me at the concert.

The night train back to London after the concert was full enough, but I did get a seat. Non-smokers, first or second class, were all the same. Everyone smoked where they wished, and it was a waste of money to buy a first class ticket. Inspectors could not get through to punch tickets, let alone collect excess fares.

After that experience, I cancelled all engagements outside the

London and Greater London area. At the beginning of September we experienced the worst raid of all. On that night, both the London Hospital and St Clement's Dane received direct hits. In the East End it was like an inferno.

Then came a lull when raids decreased in violence. I had the interesting experience of singing at the opening night of "Stage Door Canteen." This was a social centre in Piccadilly, started by Beatrice Lillie and Dorothy Dickson. It was intended for non-commissioned ranks, both men and women, of all the Allied Forces; food at canteen rates, and nightly stage entertainment were provided. Admission was free, and a thousand people could be accommodated. Writing of the occasion, the *Evening News* reporter said: "I squatted on a crowded dance floor when the Stage Door Canteen in Piccadilly was opened last night; and as star succeeded star on the stage I began to wonder what the entertainment would cost if, say, a private hostess had to foot the bill. I made it somewhere about £2,000."

It was certainly a night, and it gave the Canteen a wonderful start. I was the only classical artist among a bevy of famous names which included Beatrice Lillie, Bing Crosby and Fred Astaire, both of whom had come in from America to entertain U.S. troops, Jack Buchanan, Nervo & Knox, Naunton Wayne, and another V.I.P. from a completely different sphere—Anthony Eden.

The concerts were a real mixture; there was something to make everybody happy. The Canteen filled a great need, and helped many a lonely person to find companionship. It was a haven of good fun and relaxation for those who sorely needed it.

Early in September I left for an ENSA tour at Scapa Flow. Gerald (Moore) was the accompanist. A very amusing, excellent tenor, Francis Russell, and a 'cellist, Antonia Butler, made up the party. We went by train to Inverness, and from there an R.A.F. aircraft flew us to Kirkwall. We gave two concerts daily in Orkney, mostly for the Navy, but also for the R.A.F. camp and hospitals.

On one occasion we were driven twelve miles in an open truck and then taken on a drifter to Lyness. "Was our journey really necessary?" we asked each other afterwards. The hospital and the concert in the local cinema to an audience of mixed troops were accepted, but not with any degree of enthusiasm, as were the others. We gave two concerts aboard a ship on which the Commander was drunk and insulting—this was an awful experience. I was afraid that Frank Russell might lose control of his temper and knock the Commander about. Frank was a big chap and stood no nonsense from anyone. Both he and Gerald were upset that Antonia and I should have been subjected to such behaviour.

The Flagship H.M.S. *Duke of York* was in harbour at the time, and the difference aboard this ship was enormous. It completely restored our faith in, and great respect for, the British Navy.

I was now singing a minimum of three times a week, and often every day of the week, combining ENSA, charities, and normal engagements.

My first performance as Marguerite in Gounod's *Faust* was in September, a Carl Rosa occasion. What an aeon it seemed since I sang Siebel in the same opera in Sydney!

The artist A. L. Grace had been commissioned by H.B. to sketch me for large, unique posters for the Carl Rosa. The sittings were short as he worked with great rapidity. This was a tribute to me by H.B. My name now filled the theatres for him, and he wanted something special for the London season at the King's Theatre, Hammersmith. I felt very honoured that he did this.

At this time I bought my first car. It was a second-hand Hillman Minx; the price was £475, and it was the largest cheque I had ever signed. I can truthfully say my hand was shaking. Of course, petrol rationing curtailed my enthusiasm somewhat, but what a difference it made to some of the journeys!

My first concert calamity happened on 21 October that year. I had been booked to sing in Middlesbrough, and the contract from Harold Holt's office gave the time as 7 p.m. I caught a train which got me there at 3.30 p.m. I was in no hurry and I knew the hotel was near to the station. I was wandering across to it when my eyes were suddenly riveted to a large poster advertising the concert and my name, but the time read: "2.30 p.m."! For a moment I was transfixed. I rushed back to the station to try to get a taxi, but as usual, none was to be had. A porter directed me to the hall, and I ran—literally ran. The organisers were relieved to see me. All explanations were swept aside as I changed in double-quick time. I sang my three groups of songs in the second half.

When the concert was over, I produced my contract showing the time, and the organisers showed me their correspondence. Without a doubt, an error had crept in at my agent's office. This shocked me. I just could not believe that a mistake in time could happen.

A few days later the press cutting arrived. There it was splashed across the paper: "Joan Hammond arrives at interval. The famous singer, Miss Joan Hammond, mistook the time of the concert at the Town Hall yesterday. She thought it was an evening concert. This careless attitude sets a bad example to other artists . . ." etc.

I was incensed. I took the clippings in to Harold, expecting him to say: "Don't worry—we'll send a letter to the Editor asking for an apology and explaining the situation and how it arose."

But Harold just shrugged his shoulders and referred again to that small writing at the bottom of the contract, which read "The Agent cannot be responsible", etc., etc.

The whole incident upset me. I felt it was an injustice that I should be blamed for something for which I was not culpable. It was a hopeless situation, an artist can only go by the information on the contract. We have no means of checking bookings unless the organisation engaging us writes personally. Another hard lesson learnt.

I have already mentioned that a number of the best instrumentalists drifted away from symphony orchestras to bands, such as Geraldo's, Jack Payne's and Carrol Gibbons and his Savoy Band. I did a great number of B.B.C. shows with Geraldo and his band, which at times became augmented into an orchestra. These concerts and broadcasts were mainly for the Forces.

Geraldo had a brilliant pianist brother, Sid Bright, who used to do a lot of accompanying. He was first class, just as Geraldo was and his band. I found that the accompaniments to arias, especially those of Puccini, were more artistically performed under Geraldo's baton than that of many a symphony orchestra conductor. There was no rigidity. Geraldo heeded the dynamics and was prepared for an accelerando, pause or rallentando whenever the singer wished to phrase in this way, whereas so many classical conductors and players missed them, and one had to draw their attention to the composer's markings.

Geraldo asked me to go with his band to Paris and Brussels, to sing my usual material, of course, which was operatic arias. I had no desire to offend him as he had become a good friend, and he was genuinely a great admirer of my voice.

It so happened that I had my time fully booked and it was impossible for me to accede to his request. He knew my feelings and how dedicated I was to the classics. He also knew my desire to keep rigidly to the other side of the fence—the operatic and concert world. There is a distinct barrier between classical and jazz work in the United Kingdom. Normally I would never have had occasion to meet and work with the jazz kings, but during such a war we worked everywhere and with everyone. We were all lumped together and rightly so. Entertainment had to provide relaxation for all sorts of musical tastes. Artists and entertainers were thrown together in the general melting pot, and surprisingly everyone made the best of it and mixed happily with everyone else, no matter from where they came, or what their positions in life were before the War burst upon them.

Early in November I had the pleasure of meeting Benjamin Britten. His manner and general outlook on life and music impressed me. I was rehearsing his "Les Illuminations" at the time, and he went through it with me. I sang it for the first time on 9 December with the Boyd Neel orchestra.

The work appealed to me, as I had long admired the poems of Rimbaud, and I found Britten's music a new and interesting experience. I regret to say that I did not do this work justice on the first occasion. The critics enjoyed it, but I knew that I had not dug deep enough beneath the surface, and this annoyed me. The fact that I had so many engagements and new works to learn was all the more reason for getting down to it and delving into the depths of the words and music. It was inexcusable, and I felt I had let Benjamin Britten down.

He and Peter Pears came to a performance of *Il Trovatore* two days after this concert with Boyd Neel. The Carl Rosa were having a season at Wimbledon. Benjamin told me how much he loved old "Trovi" as we called it, and most of the Verdi operas. I always felt that he was influenced by Verdi's handling of the storm music in *Rigoletto*. In *Peter Grimes* this was evident. What a prolific, original composer Britten is! Many musicians are unaware of the varied amount of work he has produced. He could not have had a more musicianly, delightful tenor than Peter Pears to sing his operas and songs.

ENSA had planned for a number of artists to tour for three weeks in north-west Europe. I was booked to appear with the Hallé Orchestra under John Barbirolli, together with Jacques Thibaud (who, in the event, was unable to appear), Arthur Grumiaux, Evelyn Rothwell and Nancy Evans. Later, Gerald Moore was to join Nancy and me, and we were to give a series of concerts. At ENSA Headquarters in Drury Lane, I had been given two injections against cholera and typhoid fever which laid me low and caused me to cancel a performance of *Madam Butterfly* at Wimbledon. This was a great disappointment to me, as dear Lady Gowrie was on a short visit to London, and she was coming to hear me.

A few days later, I was given a further injection and an ENSA uniform at the same time! I came off duty from the Ambulance Station two mornings later with a dreadfully sore throat and a high temperature—and I had a performance of *L'Enfance du Christ* by Berlioz that night.

I telephoned Dr Sargent as soon as I got home and he could hear there was very little voice, if any. The rehearsal was at 10.30 a.m. The event was to be the first of the London Philharmonic Orchestra's Sunday Concerts at the Royal Albert Hall, an enterprising venture and a special Christmas Eve performance.

The oratorio was virtually unknown, but it attracted a large audience. The other artists were Parry Jones, Owen Brannigan and Swayles Atkinson.

My illness created a crisis, as no one else could be found who knew the soprano part. There was one soprano who could have read it by sight. It was that gifted singer Olive Groves, wife of another great artist, George Baker.

Olive was singing in the North of England somewhere, so our last hope was gone. If I couldn't struggle through, it meant the cancellation of the entire concert. I thought of the orchestra and of the soloists, the audience—of course I had to try. It was on occasions like these that the true, great, sympathetic character of Malcolm Sargent shone forth. If ever a conductor helped, he did, and this happened on a few other occasions much later in my career, when he had become Sir Malcolm. I shall remember him not only for this, but for his sincerity of thought, his kindliness and consideration for those working with him.

The next day I was ill with bronchitis. Everything, including the ENSA tour had to be cancelled. It was the coldest winter of the war, so Christmas and New Year were miserable times. Bed was a waste of time to me, but I had to remain there. I began work again in January 1945, but I was not happy vocally.

The weather was freezing and water pipes were bursting—most inconvenient. By the end of January, the weather people informed us that it was the coldest winter for seventy years. There was no heating in trains and no fires in the waiting rooms. It was grim.

I was busy studying *Tosca*. The première was on 20 March at Newcastle. Walter Süsskind conducted, and I had the pleasure of singing with the Czech-born baritone, Ottaker Kraus. This was the beginning of a long association with Otto. We sang together in many other operas, but his portrayal of Scarpia was, for me, the best. He really was the sadistic villain on stage, and he never gave a bad performance. He is an intelligent singer and a very sympathetic man with whom to work. I used to enjoy watching him as Dr Miracle in *The Tales of Hoffmann*. He is certainly one of the great artists with whom it has been my pleasure to sing.

Another happy meeting in this production of *Tosca* was with

K

John Moody. He is a most sensitive producer with a well-earned reputation gained through long years with repertory work and opera. His productions are always in good taste and nothing is overdone.

The costume designer, Hamish Wilson, was also very gifted and skilled at his job. I have seen some beautifully dressed productions by Hamish. *Tosca* was no exception—the costumes were elegant and the colours richly superb. It was altogether a happy cast, which included Frank Titterton as Cavaradossi. Frank had such an easy, pleasant vocal production, and he was extremely easy to work with. He had a great sense of humour, and was generous and warmhearted.

It was a busy time vocally and otherwise, particularly as the owner of the small house I was renting wished to return to London, so I had to find another roost. There was no lack of houses available as the raids were keeping people away and many had no wish to return and were selling their bases. There was a tall, terrace house around the corner in Eaton Terrace which was virtually going for a song, as it had been badly damaged in a recent raid. I needed more room as my career was progressing rapidly.

In April, Estrées helped me to set up house with very little furniture. The builders had begun work on the repairs. The ground floor had to be re-done entirely, which meant the ceiling of the basement where the kitchen was! Every window had to be renewed, and shrapnel holes repaired. The outside walls had to be shored up—it was a real picnic. One opened the front door and looked down through planks to the front basement room, formerly the staff dining and sitting room. This house had once belonged to the famous Lily Langtry, known as the Jersey Lily, and her husband, Sir Hugo de Bathe.

The house also had to be rewired, and chaos reigned for weeks. We lived on the two top floors and did our bits of cooking on a small gas ring.

On 8 May 1945, V.E. day, I was singing in *Tosca* at Glasgow. During the second interval, the news was announced from the stage. We expected the audience to leave and join in the gathering celebrations that were starting up as the news spread from street to street. No one budged. It was all we could do to concentrate on the last act, so Tosca leapt off the battlements, on to that old mattress with a cluster of dusty cushions, seething with restrained excitement.

When the opera ended the applause began for us, and then the realisation that war was over seemed to explode in the audience, and a veritable clap of thunder reached us. Strangers hugged one another, laughing, crying and shouting with relief—utter unadulterated relief.

Churchill's speech was very moving on the night of the 8th. It was followed by King George VI, who sounded very quiet and strained. Both speeches came over the Tannoy system in the theatre during that unforgettable interval.

The next day celebrations continued all over the United Kingdom, and what resounding hilarity we heard in Glasgow! It was tremendous.

My brother Tony left for Australia at the end of June. He had become very attached to England and its people, so it was a big break for him to go back. We missed him very much, for he had spent all his leave with us during the time he had been in the British Isles. Two remarks of his remain in my memory. We were walking the dogs one evening in Eaton Square when the first of the "doodle bugs" came over. The air raid warning had sounded, but until then everything had been quiet. This extra-ordinary thing came into sight with its strange sounding engine. From afar it looked like an aircraft flying lower than we'd ever seen one. Tony said: "The pilot must be mad, or wanting to commit suicide coming this low—the fool—wait a moment— what in hell is that red nose on the thing?"

"Looks as though he has a radiator to keep him warm," was my banal reply. Within a matter of moments it had passed over us, and then we heard a sickening crash. Smoke, dust, and the sound of screams and shouts, followed by the familiar fire, ambulance and police bells as the vehicles raced to the scene. It had come down just off Sloane Square.

Another night we were walking again in the gardens of Eaton Square. The sirens wailed and aeroplanes roared in. Soon the holocaust was upon us. With V.2s seeming to come from no-where and anti-aircraft guns firing from Green Park and Hyde Park, the din was deafening. There were six air raid shelters close by, but it was a fascinating sight, and I was anxious to get the dogs home, so we pressed on. Tony remarked: "I'd rather be up there sitting in my cockpit than down here waiting to be hit—at least I can have a go at them from above."

This was a bad hayfever year. I was working on *Luonnatar* by Sibelius—a most unusual score. I found it difficult to inter-pret. I couldn't like it no matter how hard I tried, and this was a rare case. Perhaps the fact that I was recording the very beautiful *Dido and Aeneas* by Purcell had some bearing on it, added to which I was singing *Tosca, Faust, Traviata* and *Il Trovatore.* Obviously fate decided I should not sing it, as I fell ill and all work was cancelled for a month. This cost me eight opera per-formances and *Luonnatar* for the B.B.C.

August 14. Peace declared. This came as an anti-climax after V.E. Day. One felt relief and joy, but there was no throwing up of hats.

I sang for the first time with the Sadler's Wells Opera Com-pany, but in Germany, not England. The tour was organised by ENSA, who booked me to sing in *Madam Butterfly* with them. Walter Süsskind conducted. There was hatred in my heart when I saw the German people, but commonsense soon drove such an idiotic emotion away. Hatred was useless. They had been caught up in it as we had, but with a big difference. They knew war would come; we didn't. It was all such a tragic waste of life and time out of life.

Soon after this, I had the pleasure of working with another Czech-born conductor, Vilem Tausky. He had the same flexible easy style as Walter, and a beat that was clear and decisive. His knowledge of opera is the most extensive and profound of any conductor I have ever worked with, before or since. Even apart from his work, he is one of the most interesting men to talk with. He lives for music. Vilem is the greatest asset to any opera company. He'll work and train his orchestra and singers with the minimum of fuss. We were all devoted to him in the Carl Rosa, and he certainly improved the standard of performances. Being reticent and unassertive made his road the harder in this world of "the louder you shout the sooner you'll get there." I should like to have him on a quiz session being asked who composed a particular ballet, concerto, symphony or song, and where and when it was first performed. His knowledge of music is limitless and his taste is catholic.

As each year passed, I tried to sum up the progress I had made. In 1944 I had been gratified to have my first entry in *Who's Who*. At the end of 1945 I had attained recognition, and a growing number of devotees of my voice, but I knew that I was lacking in so many ways. Vocally I was insecure, and when a singer is unsure of his technique he tends to become "difficult". One can give the impression of being conceited, and of lording it over others. I never felt in the least superior to anybody else. My feelings were of shame, and to hide this, I built an imaginary wall round myself. I was very unhappy about my voice, and this caused great nervousness and an unfriendly manner. When I read the criticisms I knew that I was not the accomplished, finished artist described. I felt embarrassed when I read praise. And so, at the end of a long dark tunnel of war years, at the end of which one sometimes saw no glimmer of light, I emerged having learnt a tremendous amount, but still feeling vocally insecure.

The end of 1945 ran to pattern. A London recital with Gerald as accompanist, to which I had been particularly looking forward, had to be cancelled. At the time it struck me as a tragedy, which shows that my values were rather unbalanced—doubtless due to ill health.

I was in the hands of that great ear, nose and throat specialist, Ivor Griffiths, who was both friend and saviour as far as my voice was concerned. If Ivor advised me to stop singing, I would stop—I had absolute faith in him. I could consult him about anything, and for a singer to have such a throat specialist is the greatest good fortune. I had a troublesome antrum as a result of a chill I'd caught. It ended up as bronchitis, so yet another Christmas was spent in bed.

I, together with thousands of others, no doubt, was glad to see the end of 1945. During the War years I'd given 455 performances of which 71 were for charity. Cancellations had totalled 69.

The War over, civilians were faced with the problem of reverting to a more normal life. Families who had led such an unnatural life and who had spent many days and every night in the London Underground, were reluctant to return to their homes and pick up the threads of above ground existence. They missed the freedom from household chores, the gossip and the general camaraderie. It had been cosy down below. Plenty of light by which to read or knit and sew; no blackout troubles. The London County Council had quite a job to get these tunnel-dwellers up into the air, which though not exactly fresh, was better than the dankness of the tubes. Up above there was the smell of decayed and rotting beams, crushed bricks, cement and rubble, but there was daylight too.

Food is a subject very close to the heart of every singer, since no voice can exist for long without good inner sustenance. News reached us that artists in our former enemy countries were given a heavy labourer's ration, and also special passes for journeys, permitting them to reserve seats. But as one hungry British bass singer was heard to remark: "It's a wonder our mob didn't issue us with a baby's book of coupons."

One of the most tiring and irritating things, as far as I was concerned, was the perpetual house cleaning. It was impossible to get help, so there was an endless routine of washing, scrubbing, dusting and sweeping, in spite of which, within a few hours, the house looked as if it had never been done. With the vibration from bomb explosions and gunfire the house was shaken up, and bits of plaster would fall and layers of dust settle. It was a losing battle.

Dirt really worries me, and no matter how tired I felt, some inner force compelled me to go on and on scrubbing and cleaning.

It was a matter of hands and knees, too, as the kitchen floor and lower passage-way seemed to collect the lot.

You would never think of Blackpool as anything other than a place of fun and jollity, where the families of the large northern industrial cities flock for their holidays. To me, it will always mean the purchase of my first radiogram. As you walk along the sea-front, your ears are constantly assailed by a cacophony of sound which comes from the amusement arcades and other places of entertainment. To avoid this I used to wander along the back streets. There I found a handsome, second-hand radiogram. Until then I had only a portable machine which I brought from Australia. It had served me faithfully over the years, but as it played only 78 r.p.m. it was somewhat limited for my ever-growing collection of concertos and symphonies. I could now afford to buy this radiogram. The most obliging shopkeeper said he could easily get it to London, so the deal was made.

It was a most exciting day for me when it finally arrived and I had it working. How different my orchestral records sounded! A very joyous asset, but I still clung to my original portable—in truth, I did not part with it until 1966, when I returned to Australia after my retirement. I should really have brought it all the way home again!

My new purchase afforded me pleasure until it suddenly blew up and very nearly caused a fire in the house, not to mention giving me a fine old shock. It was a complete write-off, but an ingenious little man in a dingy old "shop around the corner" doctored the case and lined it with felt. It served as a record container, and it is still carrying on in that capacity in the home of a friend in London.

PART IV

Breakthrough

Early in 1946 I agreed to tour in Australia under the auspices of the Australian Broadcasting Commission. The terms seemed right until I was told that I should have to pay double income tax. This unnerved me somewhat, but there was nothing to be done as the contract had been signed.

I had to prepare eight different recital programmes and several orchestral groups. This meant a colossal amount of rehearsing and studying in between engagements in Europe. As one half of every programme was to be broadcast, it also meant strict timing of the items.

Until I left on a flying boat on 23 June, every minute was given over to the preparation of the programmes. My selection was highly classical, and included German lieder, Italian, French and English groups. Also incorporated were such works as Britten's "Les Illuminations", "Dies Natalis" by Gerald Finzi, Wagner's Wesendonck lieder, and a cycle of Gipsy Songs by Dvořák. Very few arias were included, as I kept them for the A.B.C. orchestral concerts. At this stage, I was entirely ignorant of the popularity of "O My Beloved Father", and other Puccini arias.

My ignorance was not confined to the sale of my recordings. It extended to many other things. Clothes meant little to me. I felt that if one's work was good, clothes could be regarded as unimportant. It was just as well that my taste hadn't developed at that time, as I couldn't have afforded expensive gowns and exclusive models. My fees were beginning to increase, but not to any great extent.

I knew that a mink coat would cover a number of inferior dresses, so I bought one on the "never-never" system. It was my first plunge and never before had I signed a thing called a promissory note. It rather worried me, as at no previous time had I bought anything so costly without having the money in hand to settle for it.

Clothes and materials were still rationed in Britain, and I never had enough coupons for my needs. Once, when I wanted a simple blouse, I exchanged margarine coupons with a friend who had a few clothing coupons to spare. I gave little thought to the finer details of appearance, and put all my concentration into being absolutely prepared musically.

I had planned to do all the preliminary rehearsals with Gerald Moore in London, but these plans were soon upset. It came as a shock and a deep disappointment to learn that the A.B.C. did not agree to Gerald's terms. We had believed all was settled when their final refusal came through Harold Holt.

This was to be my first visit to my homeland in ten years, and Gerald's presence would have given me a great fillip. I was to learn the importance of touring with an accompanist who had done all the preliminary hard work prior to leaving the home base, which at this time was London. With programmes such as I had prepared, it would have been of crucial value. I stressed this point to Harold, but he said the A.B.C. had assured him there was a first-rate accompanist for me in Australia.

Later I was told that the accompanist had to play a solo group. This was another surprise. Their pianist, Raymond Lambert, had demanded the inclusion of solo piano works as he was a soloist. Both Ivor and Gerald avoided playing solo groups. They were dedicated accompanists, and the two forms of art cannot be mixed. One must either be a soloist or an accompanist, as the technique and approach are entirely different, one from the other. A good soloist is a mediocre accompanist, and vice versa.

The Sunderland flying boats were most comfortable, but slow. The flight took eight days.

My arrival in Australia was unforgettable. My mother had written to me a few weeks before I left London asking me not to give her address, as the telephone never ceased ringing, and letters were pouring in asking for information and news of my arrival. Not unnaturally she found this irritating and troublesome. The request perplexed me as I had never given her address to anyone. I could not understand who would be telephoning or writing other than my close friends.

I was met in Darwin by a young pressman. Among his many irrelevant questions was: "Where do your parents live?"

"In Sydney."

"Whereabouts in Sydney?"

"Somewhere in the Edgecliff-Double Bay area, I believe."

The young man pressed on. "But surely you have their address?"

My reply was curt. "But surely I have. And it escapes me for the moment."

My hedging was not appreciated, but before he could ask again I pipped in with a question myself. "What is your next question?"

I flew away from Darwin without giving another thought to the cub reporter.

My reception in Sydney, at the Rose Bay flying-boat base, was a most overwhelming experience. I was totally unprepared to see a mass of radiant faces all waiting to see me. Newsreel cameras were whirring and press cameras clicking furiously. What with greeting my family, friends and mere acquaintances, and trying simultaneously to answer the questions which were being fired at me like shots from a gun, I was dazed. It did not seem real. How could I know that my popularity had gained such momentum through my recordings?

When I finally reached my hotel bedroom I found a stack of correspondence that made me feel nervous to look at, and there was also the joy of seeing massive bouquets and baskets of fruit. What an unexpected welcome it all was!

The next day I had to begin rehearsing. I was still in a daze. My second eldest brother, Len, came to my aid and brought his secretary in to help me to cope with the mail before it engulfed me completely. The telephone never stopped ringing. It was chaotic. I had to do my own unpacking and sorting out of what to wear for several press interviews and three large receptions given in my honour. Meeting my accompanist and rehearsing were the last things anybody expected of me!

I was bewitched and bewildered, and I never recovered from this state of semi-awareness of just what was going on all around me. I was quite unaccustomed to such V.I.P. treatment, and the same was to happen everywhere I went—receptions, speeches (horrifying, tiring and nerve-wracking), press interviews, photographs—I was caught up in a maelstrom of the other side of an artist's career, a side unknown to me. In Britain one went to an engagement, carried it out and left again, having seen the organisers or agent, and the autograph hunters. Another facet of an artist's life was making itself known to me, and I bemoaned the fact that no one had warned me of this other side, which exists mainly in the Southern Hemisphere and the U.S.A.

When I went to bed on that second night in Australia, I noticed an evening paper on the bedside table. Then I saw it, splashed across a corner: "Joan Hammond does not even know where her parents are living, our Darwin correspondent tells me." Something seemed to hit me in the stomach. I felt sickened and disgusted.

As nearly all unsavoury newspaper titbits seemed to be cabled throughout the world, months afterwards press cuttings arrived from every city, town or hamlet in which I had ever sung, all repeating the same damaging reporter's verbiage.

One teacher on the staff of the Sydney Conservatorium of Music, who also wrote music criticisms, lashed out after one of my recitals and ended his blast with: "What can one expect when she doesn't even know where her parents live!" These words were wounding and it took me a long time to get over the hurt. It is to be regretted that people in responsible positions do not check their facts and realise that many such errors creep in with hurried reportage.

Owing to the number of arranged social functions, I had only time for two rehearsals before my first performance. I flew to Melbourne to be greeted by the same press barrage and insistence on social appearances. It was all part of the publicity campaign, but it was beyond my comprehension. I knew that the programmes were difficult vocally as well as pianistically. To give a good account of the composers' works, both singer and accompanist needed hours of rehearsal.

My first recital was on 9 July. Melbourne Town Hall was packed, as it was for the succeeding recitals. Very gratifying, but worrying. My accompanist, Raymond Lambert, was a delightful companion. Being very conscientious and an excellent musician, he did his utmost to get the desired results for me, but his battle was a mighty one as he was tensed and anxious about his solo items, and this tension was transmitted to me. His livelihood depended a great deal on favourable criticisms as a soloist and as an accompanist.

It was too late to make more time available for rehearsing. We had to plod on as best we could, always trying to give a creditable rendering of the various items.

I found the climate much colder than I had expected, so my mink coat was a cosy as well as a costly comfort. Later in the tour, when I returned to Sydney for recitals there, a great friend of mine found herself pinned by a neighbour while on a bus to the City one day. After the usual words of greeting the neighbour said: "I saw you at Joan Hammond's recital the other evening. I was at her farewell concert, you know, before she left the country."

"Oh? How interesting," said my friend.

"Yes, my dear. She was a docile creature then. We paid to send her abroad, and now she comes home flaunting a mink!" Her voice had become loud and shrill with indignation, much to the annoyance of my friend, who observed that everyone in the bus was listening. She replied angrily: "Well, if she'd come back in a rabbit fur, you'd have been the first to say 'Fancy her wearing that! You'd think she could afford a decent coat after all this time abroad!'"

Before the tour was a quarter way through, I was having trouble vocally. The strain of rehearsing in every spare minute, and using my vocal cords for the unaccustomed chatter at receptions, parties and press interviews was beginning to take its toll. After the years of absence abroad my friends were naturally anxious to see me and exchange news. I began to feel like a piece of rope being stretched to its limit in a tug-of-war. I would go to bed feeling bruised and battered, and at times voiceless. Sleep was often impossible.

A period of great worry struck me—a vocal worry of the

utmost seriousness. At many concerts I struggled through working a flagging instrument. Some concerts had to be cancelled, and social engagements too. The excellent specialist I visited warned me of the consequences. I was in a predicament from which there was little hope of escape. I looked well, and I was up and about as usual. To the layman, this means that nothing is wrong.

After Melbourne I appeared in Launceston and Hobart. This was disastrous, as the hall and theatre in which I sang were damp and the weather was bitterly cold. The audience was well rugged, but I sat in the tiny dressing room of the Theatre Royal in Hobart and watched the trickles of water running down the walls. I shuddered and hugged my mink coat closer to me until it was time to go on, clad in a thin evening gown. I was too inexperienced to cope with such situations. You may well ask: "What could you have done?" I gave the answer some years later when the A.B.C. sent me again to these very attractive cities which are blighted for artists because of the shocking back-stage conditions. I had fourteen radiators on the stage, as Walter Süsskind my accompanist on this second visit, could not feel his hands because they were so cold. I also had radiators on all day in the dressing room to warm and dry the air before I was due to sing. I sang in that same mink coat, so my body kept warm.

It is important to remember that these places of entertainment were built during an age when "theatricals", as all entertainers were called, were held in ill repute. Any accommodation was good enough for them. This attitude was prevalent throughout Britain, and many theatres there today have appalling back-stage conditions. The health authorities are doing their utmost to improve the situation. Some rooms have no windows, others have tiny ones out of reach, or so tightly closed it is impossible to open them. Toilet facilities are deplorable. It is not only the provincial halls and theatres that are neglected. At the Royal Opera House, Covent Garden, the few "star" dressing rooms at stage level were served by a toilet on the floor above. Lady choristers or anyone going up or down the stairs could have used the same convenience.

So it was not surprising that the same conditions prevailed in

Australia. We are in the process of emerging from the damp fusty odours of the past, but at least we are emerging. Theatricals are now regarded as reputable members of the community.

However, on this, my first tour, after leaving Tasmania I flew to Melbourne and caught a flight the same evening to Perth. There were strong headwinds and we were thirteen hours in the air.

When we touched down I was completely deaf in the left ear. The reception and usual chain of social activities had to be cancelled. The deafness was the prelude to a bad chill. The doctor called it 'flu. I didn't care about the title—I just wanted a wonder pill or injection to cure it.

I gave one recital and then returned to Melbourne. The Adelaide part of the tour was also cancelled. I returned to Sydney in the middle of August, feeling half an artist, but I began my concerts. My interpretation was poor, as I had to concentrate on the voice, which is fatal. I am of the opinion that a singer who has to concentrate on his tone emission is boring to listen to. One must go on stage to entertain and give out, so that the audience can feel interested and at ease. If there is a slight vocal trouble, technique should overcome it. I had yet to learn that one must be the master of one's instrument. So many things can upset a voice —atmosphere, extremes of temperature, smoke, fog, and innumerable minor irritants. You can't go round the corner and buy a couple of new vocal cords, so it is essential to train yourself to give a performance under any circumstances, and try not to think of anything other than entertaining those who come to hear you.

About this time, letters of complaint began to pour in to the press, the A.B.C. and to me. My programmes were too highbrow, and why did I not sing what everyone wanted to hear? Some letters were insulting. The battle raged both in Sydney and Melbourne. It reached a pitch where some University students rallied on my side. Before a recital was due to commence they carried boards, stating that they approved of my choice of programme.

The type of letter I received was:

L

"Dear Miss Hammond: Who do you think you are coming back here and singing stuff no one knows or wants to hear? You are making a fortune out of the sales of your recordings, but you cannot bow down so low as to sing these popular items to a public who has supported you by buying them. I for one will not waste my money on attending any future concerts."

I was able to laugh about "making a fortune" from the sales of my recordings. The royalties I received were and still are approximately $1\frac{1}{2}d$. per record for all the early war-time issues of ten-inch discs, which include the most popular one, "O My Beloved Father", and $3d$. for a twelve inch.

The A.B.C. had stressed their desire for programmes of the highest quality. They wished to set a standard and I was more than willing to comply, but the general public had other ideas. These programmes set me up for years to come, and I was glad to have had the opportunity of planning and singing them. In the meantime, I felt more and more in sympathy with the rope in a tug-of-war, and I reached a point where I dreaded opening my mail.

During this unhappy tour I had the sympathetic understanding, advice and support of that man of expansive character, Charles Moses, now Sir Charles. He was the General Manager of the A.B.C. and such a position required tact, diplomacy and charm. Charles possessed all these qualities, and it was a relief to be able to discuss my problems with him. He set a standard by which all successive managements were judged during the numerous tours I did throughout the world following this most interesting side of an artist's career—world travel.

The tour dragged on and my voice was a mixture of good and bad. I cancelled as many social engagements as possible in order to save it. Early in October I fell ill again, this time with a septic throat. It was a blessing for me that my friend Lolita Marriott was able to take over the job of dealing with mail and keeping my affairs in order. All was chaotic until she sorted things out, and she slipped into the job as though born to it. She had an excellent way with managements and fans and everybody with whom she came in contact on my behalf.

I was able to fly to New Zealand to complete that part of the tour, but when I went back to Sydney at the beginning of November I still had swollen glands. I completed the five concerts booked, one of which was a broadcast of "Les Illuminations".

My family unintentionally provided me with some light relief during this tour. My brother Len and his wife, Monti, had dressed themselves up for the occasion of my first Sydney recital. Dear Len was not looking forward to an evening of "highbrow stuff", but Monti was very keen on anything pertaining to the arts, so Len felt bound to put in an appearance. On the way to the concert they heard the clanging of fire bells, and then saw the engines roaring along in the opposite direction. Len could never resist fire engines; he'd loved them since he was a little boy.

"A fire, Monti! Let's follow and see where and what!" With that he turned the car and drove off after the fire brigade. Monti remonstrated in vain.

"We'll get to the concert sometime," said Len. They arrived just before the interval, so he did not have to endure a long night of vocal torture! I couldn't help feeling that if there had not been a fire, he would have found some other avenue of escape. One way and another he had quite an evening. A lady sitting next to him commented loudly and repeatedly on my long sleeves.

"Why does she wear them? So ugly and old-fashioned! It spoils an evening's entertainment looking at them."

Len stood up and verbally attacked her. He told her he was my brother, and then he gave her a graphic description of the injury to my left arm. He rounded off: "D'you come to a concert to criticise clothes or to listen to the music?" The poor woman was shattered and remained tacit for the rest of the evening. Len said he never felt better, and that he thoroughly enjoyed his night out!

Two of my young nieces, Julie and Jenny, asked for my autograph. They gave me two large sheets of paper.

"Please, Auntie, sign each one ten times," they requested. I dutifully obeyed, and gave them back the sheets. They seized them with glee.

"Oh goody goody! Now we can swap these for twenty tadpoles!" Their faces were a delight to see. Mine, I think, was a picture of bemused astonishment at such a strange compliment.

I left Sydney for London on 30 November. The flying boat landed in Poole Harbour on 11 December in a thick fog, but I was thankful to be back and to take stock of myself and my voice, which was always my habit as each year drew to a close.

My first appointment in London was with Ivor Griffiths, the ear, nose and throat specialist in whom I had such complete faith. I wanted his opinion about my vocal cords. Luckily all was well, despite some misuse and incorrect singing.

Vocally I had reached a cross-roads. I had not only let myself down, but those who had backed me. I had not saved any money, and the little I had been able to send back to London was almost eaten up before I returned. I had had 384 engagements during the war years, when my fees were low. Income tax was prohibitive, and I had been paying for the house in Eaton Terrace as well as the usual rates and household expenses. Ten per cent of all my fees were retained by my agent, and financially my position was still precarious. I spent freely when I had it to spend. Money came into my right hand, where it burnt like a hot potato. It was passed to the left hand and quickly dropped.

Five clear weeks with no bookings. I decided to undo and rebuild my vocal technique. The time had come for me to learn to master my voice instead of allowing it to master me.

Every day I went through a series of scales and tests. It was a heartbreaking, worrying time for us all at Eaton Terrace. At the end of each week, I went to Ivor Griffiths so that he could check there was no damage from wrongful use of the voice. I knew I must persevere with my self-instruction even while accepting work, which I must undertake in order to live. At the end of January I did a recording session, and during February I carried out five of the six engagements booked. Between dates I studied as never before, and I kept up my checking system with dear Ivor. It was vital to know if my theories were correct, and that I was now building up a vocal chart of rights and wrongs. I wanted to be able to travel, secure in the knowledge that if I felt anything untoward, I could put it right myself with the use of scales.

The process was lengthy and public appearances were a necessary part of the system. Many singers travel with their teachers, or hurry back to them if something goes wrong. This was not for me. I must know myself what corrective measures to adopt, anywhere, at any time. This eventually came about.

I studied the parts of the human body directly concerned with tone emission. The larynx, the nose, tongue and palate, the function of muscles in the throat, diaphragm and abdomen. How to regulate breath pressure. The breath is the singer's life-line.

How often, during a concert or operatic performance, have I thought of the fortunate golf champion who can have a practice swing before a shot. How perfect it would be to practice a difficult phrase or top note, and then carry on and execute it during the performance.

Complete control of the vocal organs permits a singer to articulate correctly. Clear enunciation is of the greatest importance, as words are the artistic expression of any song. One must be able to make ugly sounds as well as beautiful ones, if the words suggest ugliness. One must be able to express every emotion through the voice without injuring the mechanism. It is an endless study.

To be born with a voice is one thing, to keep it, is another. A successful singer needs healthy vocal organs unimpaired by bad habits of breathing or speech, a good ear, rhythm, intelligence, personality, an unflagging devotion to study, and dedication to one's profession. The human voice is a wondrous thing, and we who are blessed with it should never cease to preserve and cherish it.

The next three years were spent in trial and error. There were times of progress and retrogression, of happiness and disappointment, according to the success or failure of my efforts towards self-mastery. It was engrossing and rewarding.

Perhaps it was fitting that I should have learnt some invaluable lessons in my own country. The results of my first Australian tour became the basis for the future in more ways than the rebuilding of my vocal technique. Never again would I tour without taking an accompanist, and a personal representative-secretary with me. All rehearsals would be completed in London, so that there would only be a matter of a final polish up before each performance. I would stipulate that there were to be no interviews or social functions on the day of a performance; pay closer attention to dress; try to relax more and overcome shyness when meeting people; construct programmes with greater variety: these were my resolves.

Clothes are of paramount importance in Australia. Female artists are always questioned by the social columnists about their gowns, and they do not hesitate to ask what you paid for them. This accent on the cost of personal belongings, jewellery and divers things is an Australian and American custom, and one that many Europeans find distasteful.

A certain famous violinist was harshly criticised and not supported because of her meagre, unattractive wardrobe, which disappointed the great majority of female concertgoers in Australia. I heard one impeccably clad socialite discussing this unfortunate violinist with a friend who was praising the musician rather than the model. The socialite said: "But my dear, those two frocks were eyesores! How can you listen to music while gazing at such a fright!"

This made me think. The violinist was a great artist. I myself would neither have noticed nor cared what she wore, but to the women on committees who help to foster the arts, this part of an artist's equipment is of major importance.

I had found the heavy schedule of social engagements during that first Australian tour most onerous, but it has to be remembered that people wish to meet artists. It is a compliment which many of us fail to appreciate. We tend to be wrapped up in our work and study, and to regard anything outside as a waste of time. Parties can be a worry unless they are with your own intimate circle of friends with whom you can relax. Art is a jealous mistress, and our first duty is to the general public who support our concerts. Nothing must be allowed to interfere with the keeping of faith with those who book you, and with the audiences.

For a singer, parties are particularly tiring as one stands for the greater part of the function, having perhaps already stood for nearly two hours giving a recital. One is questioned unceasingly. Everyone wants to ask something special, and they cannot know that others have perhaps put the same question time and again. Nor do they realise that the same voice that has been entertaining them for two hours or more is now being raised in order to be heard over the usual babble and party noise.

I tried to avoid being entertained after a performance for the simple reason that I liked to eat a proper meal and relax. I ate very little on the day of an engagement, so dinner was a meal to be enjoyed after singing. At times, of course, I was obliged to accept an invitation, and it was just unfortunate when the meal provided consisted of a few sandwiches and biscuits. On such occasions one usually had a plate in one hand and a cup of coffee in the other, and while juggling with them unsuccessfully, different people would be introduced. It was impossible to snatch a bite —it is most inelegant to try to talk with a mouthful of sandwich or biscuit. I have a very sensitive throat, and dreaded crumbs settling between the cords and causing a coughing fit. This often happened, much to my embarrassment. A small particle of dry food would cause a tickle, and off I went! Nuts were to be avoided altogether.

At one party my host, who was an aspiring composer, asked me to hear his latest composition. The party consisted of his friends and my party of three. He had no lack of confidence, and to a hushed and expectant audience of about fifty people he announced his work, and added: "You will realise that this sonata is better than anything Beethoven wrote!" I thought at first he was being funny, but no such thing. He played a very modern, tuneless piece, and everyone flapped and raved over it. My praise was sought, so I murmured: "Excellent!" adding to myself "Liar!"

He then introduced a young poet, a protégé of his wife. As the young man launched into his third poem I set about filling the empty void within me, enjoying the opportunity of eating while being entertained. Then that sickening tickle began in my throat. I did everything I knew to quell the cough, and I felt my face redden as the perspiration oozed through my skin. A glass of water was brought to me, too late to be of any help. The poet stopped and everyone waited for the cough to subside. I apologised as soon as it was possible to speak. The poet turned to our host and said: "Professional jealousy, I suppose!" And he wasn't being funny.

In those first few weeks after the Australian tour I had plenty of time to consider the future. Financially the tour had been a flop. The taxation authorities would not allow hotel costs as deductible expenses, and over several months these were colossal.

I fought this unjust ruling. The commercial traveller was granted a substantial subsistence allowance, so why not an artist? I had spoken to the pianist Solomon and other visiting artists, and all felt very irate about the subject, and said they would never return to Australia unless the ruling were altered. I felt I entered this battle on behalf of all visiting artists.

The case of Hammond versus the Crown came up eventually, and I won. The resulting alteration in the law governing deductible expenses has been of inestimable value to all visiting artists. Hotel bills eat up the greater part of fees.

While I was assimilating all I had learnt from the tour, and also rebuilding my voice, work came in slowly. There were very lean periods when we ate yards of spaghetti, which was the cheapest form of sustenance to be procured at that time. Five bookings came in February, one of which had to be cancelled. March was no better. Just as I was getting really worried the Vienna Opera invited me to go there in April and May. The fee was acceptable and so were the operas—*Tosca*, *Traviata*, and *Bohème*. All were to be sung in German. Time was short, so it was fortuitous that little work had come in for March.

I learnt the operas quicker than it took to obtain a permit to cross the occupied zones. A most lengthy procedure.

I was given good advice before leaving London on 12 April. Take lots of cigarettes. Dangle a packet of Virginia blend and all doors would open. This was almost true.

The route was through Paris, where there was a long dreary wait at the Gare de l'Est. Customs and passport officials were fearsome men at the Swiss frontier, but even worse when we reached the Russian zone. The route by which I travelled was the only one open—Arlberg, Innsbruck and Kitzbühl, crossing the French, British and Russian zones. Those Russian officials opened and examined everything, holding on to my Russian pass as if they were afraid it would get away from them, and muttering to each other in Russian, the only language they spoke. They signed to me to get out of my berth—it was 3 a.m. when this examination took place. I thought they were going to undress me, but they contented themselves with going through the pillows and bedding. I wished I could have caught a train in the opposite direction.

I found Vienna depressing. The atmosphere was charged with a nervous, suspicious tension. The city was divided into four zones: British, French, American and Russian. I was billeted at the Hotel Sacher, known then as "Sacher's British Officers' Hotel C.M.F." It was somehow unreal to see British officers and British visitors, two of us at that time, occupying this world-famous hotel renowned for its Viennese cakes and food. I had never dreamed that I should ever stay there. When I was a student, Grace Palotta took me in once for hot chocolate and a piece of the famous *torte*.

All the glamour had gone. The food was poor, as it was under Army control. The only good place for Britishers to eat was the Kinsky Palace, which had been taken over and was run as a general restaurant and place of entertainment for all British personnel.

Rehearsals began immediately. The State Opera, which had been bombed, had taken over the Teater an der Wien and the Volksoper. *Traviata* was at the Teater an der Wien, and *Tosca* and *Bohème* at the Volksoper. Professor Joseph Krips and Kapellmeister Hans Knappertsbusch were the two leading conductors. Professor Krips accompanied me on the piano at a concert, and he was brilliant. When a conductor is a superb accompanist at the piano he is also a superb opera conductor. He breathes with you, and can make the orchestra play as a single instrument. This is a test which few can pass.

During this visit I was in poor shape vocally. I was tense and unhappy about the voice. It did not flow out easily, and the top was being forced. I sang five Toscas, three Violettas in *La Traviata*, and two Mimis, and only once did I feel that I had given a good performance.

I thought so much about my erstwhile friends in the Vienna Boys' Choir, and I had often wondered what happened to them when their voices broke and they were put out into the world to fend for themselves. Two of them I know did well in Australia— Stefan Haag, and Georg Tintner who later moved to London.

The happiest part of my stay in Vienna was seeing Alfred Komma again. We had so much to talk about. He was the only one of my pre-war Vienna friends that I saw. There were no familiar faces anywhere. I went to visit my old teacher Frau Eibenschütz, only to be told that she and her son were dead. A family living close by told me they believed the daughter had escaped the big Jewish round-up and they gave me an address, but I got no reply to my letter. I went to the Theresianumgasse and found the place a shambles. New buildings were being erected on the bomb-sites. I made persistent enquiries about the Baroness, but there was complete silence from the authorities. It would appear she had never existed!

Rector Schnitt had also met death at the hands of the Nazis. The Countess Kinsky I hope had died a natural death, but no one seemed to know anything, and if they did, they were not willing to tell me. I could not visit the Castle Wilhelminenberg because it was in the Russian zone, as were all the surrounding beauty spots of Vienna. My special Russian pass was only for entering and leaving the city.

For me it was a ghost city. It was oppressive with fear and insecurity. The country had not fully emerged from the poverty and wreckage of defeat in the First World War before being plunged into another even more devastating war. The British and Americans were treated with a surface politeness which completely lacked warmth, but there was a bitter hatred of the

Russians, under whose yoke people had been utterly stricken. The French were ignored.

There was a staleness in the air. The ghosts of all my former friends seemed to lurk everywhere. Their lives had been erased by a huge rubber—the ruthless rubber of the invader.

There was a great change in Alfred. We could not go for excursions, and there was only one place at which we could eat. I was not allowed to invite him to Sacher.

He told me how disillusioned he was. Any hope of a better future was non-existent. His outlook worried me; I felt he had an intuition of early death. He was an Aryan, so his practice and apartment had not been taken from him, and he had meticulously kept some money I had left with him, as well as some music, an umbrella and a few other bits and pieces.

Within eight months he died.

I was so glad to get away from Vienna that the day of my departure was one of great excitement; it was marred only by leaving Alfred, the one friend I had there.

I was more than thankful to see the white cliffs of Dover again.

Many contracts had come in during my absence, so the stew pot could bubble merrily again and the memory of packets of spaghetti be pushed into a corner.

The most important engagements were to be two concerts in the vast Harringay Stadium. I met and sang with Otto Klemperer for the first time, and also Rosenthal and the French National Orchestra. Klemperer I found interesting to work with, but not exciting. His gangling movements reminded me of a type of Australian straggly gum tree, called messmate, in a strong wind. His tenuous arms seemed so long that at times I felt the baton would reach me or the leader of the orchestra; but in many ways he was colourful.

All great European conductors began their careers in opera houses. It was their launching pad, and the finest training ground they could have. Their careers blossomed as a result of years spent conducting operas, with orchestral concerts filling in the spare moments. Klemperer, Bruno Walter, Toscanini, Victor de

Sabata and Koussevitzky are a few names that come to mind.

As a contrast, the majority of British conductors developed musically through positions as sub-organists rising to organists, choir masters, and combined the teaching of piano as part of the job. It was important for them to get a degree, such as Bachelor of Music, if possible.

Sir Malcolm Sargent was different from all other conductors in a unique way. If he had not been a conductor he would most certainly have been a General in the Army, a Naval Commander, or an Air Chief Marshal. Just as he prepared his work, his appearance and every facet of his art, in his own meticulous and impeccable way, so did he prepare, organise and instruct his soloists on taking curtain calls. Nothing was left to the individual. He commanded backstage, and saw that his commands were obeyed. He arranged the order of going on and coming off for the first, second and third calls. He would remain on-stage, and then the soloists were to join him. We would all leave the stage and he would take a solo call. If the applause continued he would beckon the soloists on again. The choir and orchestra also had to watch him for orders. Nothing was left to chance. Everything was neatly tied in bundles and put in place. I never worked with any other conductor who organised calls in this way. Sir Malcolm disliked indecision, and haphazard acknowledgement of public acclaim was anathema to him. When the applause rose to near frenzy he remained calm and collected, delivering his orders in the clearest possible manner.

It can be chaotic backstage when no one is in control. Often we have stood like sheep until someone says: "Go on, you lead," or, "Quick—the applause will stop if we don't go out!" or, "You go first, Maestro, they want you." "No, we'll all go together." It can be funny when we all head for the same narrow entrance!

Sir Malcolm was a most persuasive person. He had great charm, and an ability to make one change one's mind. He often telephoned me direct and asked me to sing for a reduced fee, as such-and-such a choral society could not afford the normal one. He was concerned with the solvency of these excellent societies, and, at the same time, with obtaining the services of the best available artists.

The B.B.C. put on two special performances of Verdi's *Requiem*, with Sir Malcolm and a quartet of foreign singers. Although Sir Malcolm preferred British singers for choral works, this was understandable as his usual quartet would not have been a great enough attraction. I listened to the broadcast on the first night, and I thought the performance left a lot to be desired.

Early the next morning Sir Malcolm telephoned. Always to the point he said: "Joan, I'm sorry to disturb you so early, but will you do me a favour?"

I knew what was coming. Sir Malcolm went on.

"Will you sing the Requiem for me tonight?"

I hesitated. I had to leave early the next morning for a recital in Manchester. Sir Malcolm quickly added: "There's no need for a rehearsal. Just come and sing."

Of course I did it, and I had a most heart-warming reception from the B.B.C. Symphony Orchestra and Choir.

Only once did I refuse a request from Sir Malcolm, and that was to sing Elgar's "Land of Hope and Glory" on the last night of the Proms. I gave it a good test, but I felt it was better suited to a contralto. I tried it in various keys, but somehow I could not produce the required volume where it was musically necessary.

I would have given anything to sing on that tremendous, moving last night of the Proms, but I knew my instrument too well. I love the broad stirring majesty of the melody—it brings tears to my eyes. For Elgar's sake I refused.

In 1947 another tour was on. This time I was to go to South Africa, from the beginning of October until nearly Christmas. I had plenty of work at home as well, both concerts and performances with the Carl Rosa.

The South African tour proved to be a great success, as I was relaxed and everything was well organised in advance. Lolita and an excellent accompanist, David Andrews, went with me. Unfortunately neither Ivor nor Gerald was free on this occasion.

Back again in London with plenty of work ahead, but as usual, hardly any financial reserve for the proverbial rainy day.

Petrol rationing was still in force and this was 1948! Train fares were rising, also hotel prices. I was still travelling third class and coming back to London after concerts, sitting up all night in order to save money. It was a strenuous life, but I was young and enthusiastic about everyone and everything. When I wanted to shake the soot and grime from my nose and throat, I caught a train to Beaconsfield and played a round of golf, or just a few holes if I hadn't time for more. I never put in less than five hours' study during the twelve hours of day and evening. This rule was broken for sickness only.

Apart from my debut in Paris that year, I had the honour of meeting and singing with Dr Furtwängler. There are moments in our lives which we wish we could bottle and keep for ever, and this was one. That first Beethoven 9th I sang with him was elysian. He was reticent and unassuming, and there was no feeling that there was a barrier between him and the artists. I never slept well after singing, and if a concert or opera performance happened to attain that certain indefinable electrifying quality in which music, artists and audience seem to fuse together to be transported to the highest realms, then sleep was impossible. Such a performance was that Beethoven 9th. It is the perfect work from the singers' angle because we have the opportunity to watch the conductor from the organ loft or any suitable position in front of the choir. We can watch for the first three glorious movements, before participating in the fourth. I used to note every detail of facial expression, style of conducting, and how and when cues would be indicated to the players. Thus the sincerity of the character is revealed.

An audience sees the conductor's back and an occasional glimpse of the profile, but from the singers' vantage point, the whole can be seen without interruption.

There is very little singing for the soloists in the Beethoven 9th, but what there is, happens to be vocally demanding. The final *fortissimo* with chorus and solo voices "Alle Menschen werden Brüder" (All men are brothers) was interpreted in a variety of ways by different conductors. I used pencils of different colours to mark the phrasing according to their wishes, as it was of the utmost importance not to confuse them. There were five in particular, and it is interesting to note how these five musicians could differ one from another. The five were Furtwängler, Koussevitzky, Sir Thomas Beecham, Sir Malcolm Sargent, and Schuricht. My markings in colour with the conductor's initials beside them proved to be a great time-saver, and Sir Malcolm in particular was impressed when he used my score for a piano re-hearsal on one occasion. This form of marking I also used in the Verdi *Requiem*, Beethoven's Mass in D, and *Messiah*, as they were the works I sang most frequently.

I had Sir Malcolm to thank for introducing me to two very moving pieces by Elgar: *For the Fallen* and *To Women*. It was Sir Adrian Boult who put me through my first performance of the Beethoven Mass in D. During my career I also had the supreme joy of learning and performing the same composer's Mass in C, Elgar's *The Apostles*, Bach's St Matthew Passion, "God so loved the World" and "Phoebus and Pan", Dvořák's *Stabat Mater*, "At the Foot of the Cross" and Te Deum, Handel's *Samson* and *Acis and Galatea*, the Delius "Idyll", Rossini's *Stabat Mater* and *La Petite Messe Solennelle*, Mendelssohn's *Hymn of Praise*, and *The Golden Legend* by Sullivan.

For facial expression while conducting the honours went to Sir Malcolm and Sir Thomas. Both possessed expressive eyes and muscle movements of the face. When pleased they showed it. When displeased Sir Malcolm would first look at his score, and then at the offending party, meanwhile keeping the performance together. Sir Thomas would raise an eyebrow and his beard would twitch—a sure indication of trouble. Furtwängler and Koussevitsky were more phlegmatic over a single mistake, in order not to allow it to interfere with their concentration on the whole effect. There was no facial display.

I consider myself fortunate to have sung the Verdi *Requiem* and Beethoven 9th in particular with these men, and two more besides—De Sabata and Sir John Barbirolli.

In the first week of May 1948 a most fruitful period began. I sang a Verdi *Requiem* and parts of *Messiah* in Wales, a B.B.C. broadcast of *Eugène Onegin*, *Tosca* and *La Traviata* in Glasgow, and a repeat broadcast of *Eugène Onegin*. With a rehearsal break of four days I then had a rare combination of performances and rehearsals. At the Royal Albert Hall I sang the Beethoven 9th at a matinée performance with Sir Thomas Beecham. In the evening there was a piano rehearsal of the Verdi *Requiem* under Victor de Sabata, and the orchestral rehearsal followed the next morning. The performance was the same night. Two days later I was singing in Liverpool with Sir Malcolm.

Work, work, wonderful work! How I loved it.

The whole of that year was full and varied. I appeared in four Promenade Concerts, and made my debut at the Royal Opera House, Covent Garden in *Il Trovatore*.

The B.B.C. followed up the *Eugène Onegin* success with complete broadcasts of *Thaïs* and *La Forza del Destino*. As well as concerts and opera performances all over the British Isles, I sang for the first time in The Hague and Amsterdam, and I returned to Dublin for two performances of *Tosca* and a recital.

One shadow fell across this otherwise glorious year. Sir Arthur Bliss asked me if I would like to sing the soprano role of Diana in his opera *The Olympians*, which was to be put on at Covent Garden.

He came to my home and played through the part. He was enthusiastic and so was I. He said he was delighted that I had accepted, and left me the score. I began working on it straight away. I always liked to work well ahead for all engagements in order to avoid a last-minute rush, or to find myself unprepared when rehearsals were called.

Later on, when I was rehearsing *La Bohème* at Covent Garden I saw a call on the board for *The Olympians*. A foreign artist had been engaged to sing Diana. No one had thought to tell me. I returned the score with no comment.

Later again I was approached, but by Sir David Webster. I knew that all new works were given ample rehearsal time, and that the initial cast have the benefit of full production calls, whereas singers stepping in to roles as the season progresses have little opportunity to familiarise themselves with the sets and props. I declined.

Sir Arthur's approach was absolutely genuine. And he must have been placed in a most awkward position. I realise that a secretarial error must have occurred, or a letter gone astray, in which notification about the change of artist for the role of Diana had been sent, but which was not received by me.

The year 1949 was a series of spring tides. Work flowed in and Lolita was able to set about the unenviable task of keeping me from spending aimlessly and saving instead. In this year I had two tours in the U.S.A., a recital tour throughout Britain, and many orchestral concerts. B.B.C. bookings were plentiful, and I added *Aïda* and *Fidelio* to my Covent Garden bookings, which still included *Il Trovatore*.

The degree of nervousness I felt before an engagement could be gauged by the amount of yawning I did. Yawning is an excellent way to relax breath muscles. So is deep breathing, which more often than not brings about a good old yawn.

I went through an extraordinary cycle of behaviour on the day of a performance. I was drowsy from the moment I awoke, and this drowsiness persisted until I walked on to a platform or stage. I would eat lightly at lunch time and then no more, unless I felt too empty. I would rest if possible, and the rest was always heavy. I felt drugged.

But on days when I had no public appearance, I would wake very early and be up and about, as active as a bee. The day was never long enough for all I wanted to do, and no feeling of sleepiness ever came over me. This was quite a trick to contend with, as my activities were never quiet. Ablutions were a noisy procedure, so was learning by heart. I'm afraid I disturbed the whole household, so it was more pleasant for them on the working days!

I was always nervous before a performance, whether it was to be opera, a recital, or groups of songs and arias. This type of nervousness is not for a moment to be confused with the shyness which is always near me. Pre-performance nerves heightened

M

the awareness, and sharpened the susceptibilities, to a point where I became alive to every note of the music, sensitive to the whole atmosphere of the occasion. Once on-stage I was submerged in it, involved with it, and anxious to share with the audience my part in the music, grateful that perhaps through me they would know its beauty. This I felt to be a great privilege: to be in a position to realise the composers' intentions and pass them on to those listening. To walk on to a stage or concert platform, was a release from shyness. It was an escape to a world which I knew and loved, the joy of which I wanted to share with the audience.

But if I forgot my words or music my ghoulish ghost was beside me instantly. I would feel the usual flood of perspiration, brought about by annoyance with myself for the lapse. If I were suffering from a chest cold or any vocal worry, I would be in a bath of perspiration until the performance was over. It was of paramount importance not to let the audience down. Most of them had done a long day's work. They had travelled perhaps through fog, snow or rain, maybe for many miles. They had paid their hard-earned money and had come to hear me sing. I owed them my best. If I was unable to let my voice out and had to rely on technique instead, the strain was tremendous.

I was always terribly tense during rehearsals in theatre foyers or small rehearsal rooms. I found it almost impossible to act or become submerged in the music under such conditions. This stemmed largely from sensitivity about my arm and its restricted movement, which I hoped people would not notice. I always kept it covered, even in the hottest climates. There were those who would ask: "Why do you wear long sleeves?"

So many people who have watched me play golf and who have witnessed my stage performances, have considered me to be assured and self-possessed, perhaps irritatingly so. How little they understood of me!

For a long time I had been wondering how I could make a really worthwhile gesture of appreciation in Australia for the help and support given to me to enable me to continue my singing studies. Suddenly the right idea beamed across my mind. Golfers mainly had formed the nucleus of the Joan Hammond Fund, and at that time Australian players had not been able to tour further afield than New Zealand. An International Fund would be the most helpful way of repaying the golfers for rallying to my help.

I went to Australia and gave four recitals, two in Sydney and two in Melbourne to start the ball rolling. I was very, very happy to see the project launched. It proved a great success, and the Australian, New South Wales and Victorian Ladies' Golf Unions rose to the occasion and organised everything splendidly.

It was most encouraging to have four great Australian professional golfers, Peter Thompson, Ossie Pickworth, Norman Von Nida and Eric Cremin assist the Fund by giving an exhibition match.

During my time in Australia I also gave a concert organised by the Red Cross at the Heidelberg Repatriation Hospital. I sang a short recital at my old school, P.L.C., Pymble, and that was the extent of my tour.

On the way back to Europe I went on to Honolulu, where I began my second American tour. Among the highlights of that most interesting year were two performances of the Verdi *Requiem* in the United States with de Sabata, and a further one back in London at the Royal Albert Hall. I did two complete performances of *Madam Butterfly* at the Harringay Stadium with Eugene Ormandy.

Gene Ormandy is a stimulating, vital man. He could be dynamic yet malleable, fiery or peaceable. You never knew. A short, stocky athletic figure, dancing, inquisitive eyes, and a super-abundance of energy. His nervous habit of sniffing was somehow attractive—it just seemed part of his lively make-up. He is a fine musician, and sensitive to those around him.

I was presented to Her Majesty The Queen, for the second time, at a large reception given by the United States Ambassador at the U.S. Embassy.

The late Princess Marina, Duchess of Kent, attended the second performance of *Madam Butterfly* at the Harringay Arena. When Gene and I were presented to Her Royal Highness my curtsey was, I regret to say, conspicuous by its absence. My head

was still full of words and music, and I was carrying out my usual
port-mortem. Gene, who never missed a beat, came over to me
with a gleam in his eye.

"You didn't curtsey to Her Royal Highness, Joan. Isn't it
correct to do so?"

I glossed over the fact rather breezily with Gene, but secretly
was upset, as I'd rather have died a thousand deaths than show a
discourtesy to that charming, artistic, natural yet utterly regal
person.

One of my unhappiest operatic experiences was the first *Fidelio*
I sang at Covent Garden. To me the opera is a musical treasure of
the utmost magnitude. I approached the role of Leonora with
reverence and humility. It is an operatic peak, towering above all
others, and I never dreamed I would be privileged to sing it.
When I first heard *Fidelio* in Vienna I went around in an unearthly
state for days, so much did it impress me. The music and the whole
conception were of a quality previously unknown to me in opera.

As the date of the performance drew nearer and no rehearsals
had been called, I became panicky. I needed stage rehearsals and
I never got one!

Eventually I was given four piano rehearsals and one orchestral,
but no stage call. As is usual with operas already in the repertoire,
the rehearsals were held in the foyer, so this had to be regarded
as the opera house stage! Chairs acted as entrances and props in
general, and in this case they marked the spot where the grave
was to be dug.

I felt inadequately prepared for this, the greatest moment of my
career—to sing Leonora in *Fidelio*. I shall forever be indebted
to the bass, David Franklin, who had been the Rocco in the first
and subsequent performances. He gave up much of his precious
time to rehearsing the stage routine concerning Rocco and Leonora with me. He realised what a spot I was in.

On the night of that first *Fidelio* I was really nervous. I disliked
unrehearsed performances, and I had been subjected to so many.
I was once the Leonora in *Il Trovatore* on the opening night of a
season at Covent Garden, and the entire cast met to rehearse for

the first time one hour before the performance! Some of us had sung in the Covent Garden production before, but the tenor and baritone were new to the cast, and came from abroad. They had agreed to sing in English, but when it came to the point, they found it was too much for them, so they sang in Italian.

But to return to the Leonora in *Fidelio*. David and the other members of the cast had all had the benefit of being in the première and rehearsals had been plentiful. "I'm all right Jack, how are you?" can be as applicable in the opera house as anywhere in the world. The original producer had been a guest, so he was not available. The resident producer had taken over. Everyone, except the new Leonora, was musically and stage sure, so why should they have to rehearse? This I could understand, but I expected understudies to be called, so that I could have a full cast. But no understudies were available, it seemed: the resident producer had to fill in all the missing stage positions and cues as best he could.

Preceding and during the great aria "Abscheulicher", I was preoccupied about an exit. I had never seen the set before. During the last run-through in the foyer the producer had said: "After the aria, poppet, just go off stage prompt side." Poppet would have preferred not to go on stage, such was her state of nerves.

I looked in vain for an exit on the prompt side. I was desperate, and instead of concentrating all my efforts on the vocal interpretation of that mammoth aria, I was positioning myself to view a way of escape, as a hurried exit was necessary before the next scene began.

To this day, I don't know what led me to the only possible opening. It must have been my guardian angel. I went blindly towards a section of scenery and found I had reached the wings without being baulked by a false wall, turret, locked door or any other stage hazard. I was greeted by a voice saying: "That was great, poppet. You knew where to come!"

That was a night to be forgotten, but it had many repeat performances in nightmare form while sleeping.

There is always much speculation about the flare-ups which are supposed to occur between opera house administrators and their principal singers, and I did not escape.

I had had a discussion with Sir David Webster, past administrator of the Royal Opera House, Covent Garden, about something so trivial that I cannot now remember what it was. Immediately a rumour rattled around the walls of the opera house and then swept through the musical world. The rumour was that I had first thrown an inkwell at Sir David, and then, in an absolute rage, had picked up a chair and broken it over his head.

What had actually happened was this. When I went into Sir David's office, he offered me a chair at the other side of his desk. When I sat down the chair gave a loud miserable grating groan and collapsed. The next ten minutes was spent in my being restored to my feet by Sir David, amid profuse apologies, and then both of us testing the chairs so that the performance would not be repeated. Our laughter evidently sounded like a nasty row, which in fact we never had. When I left, the broken chair was put outside the door of the office for repair, and thus the rumour started.

During my second tour of the U.S.A. I gave a recital at Danbury, Connecticut. It had been my pleasure to meet that great singer Marian Anderson in London, and now I was visiting her home town. She and her husband gave me a delightful party at their house. As an artist I had always held her in the highest esteem, so it was with increased respect that I saw the homely, happy and highly intelligent artist off stage.

It was during this tour that I was introduced to the most extraordinary way of warming up the voice before singing. I had given a recital at a college, and the resident singing teacher asked me if I would hear his two most promising pupils. I agreed most willingly, and when I arrived at the appointed time in the same fine hall in which I had given the recital, the teacher, who was a most ebullient young man, asked me to wait while the girls warmed up. I thought this an odd request, as the girls should have warmed up beforehand, but this was the New World, with different ways.

I could hardly believe my eyes when the first girl solemnly

picked up a sort of clothes peg from the piano and placed it on her nose, pinching the nostrils together and shutting off the entrance and exit of air.

"Good. Now your scales as usual," said the teacher, and he played the chord of C major. The poor girl endeavoured to follow him up in semitones until no more sound came from her. It was excruciating.

Even more excruciating was the sound which came forth when the second pupil pulled her tongue out and held it while she attempted to sing scales. I should have laughed until the tears rolled down my face if this performance had been a skit in a film or stage show, but I realised that the entire procedure was of the utmost seriousness. Any sign of ribaldry on my part would have been inexcusably ill-mannered.

After half-an-hour of this pantomime the two girls sang two songs and two arias. One had a very promising contralto voice, but the other, who was described as a rich contralto, was in effect a pushed down soprano. The young maestro had not learnt the A.B.C. of singing, and these unfortunate pupils were being crucified.

I made the greatest effort to conceal my real feelings, but I am never happy trying to be false. I truthfully expressed an interest in the first voice, and then tried to wrap up as diplomatically as possible, my view of his teaching method. I asked:

"What's the object of the peg and tongue business?" He looked at me in amazement. "*You* are asking *me*! Surely you use one of those methods yourself?"

"Most definitely not. And what's more, if you continue to use such cranky ideas on your pupils, not one will ever get beyond the 'warming up' period." I myself was getting warmed up, as there is so much charlatanism in the world of singing teachers, and here was a big fake before me.

"Where did you learn to sing?" I asked him. He glared at me angrily. "I don't sing."

"But surely you have studied the art?"

"I have played for the pupils of one of our finest teachers, and I am carrying on his methods."

"After my recital last night you paid me some very fine compliments, and you remarked on my pianissimo singing, diction, and ease of breath control. This morning I imagine you've altered your opinion because I disagree with your teaching method. Am I right?"

I sensed his antagonism. The conversation ended abruptly. He stalked off, first gathering up the music and nose-peg, and the two pupils. There were a few questions I should have liked to ask; for example, did all his pupils use the same nose peg? I'll never know.

The outcome of this merry meeting hit me in my agent's office in New York. I had barely put my foot in the door when I was asked: "What on earth did you say when you were at the —— College down South?" For the moment I was puzzled. I had been all over the place in the interim, and I had to recall the college and incident. It rushed back to my memory and I laughed, but my laughter was cut short. The agent was not amused.

"These people will not engage you if you fall foul of them, and they're among our best clients. They pay the top fees and we send them top artists. The report that's come in about you is disquieting."

This was a rebuke, and I had never received such a report anywhere else. The truth of the situation dawned on me—the charlatan was having his revenge.

In the United States, artists are sold like a can of baked beans or any other commodity. The agents send their staff out to the various cities, towns, universities and colleges, and they really work hard to sell you. In Europe you are "asked for"; in America you are "sold" all the way.

I could readily understand the agent's position. I explained exactly what had happened, and we ended up in laughter, but I knew below the surface that if I wished to work in America I should have to go along with their way of life.

In the agency concerned, I was under the aegis of one of the greatest characters I have ever met—Elsie Illingworth. Elsie was an artist in her own right, so her powers of perception and her sympathy and understanding of an artist's problems were a big part of her mental equipment. She was, as she still is, a load of dynamite. She has a great heart, and her kindness to visiting artists such as myself was of inestimable value. She lent her piano and room for rehearsals in one of the most delightful apartments that I ever visited. Her friendship caused the irritants to fade away, and I always left New York knowing that a welcome awaited me on my return. As things worked out, our business relationship ended sooner than expected, as the following third tour, which Elsie had arranged, had to be cancelled. I had a physical breakdown. Soon after this, her boss sold the business, and Elsie was invited to join the Sol Hurok organisation. The old firm was not the same without her.

I was booked to sing at one of the renowned Morning Concerts in the Waldorf-Astoria. I had a special short dress designed for the occasion. Elsie had asked me what I intended to wear, and I noticed that she was a little put out when I said: "A short dress". I duly appeared and sang. My voice went down well, but my appearance was a dead loss. All female artists were expected to wear full-length evening gowns. They conformed.

These upsets provide lessons to be learnt, and one should never have to learn a lesson twice. Do in New York as the New Yorkers do.

Another important American way was pointed out to me. If you have to cancel through illness, which happens to us all, that particular booking will not be on your next itinerary. In other words, you have let them down, and that's that. I had been accustomed to a cancelled date being re-booked immediately. These differences in approach to dates and cancellations are very interesting, reflecting as they do the attitude of mind in the Western and European worlds. A two-month tour booked for February 1951 had to be cancelled. Not one of those organisations re-booked me for the next tour.

The fees earned in the United States were astronomical, but by the time the agent's fees were paid, and numerous extra deductions for working permit, musical association, and an assortment of accounts for photographs and publicity were lopped off, the remaining money almost reduced one's efforts to a costly working holiday without pay.

Another striking variant from British customs was the importance of the woman in all matters concerning the running of concerts, etc. Her word is law in most instances, and how businesslike and capable she is! The wife of an impresario said once in my presence: "If you book So-and-So I'll leave you." She meant it. The artist concerned had been mixed up with the Nazis, and a few unsavoury rumours were afloat. The impresario did not book her. I heard many such discussions, and in every case the female had the final word.

I enjoyed the stimulation of American conversation, and I made many lasting friends. Personally, I did not like the Americans' method of selling artists, but it is obviously right for them. Life would be boring indeed if we were all turned out from the same human mould.

I sang *Aïda*, *Tosca* and *Madam Butterfly* with the City Centre Opera Company during the 1949 tour. After the New York season, I went with the Company to Chicago and Milwaukee. From there I flew to Dublin, where I gave a recital, and a second one in Belfast. Then home, to finish the year in a B.B.C. "In Town Tonight" programme with Robert Donat, Anna Neagle and Michael Wilding.

Lord and Lady Gowrie were now living at Windsor Castle, where they had settled themselves in the Norman Tower. I visited them often, and it was quite a joke that we were now near neighbours. On one such visit I had the pleasure of meeting the late Eleanor Roosevelt. Her interests were widespread, and included the arts. As soon as she heard I was going to America again, she asked for my New York dates and said that she would look forward to hearing me. True to her word, she attended my second recital, and expressed pleasure and interest in my voice and career. After going down South to give recitals and sing in orchestral concerts, I returned to New York to sing *Tosca*. On the day of my first performance, Mrs Roosevelt had asked me to a luncheon, at which I was to sing for her guests. A final orchestral rehearsal was called for that morning, so I wrote explaining and expressing my regret at having to refuse her invitation.

I was ignorant of American protocol. I should have discussed
the matter with the Musical Director, who would have released
me from rehearsal. I should never have refused such an invitation.
I was also considering the performance at night, and how tiring
such a luncheon might prove for me. I was not offered a second
chance, and rightly so. The guest had been specifically chosen, and
this great, charming lady was hoping to spread my name and
fame.

This was another of life's spent arrows that never came back.

During the next decade, a series of wonderful tours and opera
performances took place. Early in 1950, I overcame the last vocal
worry—breathing. At last I had succeeded in erasing bad habits,
and abdominal breathing became natural and easy. Clearing this
last vocal hurdle set me up for the busiest and most rewarding
years of my career. I could now sing for any unlimited period
without tiring vocally. The slightest sign of trouble could be
rectified by a few scales. This was the fulfilment of years and years
of work.

The voice can often run off the rails, so to speak, when learning
a new work or role, and it is essential to know how to put it back.
This vital lesson I had now learnt, and the result was ease on the
platform, and ease with the audience and fellow artists. There is no
need for nervous tension when one is vocally secure. This phase
altered my manner considerably. Tenseness vanished, and I was
no longer irritable if some mishap occurred during a recital. I
could make a joke of and tell the audience if necessary—how
often did I bring them into the picture of what was going wrong:
a squeaky board; my accompanist stepping on my train, pulling
me up with a jerk and a nasty ripping noise behind; a clock
clanging overhead which caused me to time my groups to miss
the longer strikes; my train—all my gowns had trains—catching
on a large splinter, and various other small mishaps which
formerly would have worried me.

Many new roles were added to my repertoire, and others were
re-learnt in another language. I had formerly sung Elisabeth in

Don Carlos and Agathe in *Der Freischütz* in German; now I sang them in English. Turandot I sang in English and Italian, and Manon Lescaut and Thaïs in French and English. Two I learnt in Russian. These were Tatiana in *Eugène Onegin*, and Fevronia in *The Invisible City of Kitesh*. Also I learnt *Dalibor, Otello, Salome*, the Marschallin in *Der Rosenkavalier*, and Berlioz' *Damnation of Faust*. Another one was the little known Schubert *The Conspirators*.

I completed my longest recital tour of the British Isles. I gave three performances a week for four consecutive months—forty-eight performances in all, without a cancellation. My life was full to the brim with activity, and I made further tours in Scandinavia, Europe, Malta, East and Central Africa, Russia, Australia, India, Malaysia and the Far East, and later in America and Canada, Portugal and Spain.

When not touring my time was fully occupied with work at home: orchestral concerts, recitals, Prom concerts, and a great number of recording sessions.

A very unusual B.B.C. performance took place. I was booked by Robbie (Stanford Robinson) to sing the title role in *Turandot*. The first two bookings were for excerpts, and the second two, which were to follow two months later, were for the complete opera. The first night of the complete opera went according to plan on 1 December 1956, but the second date, 4 December, saw me in bed with a bad bout of 'flu and running a high temperature. Robbie conducted a brilliant performance of *Turandot* without Turandot being present. I was lying in bed wondering who had stepped in for me when I heard the cast given, and my name came over as the Turandot. I thought I must be so ill that I had gone cuckoo, but Lolita, who was in another part of the house, also heard the announcement. This really shocked us. Lolita telephoned the B.B.C. They said: "Tell Joan not to worry. Robbie decided to use the tape of the first performance with Joan's voice, and he is cueing in the other artists in the studios for the rest!" The connections between the tape recording and the live performers in the studio were undetectable, and for once no one knew that I was ill. Some kind people even thought that I had sung better on the second night!

I was singing Butterfly, Aïda and in *Il Trovatore* at Covent Garden during this period, and it was most fortunate that the bout of 'flu was over without a cancellation at the Opera House.

Production rehearsals for *Don Carlos* were taking place at Sadler's Wells, and I had the pleasure of working with that gifted actor-producer George Devine. The première of *Don Carlos* took place on 16 January 1951; it was the first time I had sung at the Wells. I was able to renew my friendship with the Director, Norman Tucker. These were happy days, and I thoroughly enjoyed working with the Company.

Not once, but many times members of an audience in various places would come round to see me after a recital or opera. They would look at me keenly and say: "D'you remember me?" This guessing game, after my head had been remembering words and music of twenty songs or arias or a complete opera, always confounded me. In the course of a career you meet people all over the world, but you are expected to remember someone who perhaps was introduced on one occasion and never seen again until that moment. I liked the people who came up, said their names and where we'd met. It saved time and embarrassment.

Much confusion arose in the early stages between the famous soprano Joan Cross and myself. It was a case of mistaken Joans. I was flattered, as I admired the voice and artistry of this great singer. Men in particular have said to me: "I remember hearing you when I was a boy." I'd look at them and see that they were of my own age group, and this puzzled me. "When did you hear me?" I'd ask, knowing full well what was to follow. "At the Wells." "When would that have been?" "Oh, years ago— before the War." Then came the dénouement: "I'm sorry, but you're confusing me with the other Joan, Joan Cross. My first appearance at the Wells was in 1951."

Another man assured me that he'd heard me when he was in knickerbockers. It had been in opera in the Midlands, he told me, in the early thirties. I told him I hadn't left Australia until 1936.

He became rude, and almost called me a liar. He refused to believe me, and as he left the artists' room he said bitingly: "I'll say this for you—you're wearing well!"

A mother brought her seven-year-old daughter backstage to meet me, and asked me to hear her sing.

"My little girl has a glorious voice just like yours, and she sings 'One Fine Day' just as you do. She's copied your recordings."

What can you say to such people! When I told her I would prefer to hear her daughter at a more mature age, the mother evinced shocked surprise.

"But my daughter is singing professionally already."

"Does she sing 'One Fine Day' in public?" I asked.

"Of course, and 'O My Beloved Daddy'."

"When she sings in public is a microphone provided?" I enquired.

"Oh, yes! All the cinemas and theatres have them. You ought to know that! They improve the sound of your voice."

"You realise there were no microphones tonight?" I replied.

"Weren't there?" was her answer.

This time-wasting conversation had to be stopped, so I took her name and address and said I would keep an eye open for her daughter's name on placards. I made a note of the age, seven years, and when the child must have been eighteen or so I remembered to keep a watch for her name, but it never appeared. Anything could have happened to her, but one thing is certain: her voice would have been ruined before it had a chance to flower.

Just as confusion arose between Joan Cross and me, so in the latter part of my career did another confusion arise between Joan Sutherland and myself. The press and public alike continue to confuse us. It must be the Christian names which muddles the different generations.

Joan Sutherland, the possessor of a lovely liquid voice, was my understudy for a short time in the role of Aïda at Covent Garden during the 1959-60 season. Understudies are required by contract to remain until the last act before leaving the theatre. Due to the inevitable 'flu in the heart of winter I had to cancel a performance, and Joan stepped in.

At the next performance, while I was singing the Nile scene, Lolita, who was standing near Joan in the wings, said to her: "I've heard on all sides what a lovely performance you gave ten days ago." Joan replied very simply: "Thank you." Lolita then asked her: "How did the Nile scene go?" Lolita asked this question because she knew how I approached this vocally testing scene—always with an initial nervousness until I began, and with a silent prayer that I would be in good voice and that I'd sing it as Verdi wrote it. It is the greatest moment for a soprano, and her vocal ability can be judged accordingly. Joan with utter simplicity replied to Lolita's question. "I enjoyed it," she said, meaning that it caused her no worry or preoccupation.

This interested me immensely, for it showed our opposite reactions and nervous differences. To dissect a voice and its possessor is endlessly fascinating. We vary so greatly in respect to performance-nerves. I haven't had the opportunity to discuss this with Joan, but I believe she, like Ida Haendel, the brilliant Polish violinst whom I know well, feels no qualms. This could arise from total assurance and confidence in their art and themselves. I did not lack confidence in my work, voice or interpretation, but I always feared the unknown quantity, something that might mar the entire performance for me. I could forget a word or make a musical error, or fail to carry out the dynamics as written.

Ida used to tell me that she never felt nervous. On the contrary, she didn't know the meaning of the word.

I believe in nerves and nervousness. In most cases they tend to sharpen the faculties and put you on your mettle. The finest performances have always been, in my experience, when the entire cast felt apprehensive, and on tiptoe with that right amount of nerves.

During this decade two opera engagements were cancelled. I was booked to sing in *Oberon* at the Florence Festival, and only three weeks before I was due to go there, the organisers decided to drop *Oberon* from the repertoire. No remuneration was received in the circumstances. The other booking was for *Simone Boccanegra* and

Nabucco at the Colon Opera, Buenos Aires. I mention this to show how an artist works up operas for accepted engagements, and then is left high and dry with no other work when they fall through for no specific reason.

One very important change occurred for me in 1951. I moved out of London to a 16th-century house in Burnham Beeches. After the two months of enforced rest when I had had to cancel the American tour, I became conscious of noise and the smell of crude oil from the exhausts of the London buses. When I lived in Eaton Terrace, there had previously been little traffic-noise or gaseous odours. A change took place when the Green Line buses were re-routed along Eaton Terrace to relieve the ever-growing congestion in London. The noise and smell became an irritant, and my doctor advised me to quit London before they got worse.

The Old Cottage, situated in a corner of the Beeches known as Egypt (it derived its name from the fact that the first gipsies to come to England were encamped there), was ideal. The original old cottage had had two large wings added, and though they had not been constructed at the same time, both had been expertly designed to blend with the old building. A hundred years had separated the addition of those two wings, but the demarcation lines could only be detected under close scrutiny. Old Buckinghamshire tiles had been used on both wings, and the same type of old window frames in a larger design made the whole blend perfectly.

There was the most entrancing low-ceilinged attic in the original old cottage with beams showing their age, but still solid, and a small putty window inset in the eaves. A narrow spiral staircase led up to it from the first floor. The story has been handed down over the years that Sheridan wrote a part of *The School for Scandal* in this very attic. I could sense great atmosphere when sitting there. The hand-plastered ceiling, bearing all shapes of hand imprints, which remain to this day, was fascinatingly uneven. It was very low according to our modern standards, and you could give your head a crack if you forgot to remain stooped from the time you arrived on the landing leading in to this capacious hide-

Durban: with Bobby Locke, the golfer

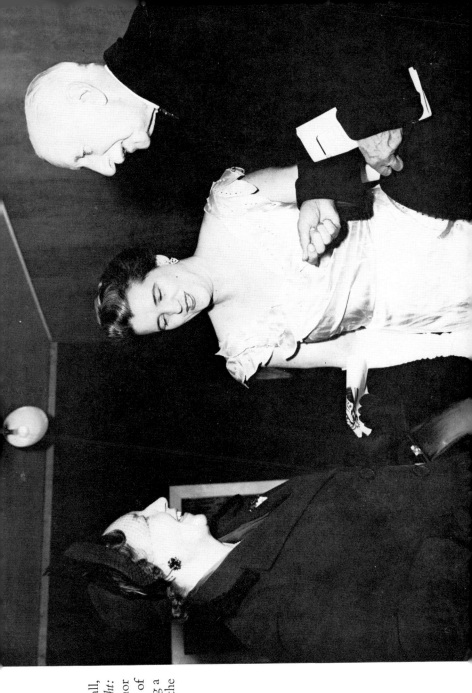

Royal Festival Hall,
1953. *Left to right:*
Ivie Price, the author
and the Earl of
Gowrie, following a
recital given for the
Opera School

Johannesburg, 1947: The author and Lolita Marriott inspecting a gold-mine

Moscow, 1957: *Left to right:* Ivan Koslovsky, Constance Shacklock and the author

London, 1969: Chatting with John Whittle of E.M.I. and Robert Leslie (editor of *Records and Recording*) following the presentation of the Gold Disc

The author at The Old Cottage, Bucks, with some of her pets

Australia House, London, 1964. *Left to right:* Lady Harrison, Sir Robert Menzies, Joan Sutherland, the author, Dame Pattie Menzies, Sir Eric Harrison (High Commissioner for Australia), at a reception for the Australian Prime Minister

The author setting off for a bird-watching picnic in Australia

away. It was in this attic that I kept all my operatic costumes and props.

Our dogs, cats, hens, and a pheasant which had adopted us had seven acres of beautiful woodland to roam in, and life was good to me. After I suffered the coronary, and subsequent angina attacks, and medical advice was to give up any idea of continuing my career, I sold the Old Cottage in 1966. I said at the time: "I hope that a Mr Right buys this home." I am very happy to say that a charming couple and their family did buy it. The purchaser's name was Wright!

The last occasion on which I sang with Sir Thomas Beecham was at a concert at the Kilburn State Cinema early in December 1952. I was the only soloist. At the morning rehearsal the fog was already dense, and as only half the orchestra turned up, nothing much could be done. None of my arias could be rehearsed, so after a long discussion with Sir Thomas and the organisers as to the best course of action, I returned home. The house was sold out and postponement was impossible owing to our commitments.

Cancellation meant a financial loss to us all. The gentlemen gave me the decision and I thanked them for their thought and consideration, but I felt the rightful person to decide, because of age and position, was Sir Thomas. He said: "If the orchestra can be here an hour before the concert, would you be agreeable to a quick run-through then?" I agreed. At the Old Cottage we were well out of the fog.

I had lunch, and then Lolita and I decided that I must forgo my rest and set off immediately, as we had heard that the fog was worsening. Fortunately it was still fairly thin on the Oxford road approach into London, but many members of the orchestra had not arrived by 6.15 p.m., nor had Sir Thomas! Ten minutes later there was a great noise from the main road, and then Sir Thomas appeared. He had been forced to travel from the West End by tube, and a torch-light procession escorted him from Kilburn station to the cinema.

The auditorium was filling rapidly as the orchestra assembled on the platform. Some players were still missing; their parts had to be

N

cued in by other instruments. We only managed to skim through Tatiana's Letter Scene and one of the three Puccini arias before the concert began. How the members of the audience found their way in that smog was incredible, but not a seat was empty. Sir Thomas asked me if I minded singing the unrehearsed arias. My reply was: "Look, if the smog became so thick inside here that you couldn't see the score, I'd still feel perfectly content with you on the rostrum." Incidentally, Sir Thomas conducted "O My Beloved Father" unrehearsed as an encore, better than any other conductor with whom I've ever worked.

The smog was so thick in the cinema by the interval, that I could not see beyond the first rows of the stalls. The concert went wonderfully, and the audience gave us a tremendous, ear-shattering reception. Sir Thomas was escorted back to the tube and to his West End flat. Lolita and I took four and a half hours to do a journey that normally took fifty minutes at that time of night. I worried about Sir Thomas, and feared he might contract a chill, but all was well, and he wrote me a letter to be treasured.

An extraordinary film contract was arranged for me. A film of Melba. The orchestral items were to be recorded in November 1952 with Sir Adrian Boult and the London Philharmonic Orchestra. The discussions had taken place, and terms and dates were settled several months beforehand. On the day of the first rehearsal, a director telephoned to say that the rehearsal would not be taking place, and he would get in touch with me later. I thought that perhaps Sir Adrian was ill, or that studio arrange-ments were disorganised. Naturally I had had to keep several weeks clear for the filming. Days passed and there was still no rehearsal-call. The office concerned kept stalling and saying that the directors were having meetings. Then came the bombshell. The entire project had been scrapped as news had reached them that an American company had begun work on a film of Melba. I could not get a penny compensation. It was the busiest time of the season, and I had refused a great deal of work because of this proposed venture into filmland.

To go to Court was a costly business, and unpleasant. A Liverpool agent had once booked me through Harold Holt's office and had failed to pay for four recitals. Harold Holt had advised me to "forget about it, unless the agent starts up again." The man had declared himself bankrupt. Such unsavoury monetary losses were best forgotten.

Instrumentalists have many advantages over singers. They can practise long hours, and the muscles of their hands and arms will become accustomed to the exercise and gain in strength all the time, whereas a singer is limited. Vocal cords are vulnerable to changes of climate, the atmosphere in halls and theatres, and to any digestive trouble. They take great punishment, as you realise when you consider the pressure of breath passing through them. They are affected by shouting, laughing or crying. Damage can be irreparable. Complete rest sometimes works wonders, but a roughness or huskiness often remains, and can be heard in the speaking voice.

Language is another problem for singers. This question arises endlessly during a singer's career. There have been famous Italian singers who have refused to sing in any language other than their own, but generally a first-rate artist takes pride and pleasure in learning other languages.

I always learnt every role and song in its original language before attempting it in any other. In this way I learnt the correct phrasing, and I was able to change a word here and there to keep the phrase as near to the original as possible. Many translations distort the musical line and rhythm. This is difficult to avoid, and librettists have to be musical as well as practical if they are to produce a credible translation in the idiom of the times.

Instrumentalists have another advantage in the choice of music to be performed. A pianist or violinist knows very soon whether his technique is good enough for certain works. He leaves them alone if his execution falls short. A singer is told to learn a certain role, and if he is a member of a Company he has little or no choice, even if the role does not suit him vocally. Conductors and administrators have been responsible for ruining many a good voice because they have misjudged a singer's weight of voice and technique. When young and enthusiastic, one accepts everything without question, and this is when one needs guidance.

To revert to the instrumentalist, he also has the advantage of being able to select a teacher capable of giving him the basic fundamentals of his art, and then he advances to another teacher who takes him to a higher grade. But all his teachers will have been executants themselves, whereas there are many singing teachers who have never sung a note in their lives. With much publicity and slick talk the charlatan gets a goodly number of pupils. The pupil is easily hoodwinked if he is ignorant of music in general. So few really love music. They love the sound of their voice, and the lure of the footlights is strong. They believe the road to fame is short and easy, but in effect there are no short cuts. Those who get a lucky break usually deserve it, for they have probably worked hard and long. When an opportunity comes their way, they are fit to make the most of it, and rocket to fame overnight, or so it seems to the envious ones; but it is never really overnight at all.

Early in 1953 Kathleen Ferrier was ill and I stepped in for her at short notice at a city in the North of England. Gerald was the accompanist. A long recital-programme without a rehearsal normally would be unthinkable, but with Gerald or Ivor as accompanist it was possible. We had a short talk about each group, and everything went smoothly and perfectly.

The reason for mentioning this concert is Kathleen. This was the beginning of a series of cancellations for her, as it was also the last chapter of the cursed illness which took her from us. During the interval the organiser of the recital came to thank me for stepping in. "I'll never book Kathleen again," he said. "This is the second time she has let us down."

I flushed with anger as I replied: "No artists intentionally let people down. Illness is something one has no control over. Also remember that the artist is the loser, both by disappointing the public and the loss of the fee. Kathleen Ferrier would never willingly let anyone down, and I trust you'll bear that in mind for future work." He stared at me with hard, disbelieving eyes.

"I've been in this concert game long enough to know that you singers are full of tantrums. What about that foreigner the other day who arrived at the theatre and then said she didn't feel like going on? The audience, cast and orchestra were all kept waiting while she made up her mind."

I tried to keep my temper. "Foreign artists do have different customs from ours, and if they behave like that in their home opera house no one takes any notice. There's always someone else to go on. But the British singer is neither spoilt nor pampered. We're trained to believe that the show must go on. You'd be wise to remember that, and not make comparisons."

The second half of that recital was hard work. I felt angry and saddened by the conversation. This was 14 January. On 17 February, after I had sung *Aïda* at Covent Garden in English one night and in Italian in Amsterdam the next night, I met Gerald Moore in London for lunch. He told me that Kathleen was very ill. We decided to visit her in University College Hospital, where soon afterwards she died. We had lovely, bright talks with her on a variety of subjects, and I told her about my Dutch Radames, who insisted on keeping me "in the suburbs" as we say when making love on stage. She looked radiant and laughed so much. I never saw her again. I did hope that the concert organiser in the North of England pondered deeply, and that he regretted some of the things he had said.

Stanford Robinson's brother Eric now began to play an important part in my career. I had been very wary of appearing on television, and had refused interesting offers. Then Eric and his young, talented highly skilled producer, Patricia (Paddy) Foy, talked me into appearing on Eric's "Music for You" B.B.C. television programme. My previous experience in this medium had been in two different programmes, one arranged by that delightful B.B.C. interviewer, Jeanne Heal, and the other by the great comedienne, Jeanne de Casalis. Both had been at Alexandra Palace, and Eric had conducted the second.

To my surprise I found "Music for You" a most enjoyable programme. Eric certainly has the necessary technique and ability to conduct for television. His musical versatility and ease of manner make him an outstanding conductor and personality. It is a very specialised form of conducting, and one in which many names famous in the concert hall have failed. In my opinion, the combination of Eric and Paddy has given the public first class musical television programmes, at the same time having wide public appeal.

After this introduction I found myself appearing more and more on television screens at home in Britain, and in other countries when on tour. I think my best effort was in a series called "Profile in Music", a B.B.C. programme with John Freeman, now British Ambassador to the U.S.A. I found John to be a most interesting and competent interviewer. He liked a straight answer, and he had the happy knack of drawing out the information he sought and keeping to the point. Owing to his perceptive mind and thorough knowledge of his subject there were no dull patches.

The programme ran for fifty minutes, divided into twenty-seven minutes of singing and twenty-three minutes of interview. There were no cuts. For hour after hour I rushed from studio to dressing room. I had to be in the same gown for the interview throughout, but between the snatches of conversation with John there were songs, and operatic arias in costume. Paddy was producing the series, and to me it seemed fantastic that she put it all together into a consecutive whole. On the night of the actual screening it looked so natural, unhurried and uninterrupted, but at the time of filming it had seemed, at least to me, to be completely chaotic. I didn't watch the programme myself, but reports and fan letters were more numerous and complimentary than ever.

I enjoyed another B.B.C. television programme called "Perspective". I enjoyed it because it gave me the opportunity of meeting two great poets, John Betjeman and Cecil Day Lewis. The conversation when off camera was of far greater interest than the programme, and I should have liked it to continue that way. There was so much wit and buoyancy.

The B.B.C. put on a series of "Music for All" type of programmes at the Royal Festival Hall, and through them I had the refreshing experience of singing a song linked with my name, "The Green Hills o' Somerset", and another, "Bird Songs at

Eventide", both conducted by the composer, Eric Coates. This was something I really enjoyed. He was such a quiet unassuming gentle person, and his compositions convey these qualities.

Another popular ballad writer, Haydn Wood, came into my world at that time. He and Eric Coates were not unalike, and their compositions were so English, which I mean as a compliment. One can almost breathe the delight of the English countryside while listening to their music. A sincere simplicity of style and subject was their musical symbolism. These summer orchestral concerts were most successful. The programmes were varied and well chosen.

An interviewer of exceptional qualities is Godfrey Winn. He is a man of such humanity, with expansive warmth and understanding of people's daily problems, and he combines intelligence and perceptiveness.

I was receiving more and more demands for straight recitals, and through this specialised avenue much pioneering work came my way. While touring East Africa a request came through the agent in Nairobi for me to go to the Copper Belt while I was in Northern Rhodesia. Kitwe, Ndola and Luanshya were the towns concerned. They had never had a classical concert, let alone a recital with just the singer, the accompanist (in this case Ivor Newton) and a piano on stage. I agreed to go.

The Mau Mau were still very active, and I shall never forget seeing some beautifully gowned women in the audience at Nairobi wearing revolvers as casually as a floral decoration.

We were taken for a drive to see the Rift Valley. If the car had broken down, a gruesome death could have been our fate, but the Greek impresario who was driving us seemed quite unaware of any danger. He drove like a madman, and this was terrifying enough. When we arrived at an uninhabited viewing point, Ivor asked him to let me drive back to Nairobi. To our surprise and relief he agreed willingly. I had a shrewd suspicion that he'd never driven much before. The car had been lent to him, and there we were, at the beginning of a tour, driving through Mau Mau country, and seeing these poor creatures by the roadside in groups, hugging their pangas. It wasn't funny. We found the Game Reserve far less nerve-wracking.

After Nairobi we went to Dar es Salaam for two recitals, and then to Salisbury. The theatres were packed, and the audiences very enthusiastic. This proved, if I needed proof, how widely an artist can be familiarised through gramophone recordings.

From Salisbury we were driven to Umtali, where for the first time in its history, a recital was given. The response by the people of the town and outlying districts was wonderful. Umtali has a special snug place in my memory. I was invited to buy a lottery ticket. Months later, back in England, I received notification that I had won £250—the first time I had ever won anything in a lottery. I bought my first television set with the money.

We were taken to see a large tobacco farm on the way back to Salisbury, and while in Salisbury we attended a tobacco sale. What voices the auctioneers had! I was more than interested in their vocal activities, and I asked one of them how he kept up such a rapid, clear, carrying tone (ugly but effective), and he told me that a long training had been necessary to achieve his position. The auctioneers were dependent on their voices, and they took every precaution to keep them in trim.

We spent a few peaceful hours with Sir Roy and Lady Welensky. They were a fount of knowledge about their country, and we were happy to listen to them. Time seemed to pass unheeded by us all, but events and history were vividly present.

In all my travels, the views that have impressed me most have been the Matopo Hills near Bulawayo and Table Mountain in South Africa, Mount Kilimanjaro, the Swiss Alps from the air, and the Blue Mountains of New South Wales. From Salisbury we drove out to the Matopos where Rhodes loved to wander, and no doubt ponder over the many prickly situations which arose in Rhodesia. I can well appreciate his love of it.

I felt my entire being bathed in such utter peace. A great and inexplicable serenity enveloped me—a new sensation. I understood for the first time the full force of the saying, "At peace with the world". There was a magnificence about the view of all the surrounding countryside, but I have never felt so keenly aware of great silence, a silence which forces the mind and body to become a part of that place. Such stillness I have never known. No sound, even of birds, disturbed this patch of earth. It is the kind of haven one longs to visit in times of worry and trouble.

We journeyed on to Southern Rhodesia and stayed at the Victoria Falls Hotel. The recital was just over the border in Northern Rhodesia, in Livingstone. Throughout the tour, the halls were bursting out with people, while many had to be turned away. The impresario wished he had booked us for two performances in each place instead of one.

The huge cascading falls were awe inspiring. So was our flight, in a light aircraft, over Bechuanaland, when I was afraid we should decapitate the giraffes as we skimmed just above their heads. Every kind of wild animal was visible. It was dusk, and they were all at the water holes. We then went in a boat up the Zambesi, to become acquainted with the sad but comical looking hippopotami, and to gaze with respect at the crocodiles. A trip to the Wankie Game Reserve was another adventure, for we could study the wild animals at ground level. Our guide was the renowned Ian Sussens. He would leave the huge station-wagon and take photographs for us. He had a loaded revolver in a holster in case of emergency, but what he could have done in the event of an elephant stampede I don't know!

We arrived at one of the Reserve huts at 4 a.m. It was still dark as we left the car, and as we were following Ian to the hut, I happened to look at Ivor. He was frozen like a statue, and I could see the pallor of his face.

"What on earth's the matter?" I asked. He tried to speak but couldn't. Ian and Lolita were already at the door of the hut, so I went back to Ivor.

"Something's rubbing against my legs," he gasped. "I daren't move. Tell Ian to do something."

Ian heard and went to Ivor, laughing his head off.

"That's only the camp cat. Nothing can get into this reserve. It's all cat territory."

Poor Ivor drank two cups of coffee before he recovered from the shock. You should hear Ivor tell the tale himself. He is a natural raconteur. We all laughed at his description of this warm, soft, furry thing entwining his legs. He felt sure it was a man-eating animal.

We met with nothing but kindness and hospitality and friend-ship wherever we went on this tour, and some unusual problems, such as there being no back-stage in the Ndola cinema. A very narrow steep plank was our only means of reaching the stage. Ivor shuddered, and turned to the helpful but ignorant concert organisers.

"Can't anything better be done? You'll lose both your prima donna and her accompanist with broken limbs if we have to negotiate this plank every time."

The organisers scratched their heads and showed us the difficulties they were up against. There was certainly no other way. The men offered to act as railings and help us up, and this they did. It was a most comical experience for both Ivor and me, made more perilous because of my train. We swept down the aisle and reached the plank five times in all, and then the fun began. I made my bow acknowledging the applause, and simply asked the audience to "wish Mr. Newton and me a safe and happy journey!"

After the interval the plank became rather tired, and sagged a bit, though our human guard-rails assured us it could stand the strain, and it did. The piano was an upright, horribly out of tune, but the audience enjoyed it all and showed us so in no uncertain fashion. I made jokes about it and treated it all as a bit of fun. We were sorry to leave these people. As there were no hotels we stayed in private homes, and at a house kept by one of the large mining firms for their visiting directors.

I encountered another cinema with no back-stage area. It was a recital again, which meant at least five long walks backwards and forwards down the centre aisle, and a stiff climb up rough wooden steps made specially for the occasion. I had to change into my evening gown in the manager's tiny office, which was at dress circle level. It was a sure test of breath control and leg stiffness.

We flew back to Livingstone, and our last view was of the beautiful rainbow forest created by seeing the Victoria Falls from a different angle. We all had wonderful memories of that particular tour.

During my third tour of Malaysia another pioneering booking came in. I was asked if I would give a recital at Ipoh, way up north from Kuala Lumpur. Again we were given marvellous hospitality in private homes, as there were no suitable hotels.

There was one remarkable feature about my visit to Ipoh. I felt the effects of the tropical climate. The concert organisers procured every available fan, and had them concentrated on me during the recital. The noise was disconcerting, but those fans helped to cool me and keep the piano in tune. It was a testing climate for both piano and singer—what a contrast to the radiators on stage in Tasmania.

As far as artists are concerned, the most striking thing about these off-the-map places is the unspoilt, unsophisticated attitude of the community. The wealthy and the not-so-wealthy enter into the spirit of it all, and no effort is spared to make the event a great success. We always found these recitals so revitalising and enchanting, especially after coming direct from Europe or America. We could reinforce and regale our mental outlook in preparation for our return to the world of sophistication.

It was at times unbelievable to have been at Ipoh one week and singing in that perfect, beautifully appointed San Carlos Opera House in Lisbon the next!

It was in Lisbon that Lolita and I were forbidden to land, and we were very nearly put on the next aeroplane back to London because of visa trouble with our Australian passports. We spent three uncomfortable isolated hours at the airport. Luckily Colonel Cross Brown, who had been lunching with the Chief of Police, was awaiting the flight to London on which we were to be deported. He heard of our plight, and that I was to sing that night! He rang the Chief of Police, and within half an hour we were being driven to the city, free but somewhat exhausted from trying to explain that my commitment was to sing that night.

I shall never forget my first visit to Spain, where I had been booked to sing Tatiana in *Eugène Onegin*, and Fevronia in Rimsky Korsakov's little known opera *The Invisible City of Kitesh*. Both operas were to be sung in Russian. I gave a lot of thought to this before accepting the contract, as the Russian language resembled Chinese to me. But it was a challenge, and this I liked. The Pushkin words were new Russian, but those of *The Invisible City of Kitesh* were in old Russian, which presented an even more formidable task. I bought the language records and went to a school of languages in London. I ate with and slept with Russian, and studied it to and from engagements all over the place. I cannot sing a song or any operatic role unless I know what I am singing about. I love words, and if you are to sing with conviction, you must understand what you are singing about. The great composers of song chose the most beautiful poetry to set to music.

There are some musical phrases which give immense joy, both to singer and audience. One can sense that the listener is being carried along, and is uplifted by the music. This is an exhilarating sensation. Soft, simple tunes as well as great climaxes have power to move an audience if the singer is sincere and has a voice that can thrill.

One such passage comes at the end of Act II in *La Traviata*, in the phrase "Amami, Alfredo, amami quant' io t'amo"—"Love me, Alfredo, love me as I love thee". Verdi provides another example in the liquid soaring beauty of the phrase "Rather a thousand deaths I'd die" in the last act of *Il Trovatore*. An equally glorious, rising and falling phrase comes in the same composer's *La Forza del Destino* during Leonora's aria "Madre Pietosa Vergine"—"Mother full of pity". And Verdi again in *Otello*, when Desdemona has been thrown to the ground. She sings to the jealous Otello "E un di sul mio sorriso"—"And one day you smiled on me".

Verdi left us a galaxy of beautiful music which affords all singers the opportunity to display the richness of their voices to the best effect. Both he and Puccini were masters of the theatre, and both understood vocal technique thoroughly. They knew the strong and weak parts of the voice, and composed their music accordingly. They gave breadth and scope for mighty climaxes and crescendos in the parts of the voice that can fulfil the demands.

Puccini provided the soprano with splendid music in most of his operas. Near the end of Act II in *Madam Butterfly* a cannon-shot is heard. Butterfly, standing at the window, sees the man-of-war in the harbour. Her aria builds up to a great climax with the words "He's here! He loves me!" There are many such examples.

There is no sensation more gratifying than to let the voice flow out in a superbly written musical climax which gives ample scope for interpretation. This is exciting to singer and audience alike. When the voice is at its best the singer finds nothing comparable to the magic of beautiful, expressive melodies which lie particularly well in the voice.

The Vienna State Opera gave a short season of Mozart at the Liceo Theatre in Barcelona, and this was followed by Ingrid Bergman directed by Rossilini in Honegger's *Joan of Arc*, interspersed with the Russian operas. The singers came from Paris, but the conductor was from the Vienna State Opera. This was an amazing experience. Rehearsals were haphazard, and never started before 3 p.m. No calls were put on the board; I would receive a telephone call saying, "Come now", or "You are expected at 7 p.m."

My fellow artists were an easy-going group. They seemed to regard the season as a pleasant interlude in which you sang what you wanted to sing, and cut the rest. The bass singing the role of Gremin in *Eugène Onegin* never once sang the famous and beautiful aria when he tells Onegin of his love for Tatiana. The young Viennese conductor Klobućar was at his wits' end to know how to cope with such a situation. He spoke only German, so I was used as an interpreter; not a very good one, but adequate. Thankfully, somehow orchestra and soloists began and finished together when it came to the performance.

I bought another lottery ticket and won a prize which seemed like millions, but being 500 pesetas was worth about ten shillings which I put straight into the poor box.

The performances began at 9.30 p.m., but the bulk of the

audience did not arrive until the first interval. I found it very disturbing to see people so impeccably dressed and groomed, obviously lacking nothing, yet so inordinately lax about time. It seemed such a poor compliment to the artists. The few who were on time did not seem to mind being disturbed by the continuous stream of late-comers. The opera or play often began much later than the advertised time, but I never knew why. I realised it was all part of the tradition, and one must do in Spain as the Spaniards do. Musically and aesthetically it was upsetting, though. I loved both operas and found much compensation in taking part in them.

I was invited to sing the role of Salome with the Elizabethan Theatre Trust Opera Company. I immediately got in touch with my old friend Bobby (now Sir Robert) Helpmann. He gave up some of his valuable time to show me a few steps and see how I limbered up, as I was hesitant about accepting the role of Salome unless I was found to be a good enough mover. I knew Bobby would be honest about it. Rhythm was no problem, and after our third meeting, which he refused to regard as a business engagement (but such is the man, expansive both in his art and in his dealing with his fellow artists), he told me who would be the ideal person to coach me. It was Pauline Grant, and I am eternally grateful to Bobby for this introduction. Like him she is a most gifted choreographer, especially for opera ballet. Both are indefatigable workers, and love it. Although Pauline's commitments were heavy she put me in wherever possible. Our places of work were so varied. Julie Andrews was starring in a television show which at her request Pauline was producing, so I used to go to the studio during the break to be put through my paces. Norman Tucker gave us permission to use the ballet rehearsal room at Sadler's Wells, which became another venue.

As the Dance of the Seven Veils progressed, so did my enthusiasm and desire to do it to the best of my ability egg me on to practise as often and as diligently as possible. We had upsets over the undergarment for the costume, but after much thought and careful designing the ideal pattern took shape. Pauline knew what she wanted, and where to get a thing done. Those veils gave us such fun and quite a bit of trouble.

The rehearsals of *Salome* became longer, as I had to start linking up the singing with the dance. Vocally it is one of the most demanding of all roles. Strauss created a problem by writing the title role for a dramatic soprano. Salome should be young and beautiful. She must be able to dance. Some productions have a ballet dancer waiting in the wings to slip on and do the famous dance of the seven veils. This is not the ideal solution, as the dance is an integral part of Salome's character, and no matter how well the change is executed, it jars to see another face and figure suddenly appear. There is no place in the music for Salome to leave the stage after the dance, which creates another problem.

Vocally it requires a mature voice, and there are no young, mature voices. Woe betide the singer who attempts it before she is absolutely master of her voice and technique. Also she needs to be a musician to cope with the intricate score. Strauss was not a master of the singer's art, and some of the intervals are most unvocal. Some theatrical climaxes are lost too, because of the heavy orchestration which smothers even the most penetrating voice when the notes are placed in the wrong part of the register. This role has been the graveyard of many a singer.

At this time I was also studying a new opera, *Wat Tyler*, for the B.B.C. Vocally and musically these operas are so dissimilar that rehearsing them became a matter of vocal and musical compromise. Alan Bush, the composer of *Wat Tyler*, had blended words and music perfectly.

No sooner was this production over, than a proposed tour, previously mooted, came to fruition. It was to sing *Aïda* and Tatiana in *Eugène Onegin* in Russian in Leningrad, and at the Bolshoi Theatre in Moscow, and to give some concerts. As I was the first British soprano ever invited to sing opera in Russian in Russia this was a very exciting prospect. For the moment all thoughts of *Salome* had to be dropped—there would be time for that later.

As soon as I boarded the Russian Aeroflot air-liner at Helsinki I realised I was bound for a different way of life. To begin with, there were no seat belts for take-off and landing. Seeing me fumble for one, the air hostess assured me that they weren't necessary, and just to test her theory I took a little walk up and down the aircraft during the take-off. Nothing untoward happened, and the novelty soon wore off.

Once in Russia the lack of colour in wearing apparel looked rather drab to us, but the Russians are most colourful in personality. We were treated with abounding generosity and kindness.

The Russians are hungry for classics in every field; they fill the art galleries as they do the theatres. They really appreciate vocal difficulties and the intricacy of ballet steps, and they applaud wholeheartedly when an artist surmounts a hurdle efficiently. Pianissimo singing makes a particular appeal to them. The roars of applause which follow an exit made on a difficult pianissimo note are far greater than those called forth by a more spectacular fortissimo. This is a very unusual reaction, most gratifying to the artist. The Russian conductors easily gained all the effect they wanted. The pianissimo playing was superb—never once did I hear a singer drowned. As soon as the voice entered, the volume of orchestral sound automatically dropped, thus giving even greater effect to the great climaxes. It was operatic accompanying in the best tradition.

In the U.S.S.R. artists are given every consideration, and their only worries are the portrayal of their roles. Directors, conductors and artists all enjoy the same status, and no one is lionised above another. Every opera house director I met was a professional musician, and the producers had all received a five-year training, while women enjoy equal status with men in the theatre as in all other professions.

The stage lighting system I found particularly good. The facial expressions of the soloists can be seen at all times, and there is no front centre lighting as in most countries, though there are footlights. Three or four technicians give lighting instructions during the whole performance, and artists can move freely about the stage knowing that they are seen in a soft but penetrating light. The back-stage section of Russian theatres is run with the same efficiency.

Theatre hairdressers always asked if I needed their services for my recitals, even though those concerts were outside the scope of the theatre itself. Such facilities were available to all operatic artists.

The word Bolshoi means big, and the great theatre certainly is! There is one pleasant custom apparently instituted because of the seventy-five foot wide stage. The audience, which leaves the seats at the end of each act and crowds down the aisles towards the orchestra pit shouting and applauding, is not satisfied with an artist's appearance through the curtain in the centre of the stage to acknowledge their applause. One must first go to one side of the stage, bow to those applauding there, and then walk the full width to the other side to acknowledge the applause from there. As one crosses from one side to the other extra shouts and cheers come forth. It becomes a matter of competition, with each side trying to outdo the other in appreciation.

Architecturally the halls, theatres and buildings are elegant, with a richness that is never overdone. They reflect the good taste of Czarist days, and it was interesting to note that the Soviet citizen of today takes pride in this heritage. The finest and most beautiful hall I sang in was the Philharmonic Hall, Leningrad. The auditorium is an architectural joy, being symmetrical and classical in line. The artists' rooms are also uniquely elegant and restful, with every facility and comfort. And there is a piano for last minute reference and for rehearsals—one could try the voice and know it would not be heard in the hall. This hall and the Maryinsky Theatre, now known as the Kirov, are two jewels in that lovely city. The seating, carpeting and curtains are all in a beautiful blue. One becomes accustomed to red plush, and the unusual colouring remains in one's mind as something very lovely.

The Hall of the Conservatorium in Moscow I found most excellent acoustically, and for me it had a special significance because it was in this hall that Glinka, Tchaikovsky and Rachmaninoff studied and played. It was not particularly beautiful, but it had great atmosphere.

The best performances of opera and ballet—musically, scenically and technically—that I have ever seen were in Russia. The

o

stage effects for fire, storms, battles and the burning of a city were
terrifyingly real. I have seen wonderful performances in other
opera houses, but one night would be brilliant and the next
mediocre, while in Russia every performance was uniformly first-
rate. I heard the operas *Mazeppa* and *Iolanthe*, both by Tchaikovsky, for the first time and the only time. I should have loved to
sing the soprano role in *Iolanthe*.

A short visit to Riga in Latvia was included in the Russian tour.
This interesting old city appealed to me because of the numerous
parks—very lovely parks—which compensated for the obvious
poverty of a city that had known better times, and was now tired
and neglected. The Opera Company was not of the high artistic
standard encountered in Leningrad and Moscow, but again we
met with the warmest reception and hospitality. The people gave
me the feeling that they were being whipped and suppressed.
The buildings were in need of repair and an uplift, as were the
souls and spirits of the people. The economy must have been in a
poor state for far too long. It needed an injection to revitalise and
restore it to a world of freedom. What was once a gay, beautiful
city thronging with tourists and possessing a flourishing trade is
now languishing, and slowly being deprived of all its former
attractions.

To sing in Helsinki, a few months later, brought an even greater
realisation of Riga's unhappy state. Helsinki is a lively bustling
city, and its people are industrious, content and vibrant with life.

Early in 1959 I began rehearsals of *Rusalka* at Sadler's Wells. The
producer was a very talented and competent artist, Wendy Toye,
and the designer was James Bailey, a most proficient young man.
Vilem Tausky was the conductor. I should say this production was
one of the happiest with which I had ever been associated, and it
ended in being one of the most disastrous, from the point of view
of a London première; but to have collaborated with Wendy,
James and Vilem and all the excellent cast was nothing but a
pleasure.

At 4 p.m. on the day of the première Norman Tucker telephoned me at the Old Cottage and said: "Joan, Norman here.

We're in a spot. Charles [tenor Charles Craig] is almost voiceless and feels he can't go on. Would you be willing to sing *Madam Butterfly* instead?"

"Whew!" was all I said. Norman never wasted words or time.

"I can get a cast for Butterfly, and Anna Pollak will be your Suzuki, so no worries there. Vilem is confident that the rest of the cast will be okay."

"That's fine with me, Norman. I'm sorry for you all up there."

"Thanks, Joan, and by the way, it's getting rather foggy."

"Don't worry. I'll leave here just as soon as I get my wig and costumes out. See you later."

With that the Old Cottage rocked with activity. I had not sung Butterfly since December, and then it was in Italian. I thought of it mentally while on the journey to London. By the time we reached Shepherd's Bush the fog was unpleasantly thick, and the streets dark. We arrived at the Wells an hour before the performance was due to begin. I had the English words of Butterfly well into my head and I felt mentally prepared. For any première (and Dvořák's *Rusalka* was to receive its first performance in Great Britain), rehearsals work up to a certain pitch; during the last two weeks we had all lived, slept and eaten *Rusalka*. So you can imagine the tremendous let-down one feels when such a première has to be cancelled.

I was met at the stage door by the stage manager. He greeted me: "Joan, it's to be *Rusalka* after all. Craig has decided to go through with it." What a mental switch from Cio Cio San to Rusalka, and all in a few minutes!

Poor Charles, the possessor of a lovely rich tenor voice, was most unhappy, but he managed to get through although his voice showed but a shadow of its usual brilliance.

The fog had seeped into the theatre and into our dressing rooms, and we heard that three-quarters of the audience could barely see the stage after the second interval. They gave us a wonderful acclamation at the final curtain, but we all felt rather flat because of the ghastliness of the night. Some of us managed to reach James Bailey's flat in the West End, where we had a delightful

supper party. It took us over four hours to get back to the Old
Cottage, where we arrived at 5 a.m. with stiff, sooty black hair and
clogged noses. One of us had to get out of the car at each round-
about and lead with a torch, as the "cat's eyes" had gaps where
the different roads led off. Nevertheless we often found other
motorists on the wrong road and on the wrong side of a dual
carriageway, and twice we met cars coming at us. It was terrifying. The second performance of *Rusalka* was due to take place
two days later, but this time Charles had to cancel, and we did
Madame Butterfly instead.

Soon after this I was immersed in rehearsals of Purcell's *Dido and
Aeneas* for the Bath Festival, and later at Hampton Court. Again
I had efficient, gifted artists to work with. The young conductor
Colin Davis impressed me very much. He had a very clear, con-
cise beat and a fluidity of tempo. His approach was that of a
mature musician, a fact which distinguished him from other
young conductors. He inspired confidence, and knew what he
wanted. The producer, Anthony Besch, was a most conscientious,
artistic and thorough worker. The cast would probably be
drooping and flagging visibly after a full day of rehearsing, but
Anthony would forget time and be carrying on as though we had
just begun. The costumes designed by Peter Rice were very
lovely, and the whole effect of scenery blending in colour with
costumes made a tremendous impact on the audience. This was
specially noticeable in the charming atmosphere of Hampton
Court, which was an ideal setting for the opera.

I now began rehearsing *Salome* again, as the time for me to sing it
with the Elizabethan Theatre Trust Opera Company was at hand.
I had already given two recital tours for the Australian Broadcasting Commission, and in 1957 I sang the roles of Desdemona,
in Verdi's *Otello*, and Tosca for the Opera Company. That tour
began in Brisbane, and the A.B.C. asked me if I would be willing
to fly to Sydney for the day on 7 August to sing an aria during the
initial Opera House Appeal. The Trust agreed to release me. I
chose to sing "One Fine Day"—a prophetic choice, for events

have certainly proved that the building may be ready "one fine day". The entire launching ceremony was rattling good fun. Kisses by me were sold for £50 each, amid much gaiety. Just so long as the money came into the fund that was all that mattered, and the kisses helped! We all inspected the model of the chosen design, but I was sorry that there were no plans of the interior, which would have interested me. Looking at the curves of the unusual exterior, I thought it might take off in a Southerly Buster, which is Sydney's famous gale wind. It also reminded me of the shape of an armadillo, or a number of dinghies upended on a jetty.

Someone expressed a wish that I would be invited to sing at the official opening. A newspaper reporter mentioned the same idea to me, and I replied: "I'll probably be in a wheelchair by the time this building is erected!" I was not far out, but I'm glad to say that although no wheelchair is necessary yet, I thought of the phrase when I was pushed around in one after being in a car smash, and again after I had had a coronary. Some poor jokes come home to roost, and this was one of them.

Now in 1960, I was to sing Salome and Butterfly. The tour lasted from February through to July. Putting on *Salome* for the first time in Australia was a big gamble, and one that paid off. We opened with it at the Adelaide Festival on 17 March, and from that time on the tour was a sell-out. An extra performance was given in Melbourne, in the vast Palais Theatre at St Kilda.

I had trouble with veil number six, which would come off before its time, but apart from that all went as well as I dared hope. My one regret was that Pauline was not with me for the final rehearsals on stage. She would have been able to put the final touches to the dance. I missed her, and I missed Julie Andrews, whom I had come to know quite well during the early rehearsals, when she was appearing in *My Fair Lady*. I had often popped in to see her. Julie asked intelligent questions about the voice, and she used her own with great artistry and faultless diction.

Pauline saw me in the role when we were in Sydney, as she had come to Australia to supervise her original choreography of the London production of *The Merry Widow*. Pauline has the essential attributes of a choreographer—rhythm, musical knowledge, imagination, and the ability to synchronise movement with music. It had greatly impressed me when learning the Salome dance. So often dancers are not given actions to measure up to a great musical climax.

Salome was a challenge, and I had often wished to sing the role. I had first heard it in Vienna and the music gripped me, but the story seemed horrific. Both musically and histrionically this opera is electrifying from end to end.

I had found on my previous tour with the Elizabethan Theatre Trust Company that there was a good team spirit and great eagerness to do well. The members were unspoilt by years of professional work, and most of them had to earn their livings in a variety of ways. At that time no permanent opera company existed, as there was too little work in the world of music to keep them going. Only a few were singing professionally. It was a very sad day when the Company disbanded; its members had worked so well and hard, and many of them were really talented. It upset me to know that such-and-such a promising artist would soon be sitting all day at a typewriter, or be standing behind the counter in a store, doing a milk run—any job, while they waited for another opportunity to come up for them to follow the career they longed for in singing.

In Australia, as everywhere else, there is from time to time an upsurge of protest against the star system. One performer should not be lionised above another, say the detractors. All are part of the team, working together to present the opera, play or ballet.

This is a most extraordinary attitude; one which I find hard to understand. Who wants to see empty seats every night in theatre or opera house? Personalities draw the public in. Their presence means a thrill of anticipation in the auditorium, while on-stage they raise the level of the whole production by the inspiration they give to their fellow artists. They have a certain magnetism, and we could certainly do with more of them in the field of classical music.

All forms of sport suffer a drop in gate money if there is no big name to attract the public. There is no doubt that the patrons of sport, and of the theatre arts, love the star system, and have little taste for the levelling process which essays to reduce all performers to the same status. It has been proved over and over again that there is no substitute for personalities and big names, as many organisers have found to their cost. Stars are a necessity: the yeast in the general lump of dough. Through their art they give pleasure and excitement to millions of people.

There are some works which enjoy a spate of popularity and then drift out of fashion for years, but suddenly creep back into the repertoire. This happened with such works as Berlioz' *Childhood of Christ* and *The Damnation of Faust*, Delius' *Idyll*, the Te Deums of Bruckner and Dvořák, *The Song of Songs* by Hubert Foss, and Coleridge Taylor's *Hiawatha*. Others are perennially in fashion, such as Verdi's *Requiem*, the Beethoven 9th, *Messiah* and *Elijah*.

The work for which I had the greatest demand was Verdi's *Requiem*, and each time I sang it I used to pray that I would sing it as the great Master himself wished. I think it is the crowning work of his career with regard to solo, orchestral and choral writing. It has the strength of utter simplicity, and the purity of truth, absolutely unfettered by dogma. Verdi the man was incapable of insincerity. He was a free-thinker, a man of natural instinct, down to earth, and in close touch with life. Perhaps that is why he treated the last questions of death and eternity with such intuitive vision and poetic energy.

Today this massive opus has become one of the most favoured throughout the world; it is a showpiece for all conductors, a kind of yardstick by which their talents are measured. They all like to include it in their repertoires.

Verdi was a master of vocal technique and he knew, as few other composers have ever known, exactly where to place the notes in the scale in order to get the desired effects. He knew, in fact, the strong and weak sections through the entire range of the human voice. If he had never written anything but the Requiem, he would still have been acclaimed a master.

There are many incidents in a long career which stick firmly in the memory. Once during a performance of *Tosca* I stabbed Scarpia and he grabbed the knife, but it ricocheted out of his hand and struck me by my right eye. Blood ran down my face, and for once I really did do a job with wiping the blood off my face and hands with the napkin provided. This was during the Australian tour and my tenor, Ronald Dowd, and the baritone, John Shaw, were personal friends. John was supposed to be dead, so there was nothing he could do to help me. Lolita was quickly called from backstage: "Come at once! Miss Hammond has been stabbed." Lolita is not easily rattled, and her reply was to the point. "It can't be Miss Hammond—it must be John Shaw. It wouldn't make sense if he stabbed her." She calmed everybody down and reminded them that the end of the act was near, and no one could do anything until then. It was not much of a wound, but it bled a lot.

At a performance of *Tosca* at Covent Garden a galleryite was heard to say, after I had finished singing the famous aria, "Vissi d'arte", in the second act: "I hope she will sing the other side of the record"! Referring to my early recording of "O My Beloved Father", of course.

The child Trouble in *Madam Butterfly* has been the cause of many a good story. My worst experience ever was in America. The conductor insisted on his small son filling the role of Trouble. Apart from being overweight and very heavy to carry, he behaved impeccably at rehearsals. The producer wanted the child to sit on a small wicker stool instead of cushions. In the most tragic part of the opera, towards the end, Suzuki pushed him on as rehearsed, and he ran and sat on the stool, but instead of facing me, he swivelled round on his little bottom and looked straight at his father. He poked out his tongue, and then he scratched that little bottom. It was the only time I ever wanted to smack a child.

The members of the orchestras in Adelaide, Melbourne, Sydney and Brisbane, with the conductors' consent, used to change places during the matinées in order that they could all have a look at the stage. This I found most original and amusing.

After I had sung Tatiana's Letter Scene from *Eugène Onegin* at a city in the North of England, a singing teacher came backstage with eight of her pupils. She introduced herself, and said loudly: "Hearing that Letter Song took me back to the days when I heard Chaliapin sing it!" I was about to refute the possibility of that world famous Russian bass singing a soprano aria, but remembering the listening pupils, I refrained.

One of the last B.B.C. television series I took part in was "Gala Performance". Among those taking part were Dame Margot Fonteyn and Nureyev. Richard Attenborough was our compère. The programme was being filmed, and we were in the midst of the performance. The dancers had already made one appearance, and I was singing my first aria—"One Fine Day" from *Madam Butterfly*. Paddy Foy had a very lovely set, and soon after the opening phrases, I came down the steps towards the cameras. At that moment, my eye caught sight of Dame Margot and Nureyev keeping their muscles warm and supple while waiting for their next item. All would have been well had they been keeping time with the orchestra and myself, but an aria did not seem to be a good rhythm for barre work—they were completely out of time, and I found myself in a most unhappy dilemma. I had to stop. When I explained about my gaze being transfixed by this off-beat action of legs and arms beside my set, we all enjoyed the joke. They were very apologetic. I started again and all was well, but when the session was over and we were relaxing with Paddy and discussing the programme with the conductor, Malcolm Arnold, he said: "You were lucky, Joan. After Margot and Nureyev moved away from you they came into *my* vision, and I had to force myself to keep to Puccini and not follow their timing for the entire aria. I didn't want to stop and cause you to start yet again." It was very funny.

Criticism reached my ears about my living as a recluse and refusing party invitations. The truth was that I was too tired, and functions of any description exhausted me. I needed to keep all my energy for my work. I loved entertaining, but even this joy I had to forgo, though the entertainment of close friends was never a strain. There were some exceptions, and these included invitations to luncheons or dinners at Cliveden when Nancy, Viscountess Astor was in residence. I always met people of interest there, and conversation was alive and full of significance and substance. The salient factor about these gatherings was that no alcohol was ever served, so the brain remained clear and alert. This was a rule never to be broken while Nancy Astor reigned there. One afternoon when I was walking with her she suddenly said: "Let's hit a few golf shots."

"But where can we do that?"

"I'll show you." We walked back to the house and got a bag of practice balls and a No. 8 iron each. Nancy led the way to a superbly kept lawn.

"Surely we're not going to chip chunks out of this beautifully green carpet?" I said.

"Of course we are." And with that she proceeded to hit some very fine shots. She was at that time the lively President of the Ladies' Golf Union.

The Old Cottage was just a nice distance out of London for a drive, and we were often invaded unexpectedly. Once, after rehearsing all morning, I felt the need for fresh air and exercise, so I did some weeding in the garden. It was a Sunday afternoon, and I heard voices floating across from the front of the house, and Estrées saying in a loud voice to warn me: "Oh X, how lovely to see you!" Hardly had the words reached me when our friend X came around the corner with two more friends. Escape was impossible; there I stood in the oldest, dirtiest pair of slacks, an equally worn and dirty golf pullover, and an old hat. Friend X introduced his friends, who took little notice of me, I was relieved to see, and then he whispered to me: "You know A. Blank, the famous dress designer? He wanted to meet you, so I hope you don't mind my bringing him along." I had to say, "Of course not," and then I asked X to take them inside and I would join them.

I made a rapid change into a smart dress and pushed my hair into shape, and then went to the lounge where Estrées, Lolita and Mrs Barns were entertaining them. There was a hushed silence as I walked in, and naturally X just stood up, as he had already greeted me. The youthful dress designer and friend, however, came to life visibly, and to my astonishment the dress designer said: "Joan Hammond! What an unexpected pleasure! I've heard so much about you, and I have all your records." He stood as though transfixed while I began to squirm uncomfortably. I was about to remind him that we'd already met in the garden when I realised that he hadn't recognised me, and neither he nor his friend had heard X's introduction. They were waiting to see the lady of the house, and the person they'd seen in the garden was probably the assistant gardener!

On another very hot summer day I was in the front garden when a car pulled up outside and a very Australian male voice reached me. "Can you tell me, please, which direction we go to get to the beach?"

"Well, you're now in the Beeches as from here. They extend for miles," I said.

"No, we're looking for a beach."

"You mean a particular beech, such as the Jenny Lind, or the composer Mendelssohn's tree?"

"No, Miss, just an ordinary common old sand beach where we can swim."

I stifled my giggles. "Oh, someone's been having you on. This area of woodland is known as Burnham Beeches—B.E.E.C.H. —and you're miles from the sea."

"You're not kidding?"

"I'm afraid not, but there's a swimming pool about two miles away, towards the centre of the Beeches."

A great language, and I mean it!

In the spring of 1960 I was making myself useful by moving our garden seats to new positions and varnishing and creosoting them. My right knee was a useful lever until a large swing seat dropped back on to it. There was a painful swelling, but I thought nothing of it until it became very troublesome during performances of *Tosca* and *Madam Butterfly*. The pain increased, the knee ached during the hours of rest. X-rays showed an ugly picture of osteoarthritis, for which I was given cortisone tablets to relieve the pain during performances. The result was marvellous. I could kneel in *Butterfly* and jump off the battlements in *Tosca* with very little discomfort. This happy state of affairs continued for about six months, and then I found my voice beginning to tire soon after I started singing. It sounded as though I had bronchitis, and during a recital in Manchester I had to apologise to the audience and say I had a severe cold. The voice almost disappeared. I hurried to Ivor Griffiths in London. To my surprise and bewilderment, he told me there was absolutely nothing wrong with my cords. The odd thing was that there was no sign of a cold or any chest trouble. My speaking voice was quite all right except after singing an opera or a recital, when it completely broke up. I went about my work travelling to and fro, but there was always this slight fatigue, and I was more and more reliant upon technique.

I went to Scotland to sing with the Scottish Orchestra in Glasgow and Edinburgh on two successive nights. During the rehearsal I felt as though my throat muscles were relaxed, but I couldn't think why. I was in excellent health and yet experiencing this strange vocal phenomenon. I dashed back to London to see Ivor Griffiths again, but he assured me there was nothing wrong. I was very upset, for I knew something was very much wrong, yet the cords were perfect and I had no cold. The relaxed feeling of impotency was quite inexplicable.

I left London feeling that my world had come to an end. To wake in the morning feeling fine yet not be able to sing was disastrous. I had to sing in Wales, and I had to force my muscles to emit sound. At first it was normal, but as the evening progressed it became broken and husky.

When poor dear Ivor found me once again in his consulting room he laughed and said: "Joan, you must be suffering from nerves after all these years."

"No, I'm afraid not. I've been too long in this game to be suffering from that kind of thing—whatever 'thing' it is."

When I left his room I felt as miserable as I had ever felt. I knew I could not go on facing audiences with my voice so insecure. I wept bitter tears that night, as I was sure my career must end on a very discordant note.

The next day I went to London Airport to take a flight to Holland, where I had been booked to sing three performances of the Verdi *Requiem*. I was feeling fit, but suddenly my speaking voice croaked out a sentence. I looked at Lolita. "This is it. I simply cannot set out from here with my voice in this condition. Please get in touch with Emmie [Emmie Tillett, of Ibbs and Tillett, Concert Agent] and explain what's happened."

Emmie was not only my agent, but a great and wonderful friend. She sent her love and told Lolita to reassure me, all would be well, and she would cope with the situation. Emmie is one of those few people who can be completely businesslike while giving advice and comfort to her artists. An agent among and above all agents.

When we got back to The Old Cottage, I telephoned Ivor and told him what had happened. He was too conscientious to brush me off after all the visits with negative results. He asked me suddenly: "Have you been taking any pills for anything?"

"Yes, I have. I've been on cortisone tablets for some time."

I heard him gulp something unintelligible. "Can you come in right away?" he asked. I went immediately. He had never thought to ask me if I was taking any tablets, and I had certainly never thought of telling him about my knee trouble. He explained about the side effects of cortisone, and then asked when I was next expecting menstruation. It was not due for another three weeks. He told me to cancel all engagements until then, but to keep on singing scales or anything, just to keep the muscles in use. And to stop taking the tablets.

I kept up my scales and programmes as usual, but the resultant noise was pitiful to my ears. Any person listening would have thought I was stupidly trying to sing while suffering from severe bronchial trouble. I was to give a recital on the day menstruation was due, but it was cancelled with all the other engagements. As it happened, I could have sung. Ivor was right. Menstruation began that morning, and within an hour or so my voice was normal—clear, strong and normal. It seemed like a medical miracle to me. Another hurdle cleared with a safe landing, thanks to my friend Ivor Griffiths.

Relating to this subject, it is customary for Continental singers to refuse to sing during menstruation. Directors of foreign opera houses are quite prepared for it and think nothing of it. Often such a clause is put into one's contract. This is a sensible attitude, as the voice can be affected during menstruation, and the performance suffers as a result. The natural approach and complete agreement by the management is the right and sane course. It would be useless to suggest to singers who suffer during this period to work to a timetable. All the best engagements are sure to fall at that precise time! Unless a singer is on a weekly salary with a company, or is financially secure, this arrangement would not be feasible—in Britain, for instance. Perhaps with the increasing influx of foreign artists, this important subject may be given consideration—to the advantage of all concerned.

As time passed and irresistible changes occurred, so did my own thoughts with regard to charitable work.

There are many well organised, wonderful charitable concerns, but there are also many in which the meaning of the word "charity" was to be impressed upon everyone except those closely concerned with the organisation. I often discussed this with Ivor Newton. I have always felt that a certain amount of time and work should be given to charitable concerns, but there was one incident that caused me to change my attitude as to the form of charity to which I would contribute.

I was approached by the London Opera School to donate a yearly guaranteed sum of money to their worthy school. I felt that such a commitment would be a bit rash, as no artist can foresee what the future holds in the way of engagements, and if one suffered a period of illness, the commitment would be a monetary worry. I offered instead to give a recital at the Royal Festival Hall, and give all proceeds to the School. This they readily accepted.

At the time I was rehearsing recital programmes for an Australian tour, with Walter Süsskind as accompanist. I asked him if he would accompany me at the Festival Hall recital, but I was prepared to pay his fee, as I always did for such concerts. I never thought it right that the accompanist should give his services. But Walter, without hesitation, waived his fee.

Prior to the concert, unbeknown to Walter and me, a large cocktail party had been arranged by the Opera School to be held at the home of the Countess of Harewood, who was a patron of the school. This was to interest as many people as possible, and to sell tickets. On the day of the party, the press telephoned my home to ask what I would be wearing, as they wanted to give a publicity splurge on their social page. When I said I knew nothing about a party the reporter said she must have made a mistake. Evidently she got in touch with the Opera School immediately, and in a matter of minutes my telephone rang again. It was the Opera School, expressing apologies and saying that there had been some mistake—could I possibly go to the party, even at such short notice? The press had unwittingly caused a stir. Walter Süsskind had not received an invitation either. It was obviously a clerical error, and one which no doubt embarrassed the organisers.

The concert went off most successfully, and a Joan Hammond Scholarship was established. Some weeks later I received the final statement of accounts. There was a large deduction for the cost of the party, a fee for the secretary, and several other amounts for odd items usually donated by members of a committee. The agent's fee for running the concert was also high, but this item was normal, as agencies are not run on charity.

Charitable committees usually have charitably-minded people

among their number, who donate sums to cover the cost of parties, special secretaries, artists' expenses (hotel and travel), and some even pay the agent's fee, so the Fund for which the entertainment has been arranged benefits to the full.

For some time Ivor Newton had been trying to induce me to do prison concerts, and after much thought I realised that this was another very imporant form of charity where no money whatsoever was involved. Charities such as the Victoria League, the Catholic Stage Guild, and the Australian Musical Association I continued to support.

Ivor had been doing excellent work for the "Field Lectures", instigated by that versatile, capable woman, Xenia Field. The Field Lectures included a variety of entertainments at Her Majesty's prisons during the Christmas period and throughout the year.

My introduction was a recital at Wandsworth Prison. Never have I felt so nervous, but with a different kind of nervousness. It was not the music or the words, but the circumstances. I knew that I should have to make some firm rules with myself, and stick to them. I would always get dressed as for a concert in any hall or theatre throughout the world—gloves, jewellery, and my latest and smartest gowns. I would go out and sing to the prisoners, forcing myself to forget they were prisoners, as though they were a mixed, ordinarily dressed audience. Under no circumstances would I let them think I was doing them a favour by coming to sing, but rather that they had paid to attend and therefore wanted to hear me.

Xenia always met us outside the prison concerned so that we could go in together. It was a cold wet night at Wandsworth when Xenia first led us to the huge, forbidding entrance. The locks and bolts were undone and we went into a small covered entrance with the same big gates at the other end. Here we had to sign a book and wait for our escorts. More unlocking, passing through, and the sound of grating locks and bolts being shot behind us. This part of the evening had such a chilling effect on me. I remember so clearly the shudder that ran through me as I looked around at this vast, gloomy prison. My vivid imagination made me think of the men who had passed through those gates leaving a world of light and hope behind them; some never to see the world beyond again, a world that once must have meant something to them. We rarely appreciate the things of beauty and the endless gifts of nature—the trees, birds, flowers and all that can be enjoyed free on this earth until we are deprived of them.

When I walked out on to the platform, my heart beat faster than usual and perspiration, which was always a certain indication of nerves and tension, began to form all over my head, trickling down my neck and face. When I saw row upon row of men in prison garb, I had to remind myself firmly of the rules I had made for myself. This was an ordeal: something I had never experienced before. At first the men received me with quiet, respectful applause, but as the evening progressed, this applause grew until the last item. Then one of the men called out: "Please sing the Bach-Gounod Ave Maria." This acted as a release valve; I sang it, and other men then took courage and called out for "One Fine Day" and "O My Beloved Father". I had already sung "Love and Music" from *Tosca*, Mimi's Farewell from *La Bohème*, and "O Silver Moon" from *Rusalka*.

This was a climax in my career. I felt so happy and exhilarated that the men showed their appreciation just as any other audience. The ice was broken.

My next recital was at Wormwood Scrubs. A new hall had been built and the back-stage area was as comfortable as any I had encountered. This prison had a different effect on me. I felt a great sadness and distress for the inmates, but I never felt that all hope was gone, as I did in Wandsworth. My thoughts flew to such men as Ivor Novello, who had been martyred by a judge or magistrate for possessing extra petrol coupons. All artists were subject to having coupons passed on to them by fans during petrol rationing, but poor Ivor was the one sent to prison. We all felt sick for him when the sentence was given. I remembered my second meeting with him in New York, when he came up to me in a music shop and expressed his admiration of my voice and art. As usual I felt honoured, shy, and almost speechless. I

P

always wanted to kick myself afterwards for becoming tongue-tied at such chance meetings. Ivor Novello was such a sincere, gentle person, and he was certainly not a criminal, but he was given a criminal's sentence and was forced to suffer the agonies of prison life, as did Oscar Wilde. Both men undoubtedly died as a result of incarceration. It killed them as surely as a cancerous growth, and they both gave so much pleasure to so many.

It was quite some time before Xenia broached the idea of my giving a recital at Holloway prison. After lengthy discussions I agreed. Somehow, appearing before women was a far greater ordeal than appearing before men.

Holloway is one of the coldest and dreariest prisons of all. As usual, Ivor Newton and I had to share the one room, which belonged to the prison chaplain. It was small and freezing. Xenia had asked for a radiator, but none was available. I wore a red velvet gown, and I had to walk from the first floor to the ground floor by means of a stone staircase and bleak, narrow passages— a long, icy trek. There was something far more poignant and final about this prison. I felt deeply depressed, and kept thinking: "There but for the grace of God, go I."

Something prompted me to walk down the centre aisle at the conclusion. I had first to ask permission. I saw a sea of faces, old, middle-aged, and very young. I had now created a feeling of friendship and equality, which I felt to be of great importance. I happened to see a sweet-faced woman put out a hand to touch my gown; a hand which she quickly withdrew lest perhaps she was giving offence. I stopped. "Do please feel the velvet if you would like to." I shall never forget the look in that woman's eyes, and I felt the tears welling in my own. I secretly thanked Xenia for suggesting that I might come to face the women in Holloway. Many hands stretched out to touch my gown. It was equivalent to putting a plate of food before starving animals. The look in their eyes will remain with me for ever.

It was a startling revelation to find that a great number of the inmates had been given jail sentences for failing to pay on some household hire-purchase item, or for petty theft. Some of them had got themselves embroiled with a man who set them off on the wrong track. Some of them were in for such nugatory offences, and the lightness or harshness of their sentences depended on the judge or magistrate.

The most primitive prison accommodation I encountered was at the vast Parkhurst Prison in the Isle of Wight. After the usual signing in, we walked across to one of the many grim buildings within the walls of this old, outdated establishment. Luckily I had completed my make-up at the hotel in Cowes before Xenia called for me. As usual, one or two Trusties carried my music case and any other small bag or make-up box.

This time I had agreed to give two recitals, with a fifteen- to thirty-minute break between. Not only was the hall too small to accommodate those wishing to attend, but certain blocks could not be mixed. The men in blocks A and B could not be in the hall with men from blocks C and D. I thought it prudent not to ask why.

We were led by the Trusty up an old wooden staircase to the back of the stage. Apologies had already been made about the accommodation, but we had not expected it to be quite as bad as it was. Every window was broken, so the iron bars were painfully obvious, and there was a mouldy, decayed look everywhere. Attempts had been made to spruce it up, but no amount of scrubbing or sweeping could improve it to any extent.

There was one small room. It was bare except for a little unsafe looking chair, a trestle table which wobbled ominously as I placed my make-up box on it and Ivor put my music bag at the other end. One further item of interest was in that dilapidated room—a bucket, in case either of us should require a toilet! There were certainly no mod. cons. We all smiled ruefully as we prepared, as best we could, for the concert. The men in charge, the Trusties, had made every effort to give us what they believed we should need, and they had even rigged up a spotlight for the platform. Lolita, who was as usual trying to ease our backstage discomforts by acting as table, chair and hallstand, even tested the floor in certain dubious places to see if it was safe to place anything on! Our cases became chairs, and Lolita had to hold my mirror as there was nowhere to put it.

The platform groaned under my weight as I took up my position in the bow of a small aged piano. After a few preliminary words of greeting, we began. Half-way through the first item every light in the dimly lit hall went out. The guards must have felt very uneasy at that moment. Ivor offered to try to continue without music, but I sensed the need for chatter. I spoke, of what I cannot clearly remember, but I know I said I had always longed to sing in the dark as I was not enamoured by my looks, and I made other self-derogatory remarks until a Trusty came on stage with a torch. There was much laughter as the Trusty tried to hold it in an appropriate position, under Ivor's instructions. But the prisoners' attention was held, and after ten minutes or so the lights came on. I blinked and said I preferred torchlight. What might have been a major disaster served to break the atmosphere and put us all in the right mood for a concert. The light failure had been caused by the spotlight—the ancient electrical equipment could not take the added strain.

In spite of all the inconvenience and lack of dressing room furnishings, that night was memorable. It was made much more memorable when some weeks later a beautifully inscribed parchment arrived at The Old Cottage. A prisoner, on behalf of all his fellow inmates, had expressed so wonderfully their thanks and appreciation of my visit. I had the parchment framed, and it is among my most treasured possessions. Beautifully hand painted, it says:

> For two of the finest concerts ever heard by many of us here, the inmates of Parkhurst Prison, Isle of Wight, express to:
>
> MISS JOAN HAMMOND
>
> our deepest appreciation and gratitude for the pleasure, beauty and brightness you brought here for us. Although "Home Sweet Home" would take you far from us, may you always find happiness!
>
> June 12th 1964. A night to remember!

Wormwood Scrubs Prison became my "home from home" as many of the men liked to tell me. It was the prison I visited the most often, and I got to know several of the men. Their crimes were of no importance to me. Xenia arranged for me to present the prize to the prisoner who had grown the best flower in a pot —she gave them the bulbs. I asked the winner: "How is it that you were able to produce such a beautiful hyacinth?" His reply gave me a lot to think about.

"I was lucky to be in a cell that got the most sun, and I think I may have had perhaps more patience in holding it up for longer periods between the bars." Although on that occasion I had gone there in another capacity, I sang their favourite aria "O My Beloved Father" unaccompanied before leaving.

Another time I went there as a guest to hear a debate between three Oxford undergraduates and three prisoners. Hugh Cudlipp, then Editor-in-Chief of the *Daily Mirror*, was in the chair. This was excellent entertainment, and I thoroughly enjoyed it, as did the prisoners. I willingly agreed to end the evening with fifteen minutes of song.

The men used to greet me as an old friend. They were allowed to talk to me after the night's entertainment, and I came to know some of them well.

There had been intermittent waves of burglaries in our neighbourhood, but The Old Cottage remained one of the few homes never to receive attention. The general opinion was that the word had travelled throughout the prisons, and I was on the list of "untouchables". A happy thought, and very possible.

In November 1961 the B.B.C. put on the première of an opera called *Yerma* composed by Denis Aplver. Sir Eugene Goossens was the conductor, and who better to cope with such a score!

I had worked with Gene during the 1946 tour in Australia, but during the *Yerma* rehearsals I had the opportunity to study his conducting very closely. I nearly turned down the role of Yerma as the music did not appeal to me, but it was a challenge and I accepted.

The scores were printed by duplicator. Many mistakes had

slipped in and changes made, which all added to the difficulties besetting conductor, soloists, chorus and orchestra. It was in three acts, each one of which seemed as long as a whole opera. Musically it was the most difficult role I had ever undertaken. I re-read the play by Garcia Lorca on which the opera was based, and steeped myself thoroughly in the Spanish tragedy. The libretto was excellent, but the vocal line was at times most extraordinary.

To watch Gene working with us all, day after day, when he was already a very sick man, was inspiring. What a musical genius he was! Scrupulously thorough, and with the patience of Job, few conductors could equal him. There were moments when the entire cast and orchestra tended to get out of hand because of the plot, but he controlled the mirth in such a way that we all slaved the harder to make it easier for him. We all knew that we had a veritable musical giant among us. His skill was tested to the full. He moulded a whole out of something which seemed to be broken up into fragments—the feat of a master.

On the second night he had to ask us to agree to performing the last act first as it was so strenuous, mentally and physically, and technically difficult for the orchestra. We recorded Act III from 4.30 to 6 p.m., and Acts I and II from 7 to 10 p.m.

This contrariwise decision meant an inverted interpretation which demanded intense concentration. I had to gear myself to believing that I had sung the preceding two acts and that the story was unfolding itself in the normal way, working up to the final bloodthirsty tragedy. I had mentally to die, forget about it, and begin Act I alive and vibrant. This was the only time such a situation arose.

Australia lost a conductor of the highest calibre and musical integrity when Gene was forced to leave. He had that very special gift of being able to build and create an orchestra. Knowledge and patience were the necessary adjuncts when he took over the Sydney Symphony Orchestra for the A.B.C. The unfortunate circumstances that brought about his dismissal were, without doubt, a cause of hastening his death. *Yerma* was the last opera this impeccable musician conducted. We lost a master musician, a builder of players and a conductor Australia could ill afford to be without.

I am happy in the knowledge that one of my final gestures was a recital held at Australia House for the Australian Musical Association. The Queen Mother was present, and my fairy godmother, Lady Gowrie. This was the last time Lady Gowrie heard me sing as her own health began to fail towards the end of 1964.

Sir Eric Harrison, the then High Commissioner for the Commonwealth of Australia, made one of the most moving speeches about me. While feeling honoured, I also felt self-conscious and shy beyond words. This was one of the best recitals I have given and one of the happiest. The cause was a worthy one—to help promote young Commonwealth artists.

Sir Eric and Lady Harrison were among the finest people I met during my long career. I was privileged to attend a small luncheon party at their London home, Stoke Lodge, at which the Queen Mother was again present. It was such a jolly, relaxing luncheon. Sir Malcolm Sargent was present, and in top form.

Soon after the A.M.A. recital, I contracted a bad infection in the middle ear. Three months' work was cancelled, and at one stage I believed I should never hear properly again. Ivor Griffiths assured me that all would be well, and I should have known that he'd be right! But when day after day dawned and the left ear remained completely deaf, I thought the time to end my career had come.

By the middle of August I was able to hear well enough to begin practising daily. Early in September I was almost fit again, and certainly what little deafness remained did not worry me.

My first commitment was for E.M.I. I did three days of recording, and I had never enjoyed sessions more. Brian Culverhouse was in charge of the sessions, and a more helpful, knowledgeable master of his profession would be hard to find. It was a series of song with piano, and Ivor Newton accompanied. John Whittle, the Marketing Manager for the classical repertoire, Brian and I had worked out the songs best suited for this record. The sessions were particularly noteworthy because of these men and the harmony existing among them and the technicians. The making of music was a pleasure.

I did not know it at the time, but it was to be my final record. This was September, and in November I suffered the first coronary attack.

After I had made a rather sluggish recovery by July 1966, John and Brian planned my next sessions. They were to be with organ in the glorious York Minster. The programme was settled and two or three items were to include the cathedral choir. I was looking forward to this unique recording.

I had been rehearsing and doing more and more each day when I suffered a further mild coronary. The breathing and general physical strain were too much. Although these two great friends still hoped that I could fulfil this booking at any time and date to suit me, I knew that I had made my last record—under perfect conditions and with my favourite accompanist. What more could I wish for?

My last public appearance was one of those singularly unaccountable and unpredictable occasions—a finale undoubtedly planned by fate

As soon as I was able I went to Taplow to see Lady Gowrie. I noticed a big change in her, as she did in me. She took my hand and looked at me with those clear, liquid brown eyes and said: "Tell me, Joan dear, when are you going to be able to sing again?" This was a question I had hoped she would not ask. I hedged, stupidly, because she was so quick to discern one's innermost thoughts. "Have the doctors given you any idea?" she continued. "Your voice is lovelier than ever."

I held her hand and said that no final decision had yet been made. There was a long pause in which I felt that she had guessed what I was trying to withhold. I left feeling heavy-hearted and sad, but she was as bright as ever, and laughingly told me how she had questioned the new vicar on the subject of death. Less than a fortnight later my fairy godmother died.

The young Earl of Gowrie, Grey, contacted me about the Memorial Service, for it had been his grandmother's wish that I should sing. There were two major obstacles, one being my health, and the other, the fact that the service was to be held in St George's Chapel, Windsor. No woman had ever sung in the Chapel, and special permission had to be granted by the Queen. I made up my mind to sing if it was the last thing I did. Grey was most concerned, and so was my doctor. But I felt I could manage the item requested—the Bach-Gounod Ave Maria. So on 30 July 1965 I sang in public for the last time, and I ended as I began, by being heard but not seen, as I was up in the organ loft. You may recall my debut at the New South Wales State Con-servatorium of Music on 27 May 1931, when I sang the Shep-herd's music in the Vaughan Williams Pastoral Symphony in F major. I was heard but not seen on that occasion.

After a very moving Service, I lunched in the Norman Tower. Field Marshal Viscount Slim was then in the position that Lord Gowrie had formerly held—Deputy Constable and Lieutenant-Governor of Windsor Castle.

It was a pleasure to meet Lady Slim again. I had last seen them both in Australia, when the Field Marshal was Governor-General.

The large luncheon was not a sad occasion, as Lady Gowrie had been spared further pain. I saw many members of the family whom I had not seen for years.

It was the end of another chapter.

My progress was not satisfactory and my doctors suggested a long sea voyage. I elected to go to Australia and back, and the greatest indignity I have ever suffered was being wheeled in a chair along the wharf at Tilbury and on to the liner *Orsova*. I have always had a self-conscious niggle about illness, and a dread of being thought a "malade imaginaire".

The voyage served its purpose, and I was able to fly back to England. Brian Culverhouse and John Whittle of H.M.V. had waited patiently for my return, hoping that it would still be possible for me to carry out the previously mooted recording sessions with organ and cathedral choir in York Minster. I started rehearsing and there was nothing wrong vocally, but I found the physical strain very great.

I suffered four attacks of angina pectoris. After three cancellations spread over a year, I knew inexorably that my career as a singer had come to an end. Retirement was inevitable.

It was a tremendous wrench. A lifetime had revolved round the preparation for and fulfilling of engagements. Always learning some new role, song or work. Packing for every variable climate, travelling hither and thither under all conditions by road, rail or air. Fog, snow and icy roads often caused considerable distress when travelling to an engagement, and on more than one occasion I have had to charter a private aircraft, when an airline had been forced to cancel flights.

The strain of jet age travel for artists is enormous. You must arrive at your destination looking fresh and feeling mentally alert to face press and public soon after arrival, sometimes after a hazardous journey. I particularly recall being in an aircraft which was speeding along the runway at Kennedy Airport, N.Y. Suddenly there was the mighty roar of those four great engines being plunged into reverse thrust. I realised that the pilot had decided to abandon the take-off. It ultimately transpired that a red light showing on the flight-deck dashboard had indicated that a cabin door was not properly closed, and the pilot had had to make a snap decision. I sang that night with the terrifying roar of reverse thrust still bursting in my head.

On another occasion an aeroplane window blew in with a loud explosion right beside my head. That journey was completed in deafening noise, and with an icy blast of air tearing into the cabin. But one arrived—and sang.

In lighter vein, I was reported to have sung "Fido's Lament" (from *Dido and Aeneas*) and "O My Beloved Father" from Handel's *Xerxes*!

How true it is that when one door shuts another opens! The hinge of my next door creaked and grated for a time but it is now well oiled and has opened fully, on to a new world. I am back among old friends and new interests. I am enjoying them, revelling in them, instead of giving them scant attention because of the necessity to study.

I look at life with new vision. Thinking of the thousands of miles I have travelled and the interesting places I have visited, I realise that I have in fact lived in a cocoon, cramped by the exigencies of my profession. I saw the world through the restricted area of a small window in a jet airliner. Life has swished past me because every thought, nerve and muscle was used to sing, sing, sing, and in the desire to better every performance and become ever more accomplished and proficient at my job.

By no means were the years of hard work squandered because of the inability to appreciate anything outside music. My working life was full of the joy of anticipation, the excitement of opening a new score, of running through a new song, of listening to a new recording of a favourite opera, symphony or concerto. This was an endless delight, and an infinite source of inspiration and revelation.

The very thing you love isolates you from all else. Nothing kills that love, but when the pressure is eased it becomes more temperate. It permits other facets of life to show themselves, and this brings about a change of values. There are still musical discoveries to make, discoveries to stimulate the voracious quest for musical satisfaction that has always been mine. During my working years my mind was obsessed by the fever of musical expression and appreciation. Just as a gambler is drugged by the belief that the next throw of the dice will make his fortune, so did I feel that the next performance would be better and more rewarding than any previous one.

I am learning the names of flowers, plants and shrubs, and pottering generally in the garden which surrounds our house, a garden out of virgin bushland. Weeding is my chief occupation, and I really enjoy providing breathing space for plants which are in danger of being choked. Roses are my favourite flower, so special attention is devoted to the two rose beds.

I can now give myself the luxury of listening for hours on end to my extensive collection of records. Instead of working out my own recital programmes, I work out orchestral ones. I can listen and go about my weeding at the same time. But even now, when I hear an overture or short orchestral piece, I reach for my gloves, and ask for my dress to be zipped up. I invariably sang my first item or group following the orchestral introduction.

Halcyon days are spent on our yacht, which is moored on Pittwater, my old hunting ground off Palm Beach. Traversing these waterways and seeing friends of my youth is a perfect linking of my wheel of fate, bringing me back to my beginnings. The saying that one should not retrace one's steps has not proved to be true in my case.

I am fit and life is full to the brim. Reading, writing and having endless discussions on all manner of subjects leave no time for idleness. I can swim, and play the odd game of golf. The strain of a pressure existence has gone, and I can learn about anything and everything.

When I first returned to Australia after retirement, it was necessary for me to have attention for a lower lip which had been sore for years. Lipstick, especially the stage variety, irritated it and no amount of emollient eased it. Within a few weeks, I was in hospital having it operated on. The whole lower lip had to be removed, but Mr Newing, the brilliant Melbourne plastic surgeon, made a superb job of it, and I now have a new lower lip. It is smaller, and if there are a few lumps and bumps they are only seen and felt by me. This unfortunate condition was brought about by an overdose of sun in my youth.

Now that this temporary disability is behind me, another form of public activity has come into my life. Instead of singing for charity, I am taking part in informal "question and answer" entertainment, in which the members of various organisations ask questions about my life and work. There are no set speeches, and my answers are quite spontaneous.

One of the questions asked of me most frequently is: "Don't you miss the adulation that goes with a public career such as yours?"

To say that one didn't miss it would reveal a form of self-deception. Public acclaim, whether it is for a victory in sport or a successful performance in theatre or concert hall, is a demonstration of appreciation—recognition of a person's skill and artistry. A child flowers under praise and withers under fault-finding. In maturity, we still flower under praise, but in order to remain at the top of a profession, it is imperative to be a self fault-finder, a self critic, always alert to any weakness or mistake. A public image must be respected and retained, but one must never be lured into the temptation of listening only to the plaudits.

I have no regrets. I had a wonderful innings, and now I am having a second innings, more tranquil than the first, but equally full of the joy of discovery. And if there should ever be a few moments of sadness for days that are gone, I shall bask once more in the knowledge that my signature was worth twenty tadpoles!

ENVOI

The award of the Golden Disc on the night of 27 August 1969, at E.M.I. House, Manchester Square, London, was a most memorable occasion and a highlight in my life. It is a rare achievement for a classical artist and something I never dreamed would happen to me. The surprise and excitement of receiving this magnificent large gold record was almost too overwhelming. "O My Beloved Father" (from *Gianni Schicchi* by Puccini), which is Band 1 on this record, had passed the million sales mark and so merited a Gold Disc. It was presented in the form of a book, bound in dark red leather. The record is set in deep blue velvet on one side, and an inscription on the other side which reads:

Presented to Joan Hammond with affectionate remembrance from all her friends in H.M.V. and Columbia on her retirement and return to Australia, September, 1969.

After the presentation a speech from me was expected. I had great difficulty in forming my words of thanks as tears were choking me. The Company had done it all in such excellent taste and the arrangements fitted the occasion; I wanted to express, in as few words as possible, my thanks and appreciation to all concerned. I controlled my emotions to some extent and managed a disjointed, higgledy-piggledy prattle containing but a few salient points and for the rest, unintelligent and unintelligible confusion was the result. The moment was too much for me, but I wouldn't have missed it!

APPENDICES

AUTHOR'S NOTE

To end a career as abruptly as I did leaves a sense of deep bereavement. The loss is akin to seeing the horizon vanish from sight; the unreachable horizon of hopes and ambitions intermingled with friendships and associations woven into the pattern of such a life as mine.

Although my connection with the Welsh National Opera Company came late in my career, it was, nevertheless, a binding one.

Concerts in Wales during the early part of my work in the United Kingdom were the main source of pleasure and remuneration. This beginning and ending urged me to present my operatic costumes to the Welsh National Opera as a token of my sincere attachment to the Welsh people, who showed so genuinely their appreciation of my voice.

The following letters are among my most treasured possessions. When negotiating some of the shoals of a career, these letters shone like beacons guiding me and causing me to realise that it was all so very worthwhile.

Letter from a Squadron Leader of Bomber Command, 15 September 1948:

Dear Joan Hammond,

Please accept these few flowers as a token payment for a debt of gratitude that I shall always owe you.

Some seven years ago I was one of some twenty R.A.F. officers, prisoners of war, who shared a small room in an underground fort in Poland. We were locked in this room from 5 p.m. to 8 a.m. each night with none of the normal facilities that humanity requires.

Q

But we had one asset, we had acquired from somewhere a portable gramophone and some half a dozen records. Among the records was that heavenly song that you have made your own "Oh my beloved Daddy"—the other side was an aria from Tosca.

I think you should know that this record was played in the darkness every night for months and many times during the day. It brought to us, in those few minutes at the end of the long day before we turned on our boards and slept, a real sense of freedom, not, alas, of the body but of the spirit, and restored in us all that faith in the omnipotent that would cause everything to come right in the end.

We were not alone in our admiration, for the German guards would make a point of being opposite our window at that sacred time each night when your record was played.

And so, having returned to this country again, this time from Egypt, I ask you to accept these flowers and with them my sincere thanks for all that your voice did and meant to me in those tedious times.

Should a parallel situation arise and I find myself again having to battle with the seeming "powers of darkness" I know I shall again find inspiration from your song.

Again, many many thanks

Letter from a Superintendent of Red Cross, 15 December 1945:
Dear Miss Hammond,

This is the echo of a round of applause from the most appreciative audience you have ever sung to. As it was in Dobadura in New Guinea it was quite unbeknownst to you, but I thought you might like to know how much pleasure you gave the boys in the 2/11th Australian General Hospital at a time when things were very tough for them.

We had a gramophone and one record, Mimi's aria with "One Fine Day" on the other side. I thought it would be rather over their heads, but never was I more mistaken. They played it from morning to night, and after I thought I'd locked the hut for the night they burgled their way in and played it some more. It was finally put on Routine Orders "The Red Cross gramophone may not be used after Lights Out." I ran out of needles and they cut splinters off blackwood palms and used them with passable results.

After they had been discharged they kept coming back, to see me, I hoped, but far from it. After a little polite conversation it always turned out that what they had really come for was to put the record on again.

Others who had never been in hospital used to come from miles around, saying "We hear you've got a good record, could you lend it to us? We would be very careful."

We had to move into a larger hut and the record was taken across by an escort to see that it didn't get broken on the way. In the end, of course, it went the way of all records, but not before we had managed to get a few reinforcements.

I used all this as a powerful argument against the popular idea that the troops only like rubbish, with the result that libraries of good recordings were added to all our establishments. So you see the Australian Army is not a little indebted to you.

Letter from a Yorkshire housewife, 15 November 1948:
Dear Miss Hammond,

I am the wife of a Yorkshire working man. Today it is the weekly washing day, a busy day, but I just had to spare the few minutes to listen to your talk in "Women's Hour", and for me the dreary dull fog of this bleak November day was illuminated with joy, as your glorious voice rang out in the Rusalka aria.

You have a very special pride of place in our humble home life. I will tell you why. I am 47 and almost all my adult life have taught the pianoforte, but do not do so now. Many adversities have kept my hubby and I poor in material things, but our mutual love of music has made us, oh so very rich, in our little home.

We had one son, a Fighter Pilot, who also loved music. He now lies buried in Malaya, at Kuala Lumpur, where he crashed when his Thunderbolt engine failed in 1945, but he left us a treasured legacy in the gramophone records he had taken round the world with him. They are all orchestral classical records with one exception, that of Joan Hammond singing "One Fine Day". He told us how when he played his records out in Burma, or back in India when the boys were resting there between operational tours, the pilots would come tip-toeing into the Mess, pull out their pipes or cigarettes, draw up a chair, and find joy and solace in the beauty of the music that touched the toughest and the hardest. Your record was such a great favourite that the boys formed a sort of Musical Appreciation Club, and whoever flew to Calcutta was commissioned to bring back an addition to the collection.

Our boy's collection was returned to us in the steel carrying cases he had bought, and although they are a little worn and scratched with usage, they are our dearest possessions. We can unite with him, as we sit by our fireside, listening, as so many of those pilots listened before, in so many cases, they went out on the last flight. They are a very great comfort to us, and I'm sure you will be glad to know that your lovely voice gave courage, enjoyment, and a belief that there was still so much that was beautiful in the world, to live and fight for.

Our records are our greatest happiness now we are left alone, we can only add to them occasionally, as health reasons have caused my husband to take a light job with a correspondingly light salary, and a serious operation prevents me working as I did during the War. But perhaps for that very reason, we choose carefully and appreciate them more. Your new record will be added to our Christmas list.

Forgive me taking the liberty of writing to you, but I just had to. My very best wishes to you, and may you be able to give joy and pleasure to ordinary folks like us for many a long day.

★   ★   ★

FROM SIR MALCOLM SARGENT, 9, ALBERT HALL MANSIONS, LONDON, S.W. 7.

21st Feb 56.

My dear Joan,

    If the strike is off, I hope to
see the singers next Tuesday when I
propose to hand them each a cheque
for 7 guineas as you suggest and
will read to them most of your
charming letter. You are very kind.

    With regard to the second letter,
you are naughty to have sent back the
cheque. I feel that you must be
using me as a mirror and are seeing in
me the good qualities which actually
exist in your sweet self.

In all friendship
Yours ever,
Malcolm Sargent

Miss Joan Hammond.

REPERTOIRE

OPERA	COMPOSER	ROLE
Fidelio	Beethoven	Leonora
Dido and Aeneas	Purcell	Dido
Die Zauberflöte	Mozart	Pamina
Le Nozze di Figaro	Mozart	Countess Almaviva
Die Entführung aus dem Serail	Mozart	Constanze
Don Giovanni	Mozart	Donna Anna & Donna Elvira
The Conspirators	Schubert	Countess Ludmilla
Norma	Bellini	Norma
Der Freischütz	Weber	Agathe
Oberon	Weber	Rezia
La Traviata	Verdi	Violetta
La Forza del Destino	Verdi	Leonora
Otello	Verdi	Desdemona
Aïda	Verdi	Aïda
Il Trovatore	Verdi	Leonora
Don Carlos	Verdi	Elisabetta
Simone Boccanegra	Verdi	Amelia
William Tell	Rossini	Matilda
Lohengrin	Wagner	Elsa
Tannhäuser	Wagner	Elizabeth
Damnation of Faust	Berlioz	Marguerite
Martha	Flotow	Martha
Faust	Gounod	Marguerite
Carmen	Bizet	Micaela
Rusalka	Dvořák	Rusalka
Dalibor	Smetana	Milada
Salome	R. Strauss	Salome
Eugène Onegin	Tchaikovsky	Tatiana

OPERA	COMPOSER	ROLE
The Invisible City of Kitesh	Rimsky-Korsakov	Fevronia
La Bohème	Puccini	Mimi
Manon Lescaut	Puccini	Manon
Tosca	Puccini	Tosca
Madam Butterfly	Puccini	Butterfly
Thaïs	Massenet	Thaïs
Manon	Massenet	Manon
Pagliacci	Leoncavallo	Nedda
Die Fledermaus	Johann Strauss	Rosalinde
Wat Tyler	Alan Bush	Margaret
Yerma	D. ApIver	Yerma

ORATORIOS

St Matthew Passion	Bach
God So Loved The World	Bach
Phoebus and Pan	Bach
Mass in D	Beethoven
Ninth Symphony	Beethoven
Mass in C	Beethoven
Requiem	Verdi
The Creation	Haydn
The Messiah	Handel
Samson	Handel
Acis and Galatea	Handel
Elijah	Mendelssohn
Hymn of Praise	Mendelssohn
Stabat Mater	Rossini
Messa Solenne (Petite Messe Solennelle)	Rossini
The Golden Legend	Sullivan
The Apostles	Elgar
For the Fallen	Elgar
To Women	Elgar
Te Deum	Dvořák
At the Foot of the Cross	Dvořák
Stabat Mater	Dvořák

ORATORIOS

Hiawatha	Coleridge-Taylor
Childhood of Christ	Berlioz
Damnation of Faust	Berlioz
Te Deum	Bruckner
Bethlehem	Rutland Boughton

DISCOGRAPHY

COLUMBIA 78 R.P.M. RECORDS

Where items have been reissued as 7-inch 45 r.p.m. records, the later record number is given in square brackets at the end of the entry, thus [SED5514]

DX1003   Puccini–Elkin: *Madama Butterfly*—Act 2, One Fine Day [SED5514, SCD2079]
Puccini–Pinkerton & Grist: *La Bohème*—Act 1, They Call me Mimi—Leslie Heward Orchestra [SED5514, SCD 2079]

DX1023   Bach, arr. Gounod: Ave Maria (in Latin) w/Bertram Harrison, organ.
Franck: Panis Angelicus (in Latin) violin obbligato by Harry Blech [SCD2120]

DX1039   Puccini–Pinkerton & Grist: *La Bohème*—Act 3—Mimi's Farewell, Act 3, Lovely Maid in the Moonlight, w/David Lloyd (tenor), Orchestra/Leslie Heward [SCD2002]

DX1075   Mozart–da Ponte: *Don Giovanni*—Recit.: In what Abysses (In quale eccessi): Aria—Cruel One, thou hast betrayed me (Mi tradi quell' alma ingrata)

DX1082   Mozart–Lady MacFarren: *Marriage of Figaro*—Recit.: Still Susanna delays (E Susanna no vien); Aria: Whither vanished (Dove Sono)

DB2015   Weatherley & Coates: The Green Hills o' Somerset [SCD2207]. Cavanars & Lieurance: By the Waters of Minnetonka, violin obbligato, Frederick Grinke; w/ piano (Gerald Moore)

DB2052   Puccini–Kingston: *Tosca*—Love and Music (Vissi d'arte); Puccini–P. Pitt: O my beloved Daddy (O mio babbino caro), w/Hallé Orchestra/Leslie Heward [SED 5514, SCD2120]

DB2060   Verdi–Kenney: *Aïda*—May Laurels Crown thy brow (Ritorna Vincitor); Names so Holy (Sacri Nome)

DX1134-5   Tchaikovsky: *Eugène Onegin*—Tatiana's Letter Scene, Liverpool Philharmonic Orchestra/Constant Lambert; Charpentier: *Louise*—Depuis le jour (in French), Hallé Orchestra/Warwick Braithwaite

DX11141   Mozart–da Ponte–Lady MacFarren: Grant O Love (Porgi
amor); Mozart–Schikaneder–Lady MacFarren: Ah!
'Tis Gone (Ach, ich fühl's), Hallé Orchestra/Leslie
Heward

with orchestral accompaniment unless otherwise stated.

H.M.V. 78 R.P.M. RECORDS

B9407   Puccini: *Turandot*—Oh! I entreat thee, Sire (Act 1);
Thou who with ice are girdled (Act 3), London Symphony Orchestra/Walter Süsskind

B9445   Sibelius: The Tryst—Black Roses, w/piano (Gerald
Moore)

B9486   Massenet: Elégie—w/piano and cello (Gerald Moore,
Anthony Pini), Tchaikovsky: None but the Weary
Heart—w/piano and cello (Gerald Moore, James White-
head)

B9503   Chesterton–Hageman: The Donkey—w/piano (Gerald
Moore), Kingsley–Lehmann: Magdalen at Michael's
Gate—w/piano (Gerald Moore)

C3378   Puccini: *Madama Butterfly*—Ah, love me a little (Love
Duet), Liverpool Philharmonic Orchestra/Sir Malcolm
Sargent

C3471–7 Purcell–Tate–editor E. J. Dent: *Dido and Aeneas*—
Act 1: Ah! Belinda—When monarchs unite [C4371]
Act 1: Whence could so much virtue spring—See, see
     your royal guest appears [C3472]
Act 2: Behold upon my bending spear [C3474]
Act 3: Your council all is urg'd in vain [C3476]
Act 3: Thy hand, Belinda [C3477]
Act 3: When I am laid in earth (Dido's Lament) [C3477]
w/Isobel Baillie, Joan Fullerton, Dennis Noble, Sylvia
Patriss (in above extracts)/Philharmonia String Or-
chestra/Constant Lambert, Harpsichord, Boris Ord

C3419   Verdi: *Il Trovatore*—
Act 1: No star shone on the Heav'nly vault
Act 4 Recit.: Why fear for me; Aria: Love fly on rosy
pinions
London Symphony Orchestra/Walter Süsskind

C3486   Verdi: *La Traviata*—
Act 1: Oh! Folly, Oh! Folly
Act 1: How wondrous, how wondrous
Philharmonia Orchestras Walter Süsskind

C3493   Weber: *Oberon*—Ocean thou mighty monster, Philharmonia Orchestra/Vilem Tausky

C3510   Weber: *Der Freischütz*—Softly Sighs (Recit. & Aria), Philharmonia Orchestra/Vilem Tausky

C3562   Wagner: *Lohengrin*—Elsa's Dream (Einsam in trüben Tagen)
Wagner: *Tannhäuser*—Elisabeth's Greeting (Dich teure Halle), Philharmonia Orchestra/Warwick Braithwaite

C3674   Gounod: *Faust*—Act 3, The Jewel Song, Ballad of the King of Thule/Philharmonia Orchestra/Warwick Braithwaite [7R166, 7P220]

C3724/5   Leoncavallo: *Pagliacci*—How fierce he looked (Ballatella)
Gounod: *Faust*—Love Duet & Trio (Garden Scene) w/Heddle Nash (tenor), Owen Brannigan (bass)/ Philharmonia Orchestra/Walter Süsskind

C3735   Verdi: *Aïda*—Act 3: Heav'n! my father, w/Redvers Llewellyn (baritone), Philharmonia Orchestra/Warwick Braithwaite

C3387   Verdi: *La Traviata*—Act 2: Ah! say to thy daughter, dear—Now command me, w/Dennis Noble (baritone), Liverpool Philharmonic Orchestra/Basil Cameron

B9705   Puccini: *Manon Lescaut*—In quelle trine morbide, Philharmonia Orchestra/(L. Collingwood)
Puccini: *Tosca*—Non la sospiri la nostra casetta Philharmonia Orchestra/Walter Süsskind; w/Heddle Nash (tenor)

B9747   Puccini: *Madama Butterfly*, Do you know, my sweet
Puccini: *La Fanciulla del West*, Oh, you've no notion Philharmonia Orchestra/Warwick Braithwaite

C3720   Puccini: *Manon Lescaut*—Act 4: Sola perduta abbandonata
Giordano: *Andrea Chenier*—Act 3: La Mamma morta Philharmonia Orchestra/Cond. Lawrence Collingwood

C3771   Verdi: *Un Ballo in Maschera*—Ma dall' arido stelo divulsa

Mascagni: *Cavalleria Rusticana*—Mother you know the story.
Philharmonia Orchestra/Walter Süsskind

C3879   Verdi: *Un Ballo in Maschera*—Act 3: Morro, ma prima in grazia
Verdi: *La Forza del Destino*—Act 4: Pace, pace mio Dio
Philharmonia Orchestra/Warwick Braithwaite

C3901   Ponchielli: *La Gioconda*—Act 4: Suicidio!*
Cilea: *Adriana Lecouvreur*—Act 1: Troppo, Signori**
Philharmonia Orchestra/* Warwick Braithwaite/** Walter Süsskind

DA1958   Moore-Trad: The Last Rose of Summer; Payne-Bishop: Home Sweet Home, piano (Ernest Lush)

DA1988   Puccini: *Turandot*—In questa reggia, Philharmonia Orchestra/Stanford Robinson

DA1998   Massenet: *Thaïs*—Ah! Je suis seule, Dis-moi que je suis
7ER5077   belle, Philharmonia Orchestra/Stanford Robinson

DB21019   Verdi: *La Forza del Destino*—Act 2: Recit.: Son giunta!
7ER5077   grazie, O Dio! Aria: Madre, pietosa Vergine (w/chorus)
Philharmonia Orchestra/Walter Süsskind

DB21451   Dvořák: *Rusalka*—O Silver Moon
Tchaikovsky: *Pique Dame*—'Twill soon be midnight now (Lisa's Aria) Philharmonia Orchestra/Vilem Tausky
[7ER5118, 7P243]

C3923–4   Leoncavallo: *Pagliacci*—Act 1: What! Thou? I thought that thou wast gone to market (Nedda-Tonio duet) w/John Hargreaves (baritone)
Nedda! Silvio at this hour, No! you do not love me! (Nedda-Silvio duet) w/John Hargreaves (baritone)
Act 2: My husband, Punchinello (Harlequin's Serenade), w/Heddle Nash (tenor)/Philharmonia Orchestra/Walter Süsskind

DB9780   Verdi: *La Forza del Destino*—Act 2, La Vergine degli Angeli w/N. Rossi-Lemeni, Royal Opera House, Covent Garden Chorus/Philharmonia Orchestra/Cond. Anatole Fistoulari

DB21098   Mascagni: *L'Amico Fritz*, Suzel, buon di (Cherry Duet), w/Rudolf Schock (tenor) Philharmonia Orchestra/Issay Dobrowen

DB21558   Verdi: *Otello*—Willow Song, Ave Maria, Philharmonia
           Orchestra/Vilem Tausky
DB21625   Boito: *Mefistofele*—L'Altra notte in fondo al mare. Korn-
           gold: Die tote Stadt, Glück, das mir verblieb, Philhar-
           monia Orchestra/Walter Süsskind
DB21580   *Verdi: *Aïda*—O patria mia
           Catalani: *La Wally*—Ebben? ne andro lontana
           Philharmonia Orchestra/Walter Süsskind *[7R172]
DB21510   Verdi: *Don Carlos*—Tu che la vanita Conoscesti del
           mondo (Elisabeth's Aria), Philharmonia Orchestra/Vilem
           Tausky
DB21549   Rossini: *Guillaume Tell*—Ils s'éloignent enfin ... Sombre
           forêt, Philharmonia Orchestra/Vilem Tausky
DB21260   Giordano: *Andrea Chenier*—Vicino a te ... La nostra
           morte, w/Rudolf Schock/Philharmonia Orchestra/Issay
           Dobrowen

H.M.V. 33 R.P.M. RECORDS

ALP1076   Mozart: Scena—Misera, dove son! Aria—Ah, mon son!
           Cilea: *Adriana Lecouvreur*—Poveri fiori
           Massenet: *Manon*—Je suis encore tout étourdie
           Bruch: Avia Maria
           Weber: *Der Freischütz*—Und ob die Wolke verhülle
           Massenet: *Thaïs*—L'amour est une vertu rare
           Massenet: *Manon*—Adieu, notre petite table
           Catalani: *La Wally*—Ebben? ne andro lontana
           Philharmonia Orchestra /Walter Süsskind
ALP1407   Verdi Operatic Arias (later reissued on ENC112) (and on
           MFP2015)
           Aïda—Rittorna Vincitor—Qui, Radames Verrà ... O
           patria mia
           Un Ballo in Maschera, Ecco l'orrido campo ... Ma
           dall 'arido, Morro, ma prima in grazia [7ER5083]
           Falstaff—Sul fil d'un soffio etesio
           La Forza del Destino—Pace, pace, mio Dio
           La Traviata—Teneste la promessa, Addio del passato
           Il Trovatore—Tacea la notte placida, Timor di me? ...
           D'amor sull' ali rosee
           Philharmonia Orchestra/Glauco Curiel [7ER5015]

BLP1073   Beethoven: Scena—Ah, perfido! Op. 65
Berlioz: *Damnation de Faust*—Romance, Alone and heavy-hearted
Saint-Saëns: *Etienne Marcel*—Act 2—O beaux rêves évanuois
Philharmonia Orchestra/Walter Süsskind

BLP1086   Puccini Operatic Arias:
La Bohème—They call me Mimi—Mimi's Farewell *[7EB6033]
La Fanciulla del West, Oh! You've no notion *[7ER5085]
Gianni Schicchi—O my beloved father [7ER5085]
Madama Butterfly—Weeping? and why? . . . One fine day [7ER5184]
Death with honour (Death of Butterfly) [7ER5184]
Tosca—Love and Music [7ER5085]
Suor Angelica—Dying thus without a mother's blessing [7ER5015]
Philharmonia Orchestra/Glauco Curiel

ALP1099   Verdi: *La Forza del Destino*—Act 2: Il Santo nome di Dio
(1 side)   La Vergine degli Angeli; Philharmonia Orchestra/Royal Opera Chorus, Covent Garden/Anatole Fistoulari w/N. Rossi-Lemeni

ALP1680 ⎱   Puccini: *Madama Butterfly*—Ancora un passo or via
ASD302 ⎰   (Entrance of Butterfly)
Puccini: *Manon Lescaut*—Sola perduta, abbandonata
Puccini: *Turandot*—In questa reggia
Giordano: *Andrea Chenier*—La mamma morta
Mascagni: *Cavalleria Rusticana*—Regina Coeli (Inneggiamo, il Signor) (Easter Hymn)
Smetana: *The Bartered Bride*—Ah! Bitterness! (Marenka's Romance)
Smetana: *Dalibor*—Do I live?
Tchaikovsky: *Eugène Onegin*—Oh, what shall I do now?
Dvořák: *Rusalka*—Gods of the Lake [7ER5085]
Tchaikovsky: *Queen of Spades*—'Twill soon be midnight now; Philharmonia Orchestra/Walter Süsskind
7ER5118—Also—Oft will he linger—*Gods of the lake
Philharmonia Orchestra/Vilem Tausky/Walter Süsskind

ALP1805 ⎱   Love Duets:
ASD384 ⎰   Puccini—*La Bohème*—Your tiny hand is frozen; Yes,

they call me Mimi; Lovely maid in the moonlight
Puccini: *Tosca*—Mario! Mario! Mario!
Gounod: *Faust*—The hour is late!
Verdi *Aïda*—I see thee again, my sweet Aïda (Nile
Scene)
w/Charles Craig (tenor)/Royal Philharmonic Orchestra/
Vilem Tausky

ALP2068 ⎱ On Wings of Song—
ASD616 ⎰ Mendelssohn: On Wings of Song, Op. 34, No. 2
Coates: Bird Songs at Eventide
Bridge: Love went a-riding
Schubert: Ave Maria (Ellens Gesang III) D839 (in
English)
Ronald: Down in the Forest
Quilter: Fair House of Joy
Bishop: Home, sweet Home
Dvořák: Songs my Mother taught me (No. 4 of Gypsy
Songs, Op 55)
Hahn: If my songs were only winged.
Quilter: Love's Philosophy
Clay: She wandered down the mountain side
Haydn Wood: A Brown Bird Singing
Charles: When I have sung my songs
Hageman: At the well
Coates: Green Hills o' Somerset
w/Ivor Newton (piano)

HQM1186 *Golden Voice Series No. 16*
Pitt-Puccini: *Gianni Schicchi*—O my beloved Father.
Hallé Orchestra/Leslie Heward
Adami & Simoni-Puccini: *Turandot*—Act 2: In questa
reggia, Philharmonia Orchestra/Stanford Robinson
Boito-Ponchielli: *La Gioconda*—Act 4: Suicidio! Phil-
harmonia Orchestra/Warwick Braithwaite
Colautti-Cilea: *Adriana Lecouvreur*—Act 1: Troppo,
Signori, Philharmonia Orchestra/Walter Süsskind
Illica-Giordano: *Andrea Chenier*—Act 3: La mamma
morta, Philharmonia Orchestra/Lawrence Collingwood
Gallet-Massenet: *Thaïs*—Act 2: Ah! Je suis seule. Dis-
moi que je suis belle; Philharmonia Orchestra/Stanford
Robinson

Dvořák: *Rusalka*, Act 1, O Silver Moon, Philharmonia Orchestra/Vilem Tausky

Piave-Verdi: *La Forza del Destino*—Act 2: Son giunta! grazie, O Dio! Madre, pietosa Vergine, Chorus of the Royal Opera House, Covent Garden (Chorus Master: Douglas Robinson)/Philharmonia Orchestra/Walter Süsskind

Hersee-Verdi: *Aïda*—Act 3: Heav'n! My father, w/ Redvers Llewellyn (baritone), Philharmonia Orchestra/ Warwick Braithwaite

Bulthampt-Bruch: Ave Maria, Philharmonia Orchestra/ Walter Süsskind

ALP1658 ⎫ Tchaikovsky: *Eugène Onegin*—Act 1: Tatiana's Letter
ASD536 ⎭ Scene, BBC Symphony Orchestra/Sir Malcolm Sargent

W.R.C. 33 R.P.M. RECORD

ST933   *Sung in English and Italian*

Puccini: *Madama Butterfly*—Entrance of Butterfly

Puccini: *Manon Lescaut*—Sola perduta abbandonata

Puccini: *Turandot*—In Questa reggia

Giordano: *Andrea Chenier*—La mamma morta

Mascagni: *Cavalleria Rusticana*—Easter Hymn

Smetana: *Bartered Bride*—Ah! bitterness

Smetana: *Dalibor*—Do I live

Tchaikovsky: *Eugène Onegin*—What shall I do?

Dvořák: *Rusalka*—Gods of the Lake

Tchaikovsky: *Queen of Spades*—'Twill soon be midnight

For orchestral accompaniment see relevant items in discography.

E.M.I. Records Limited. Long Play 33⅓ rpm record.

CLP1435   *The Story of the Passion* (A Fiona Bentley Production), w/Douglas Fairbanks, Joan Hammond, Sir Ralph Richardson

INDEX

INDEX